CW00822324

YEADON'S REGISTER

of

L N E R

LOCOMOTIVES

Volume Eleven

GRESLEY J39 CLASS

ISBN 1 899624 16 3

ACKNOWLEDGEMENTS

This is the eleventh volume, and I have only just realised that no tribute has been paid to Sir Nigel Gresley who was largely responsible for providing such a wealth, and fascinating variety of engines, that I have found it a life interest to research and write about, and that you decided to pay good money to read about. Nor have I mentioned the debt that I owe particularly to three on the LNER, for their help in guiding me to documentary material, much of it personal to their own employment by the LNER.

Edward ('Teddy') Windle, Chief Draughtsman at Doncaster, granted me access to registers, drawings, and photographs kept in his private office. He also discussed with me the part that he had played in the development of engine 10000, COCK O' THE NORTH, and the smoke and steam clearing experiments, which found the ultimate solution in SILVER LINK. When he reached his retirement age, I was glad and proud that his staff considered me as near enough to them (although I was never a railway employee) to contribute to his retirement present, and to be with them when the set of Encyclopaedia Britannica was given to him.

Lawrence (Laurie) Featherstone had been the Hull & Barnsley's sole draughtsman, and when the North Eastern absorbed that line in 1922, he transferred to the drawing office at Darlington. When I was introduced to him in February 1956 he was its Chief Draughtsman, and he too provided me with unique information, both written and verbal. He also let his staff know that I could be helped further than what they might have considered the limit of their duty.

J.G.(George) Gregory was just about the only man who had made a serious study from "hands-on" experience of the locomotives of that little known line, the Hull & Barnsley, and had assembled a photographic record of them with his own camera. When, in 1885, Matthew Stirling left the Great Northern at Peterborough, to be the H&B's only Chief Mechanical Engineer, one of the engine drivers he took with him to Hull was John Gregory. Following true railway tradition, his son George in 1901 began work on the H&B at its Springhead works, and by 1934, when I met him, he was the shedmaster, with responsibility for 62 engines, 40 of which were in five classes which had been H&B owned. He knew those engines, and their state of health, as if they had been individual people, and whatever I wanted to ask about them, or those preceding them in the past twenty years, he could answer from square one. From his 1901 start until retirement in April 1950 he worked soley at Springhead shed.

Those three were primary sources that it was my boundless good fortune to encounter, and all not only gave unstintingly of their knowledge, but accorded me valued friendship. Even in retirement they continued to point me to sources from which to increase my LNER locomotive information. Tragically, none was granted more than three years of well earned retirement, but were in full possession of all their faculties when death suddenly claimed them. Indeed, to George Gregory it came whilst sitting in a carriage in Paragon station on his way to Leeds for more photographic material. I can only hope that my work on making LNER loco information widely available will prove an adequate tribute to their generous help in effectively giving me the basic material for it. My wife, and my publisher, are both doing their utmost to keep the volumes appearing, and as you keep collecting them, I can include you in my gratitude - thank you.

W.B.Yeadon, Hull 1996.

(cover picture) **1478 brand-new outside Darlington shops with the wrong identity on its buffer beam.**

First published in the United Kingdom by
CHALLENGER PUBLICATIONS
15 Lovers Lane, Grasscroft, Oldham, OL4 4DP
Printed and bound by Redwood Books, Trowbridge

INTRODUCTION

The birth certificate for this class has Gresley's signature and is dated 27th November 1925. It takes the form of Rolling Stock Construction Order No.128 addressed to A.C.Stamer for Darlington works to build forty-four 0-6-0 Goods Tender Engines, as part of the building programme for the year ending 31st March 1927. Curiously, it is the only order issued until 1942 which does not specify the Area(s) to which the engines were to be allocated. It is reasonable to assume all 44 were to have been for Southern Area, and 32 went to sheds in that Area, but that there was a change of intention for the first twelve. Although the first engine was not completed until 28th September 1926, on 20th August North Eastern Area had begun transferring twelve of its superheated J27 class to the Great Eastern Section of Southern Area, and the register of transfers marked each one as "in exchange for J39". Because this was a new design, very much Darlington based, it was probably thought prudent to have the first ones built assigned to work where they could be closely watched, and where they could easily be called into the works which had built them should any teething troubles be found. Those twelve would also then be in the care of drivers accustomed to using steam operated reversing gear, thus cutting out any unwarranted complaints from Great Central and Great Northern drivers to whom it might be strange, and so "damn the engines with faint praise".

Ordered as "goods engines", they closely paralleled J38 class, built for main line haulage in Scottish Area, but differed by 6" larger diameter wheels, and that soon led to J39 class being used as a mixed traffic, and not just as a goods engine, especially as they had the necessary braking facilities fitted. In whatever light they were regarded, in every year from 1926 to 1938, the L N E R added to their stock of them, and on 17th January 1940, Darlington were given another order for eighteen more of these engines and tenders. When that order was completed on 21st August 1941, there were 289 in J39 class, a total which remained constant until the first withdrawals were made in 1959. Doing things on a large scale seemed natural in J39 class; from the first withdrawals, in May 1959, all 289 had been taken out of running stock by December 1962! One, no.64747 survived in use as a Stationary Boiler at Woodford shed until October 1964, but was then sold in December and cut up by T.W.Ward at Killamarsh.

It is interesting, and useful, to see how the last one, 3098 built August 1941, differed from the prototype 1448 built in September 1926. In fairness, it must be stressed that they were only differences of detail, the basic design needing no significant alteration. The items subject to change (and not dealt with here in any order of importance) concerned reversing gear, whistle mounting, cover around base of safety valves, type of brakes

No.1448 began the first batch of this class, of which twenty took numbers which were vacant from 1448 to 1498, and the other twenty-four similarly from 1233 to 1298. This is Darlington's official photograph, taken prior to final painting, and it shows items to which changes of detail were made later, such as steam reversing gear, cover at base of safety valves, type of tender, handholes for boiler washing-out, upper lamp iron, and the unusual fitting of a short standpipe for Westinghouse brake connection. The latter also caused the number on the buffer beam to be put on what was considered to be the wrong side of the coupling hook. *LNER*

The next twenty built, nos. 2691 to 2710, had screw instead of steam reversing gear, no base cover to safety valves, and tender with flush side panels, all features made standard for those built subsequently. They were also devoid of the single red lining on their black paint. *LNER*

fitted, addition of train control equipment, tender type coupled, drop grate operating gear, boiler wash-out facilities, lubrication, steam chest cover, upper lamp iron on smokebox, and (of course), numbering and liveries. All of these can be traced through the captions to the illustrations.

DIFFERENCES OF DETAIL - MAJOR & MINOR

When the prototype J39 class no.1448 appeared in September 1926, it was seen to be a larger wheeled version of the initial L N E R design, the J38 which had been put to work in Scottish Area. As well as the 5' 2" instead of 4' 8" wheels, the front buffers were to Group Standard instead of the Spencer double-case type, and the tender capacities were 5½ tons coal & 3500 gallons water, and not the 7½ tons & 4200 gallons coupled with J38 class. Superficially the boiler looked the same, but distance between tubeplates was 6" less, so the smokebox was 6" longer, with the chimney 6" further back than on J38 class. Of the 44 built to the first order, only the twelve allocated to the North Eastern Area were fitted for Westinghouse air braking, but all 44 had N.E.R. type steam operated reversing gear. On all the 245 built subsequently, screw operated reverse was fitted, and the original 44 were changed to that type, beginning in April 1935, although it took until October 1946 to complete that conversion.

The first 44, and the next 40, nos.2691 to 2730, had the whistle on a pipe which protruded from the front of the cab, and was supplied by steam from a manifold in the cab. The pipe tended to leak, even to fracture, causing inconvenience and danger to the crew, so from no.2731, new 30th May 1929, the whistle was mounted on the top of the firebox, above a valve by which it could be isolated, all subsequent engines being so fitted. By January 1933 the earlier boilers were already being changed to that safer arrangement.

As had been customary on boilers which Darlington fitted with 'pop' safety valves, the 44 to the first order were fitted with a circular cover around the base of the valves. That item was then discarded, no.2691, new in July 1928, being without it as were all the rest. The original covers then had a chequered career when the boilers carrying them were fitted to other engines. Many were removed and discarded, although some could still be seen after nationalisation, and when Inverurie works sent out 64795 as late as March 1961 from a heavy/intermediate repair, they had found one of the original circular covers to put on it. That works, and Cowlairs, certainly made some new covers for the base of 'pop' safety valves, but they could readily be identified because their shape was rectangular, 64978 showing that type clearly when ex Cowlairs in December 1950.

Until the 'Unification of Brakes Programme' of 1929 began to take effect, it was useful for engines allocated to North Eastern Area, and for those working on the Great Eastern Section of Southern Area, to be dual-braked, so on the first twelve (1448-52/54-59/81) and also 2711 to 2730, Westinghouse air brake was provided with vacuum ejector for alternative train braking. Progress on unification was such that in 1931-33, ten of the twelve North Eastern Area engines had their Westinghouse brake equipment removed, as was also done on 1459 in May 1936, the engines being changed to steam brake. The twenty on the G.E. Section however retained Westinghouse air brake through to withdrawal, but when Darlington repaired 2725 in October 1935, they converted that one from air to steam brake, which did not suit those who had to operate it. Luckily Darlington were able to retrieve their error, because 1457 had not then been converted, so it exchanged sheds with 2725, and as 4708 (64708) kept air brake to withdrawal.

Until operation of the Raven fog signalling system ceased in October 1933, it was mandatory for engines working on the main line between York and Morpeth to be equipped with the apparatus to use it. The 26 class J39 allocated to North Eastern Area to no.1483, built in May 1933, were so fitted, and the striker for it could be seen below the cab abaft the rear wheel. The Raven apparatus was removed when those engines went for repair after October 1933.

2977 to 2980 for Scottish Area were similar except for their tenders, which were the 4200 gallons type, but had already worked in that Area for six years. They had stepped top sides, because they had been built in 1926 for J38 class nos. 1417, 1422, 1423 and 1409 and when first coupled with the J39s, had kept the 2' 10½ " vertical handrails which matched those on the cab sides. *W.H.Whitworth*

The introduction of British Railways' Automatic Warning System was too long delayed to be made standard on J39 class, as by then, they were already on the withdrawal list. Some allocated to North Eastern, and to Scottish Region however were fully fitted, 64904 of Hull Dairycoates shed carrying it from a Cowlairs repair in October 1960, but it is not known how many of the class were fitted for that system because meticulous recording was faded out.

All 289 were fitted from new with the ability to drop the front portion of the grate for easier cleaning out of ash and clinker. On the right hand side an inclined operating rod from the front of the cab had part of its mechanism protected by a semi-circular casing on the running plate. That arrangement was used on the 123 engines built to no.2788 in February 1930. A simpler and more effective system was then devised and fitted to the remainder, starting with no.2962, new in September 1931. The operating rod was more steeply inclined, and passed through the running plate, and no semi-circular cover was needed. The earlier engines were duly changed to the improved type, but not all had the redundant cover removed. Some of them were still to be seen in British Railways days, and at least no.64798 carried one to its September 1962 withdrawal.

In accordance with Darlington custom, two handholes were provided on each side of the firebox, just above the handrail, to facilitate flushing out deposit from the top of the inner copper firebox. In November 1930, Gresley decided to have four washout plugs fitted in lieu on each side, and on J39 class that became effective first on no.2972 to traffic in January 1932. Then in April 1933, Gresley reversed his decision and reverted to handholes, which were used on all J39 boilers built from March 1934. So when they were new, only 2972-80, 1453, 1469, 1471, 1480, 1482 and 1483 originally had the four washout plugs on each side. Boiler exchanges did however cause others of the class to be seen with washout plugs fitted.

Lubrication on the first 44 engines was a Wakefield mechanical for the axleboxes, and a sight feed in the cab for each cylinder and piston valve. The sight feed lubrication layout was the same on both sides of the engine, with the mechanical only on the right hand running plate. The 116 engines built from July 1928 (no.2691) to December 1934 (no.1479) had two mechanical lubricators, both on the right hand side and driven off the middle coupling pin, one supplying the axleboxes as before, but the other for the cylinders and piston valves. Those 116 engines had no sign of lubrication facilities on their left hand side other than the three feeds on the steam chest coming from under the boiler. Starting with no.2941 in June 1935, the remaining 129 were built with Wakefield mechanical still feeding cylinders and piston valves, but the axleboxes were served by a Wakefield six-feed fountain type mounted in the cab. Feeds were taken horizontally and had an inverted U-bend above each box with an air inlet to reveal any blockage. From no.2993 the feed pipes were placed 10" lower down than previously. Starting in October 1943 the pipes from the fountain lubricator in the cab were sloped quite appreciably instead of being level, and the air inlets were dispensed with, test valves between the frame near to the boxes being more effective. When Gorton works fitted new cylinders to some of the first 44, the original sight feed lubrication was replaced by a second Wakefield mechanical on the right hand running plate.

The front end of the cylinder block originally had a separate circular cover to each steam chest, but from 1475 new in October 1934, a single plate with semi-circular ends was fitted. As and when new cylinders were put into engines built prior to that alteration, they too acquired the single plate. Between the circular covers, the cylinder block carried a footstep, and that continued to be fitted on the plate.

On the J39 class, a somewhat ambivalent attitude was taken to making them "crew-friendly". In line with normal Darlington custom, the upper lamp iron was above the top of the smokebox, but to help reach it, footsteps were fitted, one on each side of the rim of the smokebox front. Beginning with no.2962, new in September 1931, the position of the upper lamp iron was lowered on to the smokebox door, and that applied to all built thereafter, but the footsteps were retained. Before the war started, the earlier engines had their upper lamp iron moved to the more accessible position on the door.

Although the commodious customary Darlington cab was fitted, strangely none ever had hinged glass sight screens added between the cab side windows. Until 1937 cab seats were no more than the tops of the sandboxes serving the trailing wheels, then over the next ten years, piano stool seats gradually took over, and from 1947 tip-up seats began to be fitted.

The vertical handrail on each cab side was 2' 10½" between pillar centres, and remained so throughout. Not so however on the corresponding tender handrails. Until May 1933, all J39 tenders (both 3500 and 4200 gallons) also had 2' 10½"

Although the order starting with no.2962 had been for 35, the trade depression not only caused the use of second-hand tenders, but led to cancellation of ten, so after completing 2980, Darlington had only six more to build. The initial four, nos. 1453/69/71/80 also had to make do with second-hand tenders of stepped top type taken from J38 class 1442/41/19/20. *LNER*

handrail, but beginning with no.1482 new in that month, all new tenders were fitted with 3' 9½ " vertical rails. The earlier tenders of both capacities and types (stepped, and flush sided) were then altered to the taller rails. However, when J39 had to make do with second-hand N.E.R. tender, they had short rails which they kept to withdrawal, cost-saving no doubt being responsible for that.

PART CLASSIFICATION

In the Diagram Book Alterations for the revision to December 1930, class J39 was divided into Parts 1 and 2, simply according to tender capacity. All had the Group Standard type, but those holding 3500 gallons water were assigned Part 1, and the ones with 4200 gallons type took Part 2. Then five engines built in October-December 1934 were coupled with the tenders released by the Raven Pacifics (class A2) being changed to higher-capacity 8-wheeled type. Those five, nos. 1475-79 were allocated Part 3, which was used subsequently for further tenders which had originally been built for N.E.R. engines, when seconded to J39 class.

To the best of my knowledge, Part number was never shown on the front buffer beam, and was used only for office records. That was both sensible and fortunate, because exchanging of tenders became quite common, sometimes unobtrusively by sheds, and not always by those of the same water capacity. I have documentary evidence of 44 of the class changing to a tender of different capacity, and indeed one engine no.1491 (64819 later) qualified for all three Parts. It was Part 1 from January 1930, Part 3 from December 1951 to May 1960, then Part 2 to its withdrawal in September 1962. When preparing the Diagram Book Alterations in 1951, it was accepted that tender changing for operational convenience would still persist, so it was then decided to dispense with class Parts for J39 class.

TENDER TYPES USED BY J39 CLASS

The first batch of 44 - those built in 1926/27 - had Group Standard 3500 gallons type with the sides stepped out at the top. The next forty, nos. 2691 to 2730, had tender of the same capacity, but flush sided, although the coping was a separate plate. The rest of that order nos. 2731 to 2742 were for Scottish Area and were the 4200 gallons type, although Darlington did remember it was useless to fit them with water scoop when there were no track troughs there. It was that batch of twelve which led to the introduction of Parts 1 and 2.

The next order, placed in December 1928, was for 27, nos.2770-85 for Southern Area, eight with 14XX numbers for North Eastern Area, and new 3500 gallons tenders were built along with those twenty-four. For the other three nos.2786, 2787 and 2788, which were for Scottish Area, the order was annotated in ink (only a month after issue) that they were to have 'large standard tender'.

On 5th December 1929 the next order was for 35, of which the 15 for Southern Area nos.2962 to 2976 with 3500 gallons tender, were in traffic by March 1932. The trade depression then caused ten of the remaining twenty to be cancelled, and for the ten that were built, only two got new 3500 gallons tender. For the other eight, 4200 gallons stepped-top type were taken from J38 class and coupled with nos. 2977-80 for Scottish Area, and with 1453/69/71/80 for North Eastern Area, their 1482/83 being those to get the two new small tenders.

The order placed in December 1929 was only completed in May 1933, and in the following December, Darlington got two Construction Orders, the first for seven engines and 3500 gallons tenders which became nos.1412/63/7/8/72/88/90 and were in traffic by December 1934. The other order was for five engines nos. 1475-79, their tenders to come from the Raven Pacifics. Those were the N.E.R. 4125 gallons self-trimming type, which had four coal rails with plating inside them, and when put with J39 class, originated Part 3. They went to traffic October-December 1934.

By the end of 1934, trade conditions had improved enough

for another thirty-nine class J39 to be ordered and for new tenders to be built with them. Twenty-seven for Southern Area with 4200 gallons tender numbered 2941-53 and 2981-94 went into traffic June to October 1935, followed by twelve for North Eastern Area, nos.1436/60/4/5/73/3/85/6, 1504 to 1506 and 1584 in October to December 1935. It is rather jumping ahead to mention the 1946 renumbering, in which date built was supposed to determine the sequence, but those 12 for N.E. Area then took 4860-71, preceding the 27 for Southern Area which became 4872-98. The lower numbers of those in N.E. Area must have misled the 'allocater' into giving them preference when it came to the number changing.

In September 1935 Darlington got the next Construction Order, which included 15 with 4200 gallons tender for Southern Area, 16 for N.E. Area, and 3 for Scottish Area, those 19 to have the 3500 gallons tender. But a month later that order was cut to only six for Southern Area, the cancelled 28 then being ordered from Beyer, Peacock & Co. Ltd, the only J39 class not to be built at Darlington works. They were then so heavily engaged on orders for B17 and K3 classes that to get the desired delivery for the J39s, outside contractors had to be used. The six which Darlington built were numbered 2995 to 3000, and went into traffic during August 1936.

Beyer, Peacock produced their 28 as had been intended on the Darlington order. In September/October 1936 they delivered the nine nos. 1803/13/24/8/54/6/7/69/70 with 4200 gallons tender to Southern Area. Next came ten others, nos. 1532/3/4/6/9/40/3/4/5/7 for N.E. Area in October/November, with the other six 1563/77/80/5/6/7 in March/April 1937, and nos.1875/80/94 for the Scottish Area in May 1937. Those nineteen had 3500 gallons tender, and as all the tenders built by Beyer, Peacock were fabricated by welding, there was no perceptible joining between tender side and coping, as was the case with the riveted tenders which Darlington built.

The next Construction Order for class J39 was within Darlington's scope and was for thirty-eight placed with that works on 2nd November 1936. Twelve, nos.1508/9/35/7/8/41, and 1542/6/8/51/8/60 with 3500 gallons tender went into traffic December 1937 to April 1938, although for its first seven months 1560 had to make do with a second-hand 4200 gallons 'stepped top' type from a J38, its own new tender having been delayed. Next came six with larger tender 1804/8/35/62/3/96 for Scottish Area in March/April 1938, and twenty similar, numbered in the 1898 to 1997 range, for Southern Area were completed April to August 1938.

Finally, for J39 class, on 17th January 1940, Gresley signed Construction Order No.1000 for Darlington to build 18 engines, and tender, 14 for Southern, and 4 for Scottish Areas. No date was entered, but that Order has written on it "To be fitted with 4200 gallon tenders and water scoop gear". The war however caused a change of plan, and when those 18 went into traffic in February to August 1941 as nos. 3081 to 3098, they were coupled with ex N.E.R. tenders, ten of 4125 gallons type taken from D21 class, and eight of 3650 gallons from D17 class. In consequence, those 18 were added to those in Part 3.

NUMBERING AND LETTERING CHANGES

The first 44 were given numbers which filled vacancies due to withdrawal of engines which had been built by the North Eastern Railway, in some cases, actually by the Stockton & Darlington Railway, and when convenient later, that method

To finish the order Darlington then built 1482 and 1483, and provided them with new 3500 gallons tenders. Even so, there was a change of detail on these tenders, and one made standard thereafter. Instead of 2' 10½ " vertical handrails, theirs were 3' 9½ " between pillar centres. They were also the last engines, when new, to have boilers fitted with four washout plugs. *W.H.Whitworth*

Nos. 2719-24 worked first from Parkeston shed and here 2721 is on a Class A up goods. Its Westinghouse front connection was the more usual one by a union under the buffer beam, but of interest is the Southern Area load class collar on the vacuum standpipe showing J39 to be in load class 5. *WBY collection*

of allocation was continued. Where it could not be used, sequential numbering took place, and ultimately ranged from 2691 to 3098. There were a couple of cases worthy of comment. The engines which came out as 1453/69/71/80/2/3 had originally been allocated 2981 to 2986, and indeed, the motion parts on 1471 were seen to have been stamped 2983. The illustration that I have included showing a J39/3 numbered 1748 on its buffer beam need not cause panic. Cab side number can be seen to have been applied correctly as 1478, and no doubt that on the buffer beam would have been put right before the engine went back to traffic at the end of September 1936. Such errors of application were rare indeed, and even more so to have been caught by a photographer.

In the 1946 general renumbering, J39 class was allocated 4700 to 4988 substantially (but not exactly) in order of date first put into traffic, but it took a full twelve months, from 20th January 1946 until 13th January 1947 to alter all the 289 engines.

British Railways' attempt to distinguish between engines carrying the same number in the different Regions by adding a prefix letter only concerned J39 class from 20th January to 14th March 1948. During that brief period, Gorton works added E prefix to fifteen, and Stratford works dealt similarly with another four. Cowlairs was the only other works then maintaining the class, but they made no E prefix additions. The change to adding 60,000 then began, and the whole class acquired it, but it was not until 20th November 1951, when 64810 completed the job.

The 44 which Darlington built from September 1926 to September 1927 had single red lining on their black paint, but the painting economies put into effect from June 1928 caused that lining to disappear at their first general repair. As so often happened, there was an exceptional case; for some reason 1481 had a general repair at Darlington as early as 16th May 1928, so would then retain lining. Starting with 2691 new 20th July 1928, all the others built by Darlington until 1937 had to be content with unlined black. When placing the order for Beyer, Peacock to build 28, Doncaster in October 1935 sent them a drawing which showed single red lining, which those contractors duly applied, although it was removed at their first repainting. Despite the considerable amount of passenger work done by the class, which could have entitled them to be regarded as mixed traffic engines, British Railways classed them only as goods engines, and so they only had unlined black through to withdrawal.

With 289 engines to maintain, at one time or another, and for varying periods, due to fluctuations in work load, all seven LNER workshops were engaged on repairing J39 class. Then after nationalisation, British Railways found it expedient to spread the load even further, no less than 159 going to the London Midland Region shops at Derby, and just one, 64918 in March 1952, actually had a casual/light repair done at Bow works in London.

In the years 1926 to 1947, whilst the LNER owned them, uniformity of their painted appearance was to be expected, the seven workshops presumably all having been given the same instructions. But some aberrations (albeit of small consequence) were noted. For example, the very first engine 1448 had its buffer beam number on the opposite side of the coupling hook to what was established custom, and there is a photograph of 2712 done similarly by Gorton at a general repair. Those were due to their being fitted with a small standpipe for their Westinghouse brake, in addition to the larger one for vacuum braking. From late 1928, or early 1929 the running number position was changed from tender to the cab side, but when Doncaster turned out 1484 from general repair on 8th March 1929, it still had number on tender. In the 1930's when Cowlairs were maintaining the 2731-42 batch, number was on the cab, but the 12" LNER they had when new was replaced by the 7½" size which that works persisted in applying. These items are only mentioned for the attention of meticulous modellers, because I appreciate they are in the "What matters about that?" class, as I was once asked by an indignant child on an entirely different matter.

Otherwise, stability reigned from whichever works a J39 was turned out, through the war period, with the complete loss of any lining, the 1942 contraction to just N E, and the 1946 slow restoration to LNER. But the 1946 general renumbering upset all that, because much of it perforce had to be done at sheds, on Sundays, and by employing outside painters. A wide variety of treatment was expected and had to be accepted, results ranging from only 6" stencilled figures, to the normal 12" shaded transfers. That change was limited to the numbers and was totally independent of any change to tender lettering.

During 1947, and in the last months of the LNER, stocks of the 12" shaded transfer figures and LNER lettering approached exhaustion, and it was decided not to spend money on replenishing them. In their place, 12" yellow painted unlined characters were made standard. Gill Sans style was intended, but on the drawing which Doncaster circulated for that change, figures 6 and 9 had been wrongly delineated, because curled tails had been added to them. It was well into 1948 before paint shops made correction, and some cast smokebox plates carried that error into the 1960's.

In January 1948 BRITISH RAILWAYS began to supplant N E and L N E R on J39 tenders. The instruction to use the new title must have omitted direction as to size of lettering because 6", 8½", and 9" examples were all to be seen before it was standardised at 10". Then, from August 1949 that lettering was discarded, and a handed, transfer-applied emblem superseded it. On J39 tenders it was normal to use the larger (28") size along with 10" figures on the cab, but when 64984 was ex Derby on 10th August 1951, it had the smaller (15½") emblem and 8½" figures on the cab, although it was the only one so noted.

Final presentation, from mid-1957, was the crest from the grant of arms which B.R. had obtained from the College of Heralds, and even that was not correctly applied. The emblem had been handed for the lion to face forward on both sides, and through ignorance of the tenets of heraldry, transfers for the crests were ordered, supplied, and applied, which were also handed. That made the lion to face to the right on the off-side of tenders, which was a gaffe in heraldry, causing the College of Heralds to demand correction. By November 1958 correct transfers were being applied to all J39s painted, or repainted thereafter.

It is not known how many of the 289 were withdrawn whilst still with emblem on tender, how many had wrong crest and were not corrected, or were with crest shown properly.

REGISTRATION

This class was so ubiquitous that it took me 16½ years to complete my recording of it, and visits to places as widespread as Aberdeen and London, Craigendoran, Carlisle, and Cleethorpes. Although I must have seen some J39s when I began regular travelling between Leeds and Hull in July 1931, I was not then LNER orientated, and my first dated recording of a J39 is on 7th May 1937, when I saw 1493 on a goods at Thorne South Junction. By their 1946 change of numbering I had seen and noted 251 of them, and then determined effort in 1947/48 added another 31 whilst they still had LNER ownership displayed. The other seven were only encountered after their B.R. numbering, one at Stratford in 1948, two in 1949, one in 1950, and two in 1951, but 64894 which did all its work from Ipswich shed, eluded me until 27th January 1955. Even then it needed a special visit to that shed where I found it having its boiler washed out.

I have already commented on the considerable amount of passenger train haulage which this class did, and after I started in January 1940 recording which engines hauled me, I was in eleven trains for which a J39 was the engine. Six were locals on the Doncaster - Wakefield - Dewsbury - Bradford line, but the others were as widely spread as Hexham to Newcastle, Barnsley to Mexborough, Wakefield to Grimsby (Town), Ipswich to Felixstowe, and Burnmouth to Eyemouth. In my photographic collection I have 41 other examples of a J39 on a passenger train, and varying as widely in location as they do from one with a single coach, to an 11-coach Sheffield to Cleethorpes holiday train. A representative selection will be included later in this volume.

J39 CLASS AT WORK

With a maximum axle load of 19 tons 13 cwt. one would expect that there would be a lot of places on the LNER system which they 'could not reach' so it is surprising to see so many photographs of them at the end of country branches. Fortunately a very representative selection is available to enable you to see just where you were likely to meet up with a J39 doing what came naturally. Silloth and Skegness, Langholm and Leadgate, Cleethorpes and Clacton, Hornsea and Horncastle, Esholt and Edwinstowe, all saw something of them. Then, on lines where you did expect to see them, loads varying from a single vehicle in service use, to packed passenger trains running with Class A headlamps were dealt with the same competence as they hauled all the various types of goods, mineral, cattle, fish, and parcel trains. The following photographs let J39s speak for themselves - I commend them to your close attention.

Overleaf: **LNER Diagram of J39 Class as issued at the end of 1926.**

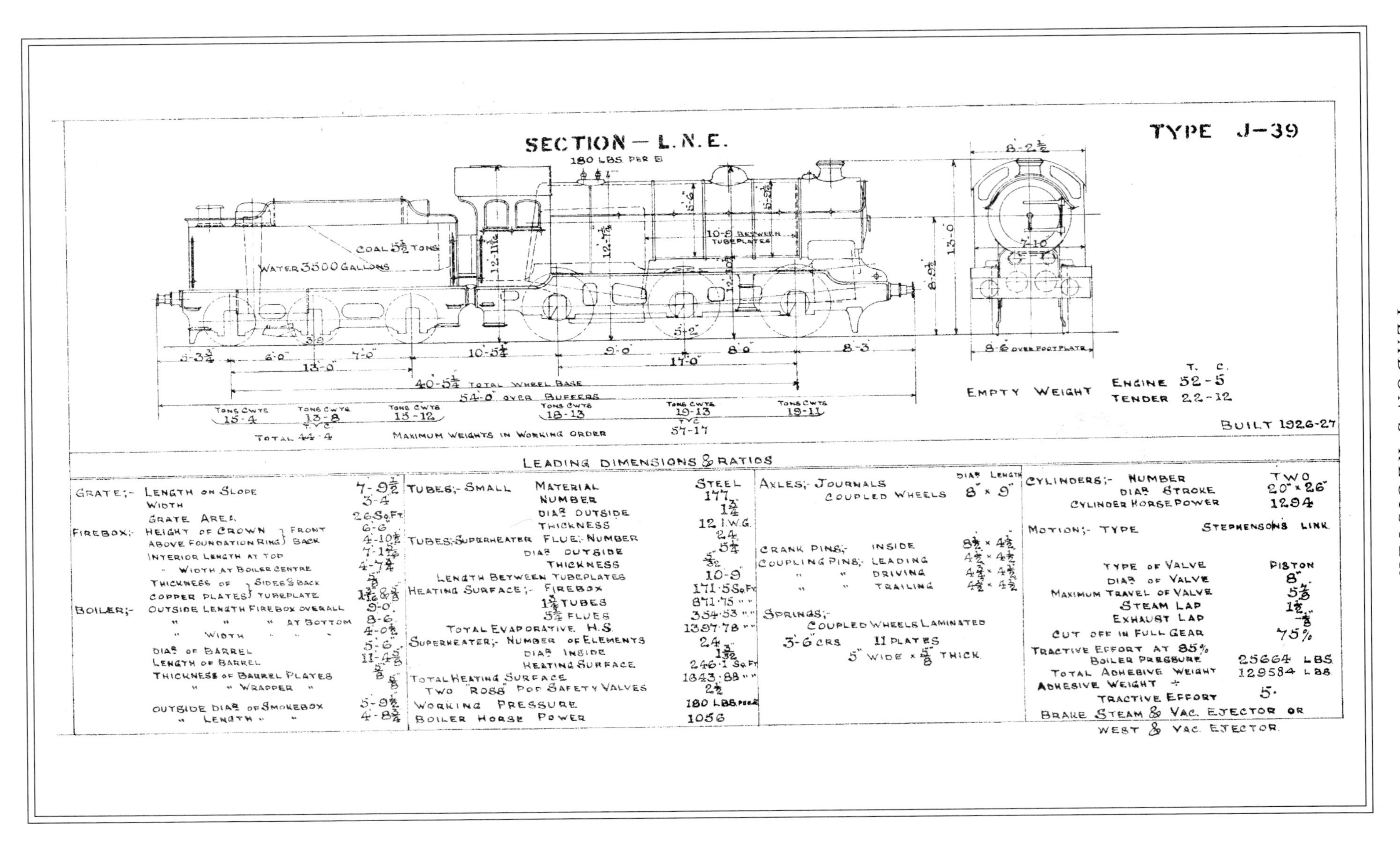
SECTION — L.N.E.
TYPE J–39
180 LBS PER ▢
COAL 5½ TONS
WATER 3500 GALLONS
10-9 BETWEEN TUBEPLATES
8-6 OVER FOOTPLATE
40-5¼ TOTAL WHEEL BASE
54-0 OVER BUFFERS
EMPTY WEIGHT
T. C.
ENGINE 52-5
TENDER 22-12
TOTAL 44-4
MAXIMUM WEIGHTS IN WORKING ORDER
T. C.
57-17
BUILT 1926-27
LEADING DIMENSIONS & RATIOS
GRATE;- LENGTH ON SLOPE 7-9½
WIDTH 3-4
GRATE AREA 26 SQ.FT
FIREBOX;- HEIGHT OF CROWN ABOVE FOUNDATION RING FRONT 6-6
BACK 4-10½
INTERIOR LENGTH AT TOP 7-1
" WIDTH AT BOILER CENTRE 4-7¼
BOILER;- OUTSIDE LENGTH FIREBOX OVERALL 9-0
" " " AT BOTTOM 8-6
" WIDTH 4-0
DIA. OF BARREL 5-6
LENGTH OF BARREL 11-4
OUTSIDE DIA. OF SMOKEBOX 5-9½
" LENGTH " 4-8¾
TUBES;- SMALL MATERIAL STEEL
NUMBER 177
DIA. OUTSIDE 1¾
THICKNESS 12 I.W.G.
TUBES;- SUPERHEATER FLUE;- NUMBER 24
DIA. OUTSIDE 5¼
LENGTH BETWEEN TUBEPLATES 10-9
HEATING SURFACE;- FIREBOX 171.5 SQ.FT
1¾ TUBES 871.75
5¼ FLUES 354.53
TOTAL EVAPORATIVE H.S. 1397.78
SUPERHEATER;- NUMBER OF ELEMENTS 24
HEATING SURFACE 246.1 SQ.FT
TOTAL HEATING SURFACE 1643.88
TWO "ROSS" POP SAFETY VALVES 2½
WORKING PRESSURE 180 LBS PER ▢
BOILER HORSE POWER 1056
AXLES;- JOURNALS COUPLED WHEELS 8" × 9"
CRANK PINS;- INSIDE
COUPLING PINS;- LEADING
DRIVING
TRAILING
SPRINGS;- COUPLED WHEELS LAMINATED
3'-6" CRS 11 PLATES
5" WIDE × ⅝" THICK
CYLINDERS;- NUMBER TWO
DIA. STROKE 20" × 26"
CYLINDER HORSE POWER 1294
MOTION;- TYPE STEPHENSONS LINK
TYPE OF VALVE PISTON
DIA. OF VALVE 8"
MAXIMUM TRAVEL OF VALVE 5⅜
STEAM LAP 1¼
CUT OFF IN FULL GEAR 75%
TRACTIVE EFFORT AT 85% BOILER PRESSURE 25664 LBS
TOTAL ADHESIVE WEIGHT 129584 LBS
ADHESIVE WEIGHT ÷ TRACTIVE EFFORT 5.
BRAKE STEAM & VAC. EJECTOR OR WEST & VAC. EJECTOR

J39 CLASS

1448

Darlington.

To traffic 28/9/26.

REPAIRS:
Dar. 29/5-5/6/29.**N/C.**
Dar. 7/1-21/2/30.**G.**
Dar. 25/9-30/10/30.**H.**
After derailment.
Dar. 20/4-1/6/32.**G.**
Dar. 12-18/7/32.**N/C.**
Dar. 29/6-13/8/34.**G.**
Dar. 24/9-2/10/34.**N/C.**
Dar. 16/10-27/11/36.**G.**
Dar. 22/3-10/5/39.**G.**
Dar. 28/4-27/5/41.**G.**
Cow. 23/10-10/11/43.**G.**
Ghd. 28/10-14/11/44.**L.**
Cow. 1-22/9/45.**G.**
Cow. 2-9/4/46.**N/C.**
Cow. 15/3-12/4/47.**H.**
Cow. 9/6-12/7/47.**L.**
Cow. 1-27/12/47.**L.**
Cow. 2/7-13/8/49.**G.**
Cow. 16/5-2/6/51.**H/I.**
Cow. 21/8-2/9/52.**H/I.**
Cow. 12-18/12/52.**N/C.**
Cow. 4/3-8/4/54.**G.**
Cow. 30/8-10/10/57.**H/I.**

BOILERS:
1902.
2303 *(ex1425)* 13/8/34.
1913 *(ex1453)* 27/11/36.
2617 *(ex1478)* 10/5/39.
1905 *(ex1489)* 27/5/41.
BP132 *(ex1418)* 10/11/43.
2843 *(ex1560)* 22/9/45.
BP137 *(ex2737)* 13/8/49.
BP137 Reno. 27521 2/6/51.
27498 *(ex64843)* 8/4/54.

SHEDS:
Newport.
Middlesbrough 7/4/30.
Newport 23/1/36.
Darlington 23/3/43.
Blaydon 3/8/43.
Borough Gardens 4/1/53.
Gateshead 14/6/59.
Sunderland 1/11/59.

RENUMBERED:
4700 3/11/46.
64700 13/8/49.

CONDEMNED:
17/4/61.
Cut up at Cowlairs.

1449

Darlington.

To traffic 5/10/26.

REPAIRS:
Dar. 2/2-19/3/30.**G.**
Dar. 13/10-22/11/32.**G.**
Dar. 9/5-5/7/34.**H.**
Dar. 18-21/7/34.**N/C.**
Dar. 14/2-20/3/35.**G.**
Dar. 27/3-27/4/37.**G.**
Dar. 4/5-17/6/39.**G.**
Dar. 21/4-23/5/41.**G.**
Cow. 21/3-20/4/44.**G.**
Cow. 2-16/6/45.**L.**
Cow. 26/1-2/3/46.**G.**
Cow. 12-16/3/46.**N/C.**
Cow. 6-27/7/46.**L.**
Cow. 20-30/11/46.**L.**
Cow. 7/4-5/6/48.**G.**
Cow. 27/9-27/10/50.**H/I.**
Cow. 1-27/2/54.**G.**
Ghd. 11/10-17/12/54.**C/L.**
Cow. 24/6-12/7/58.**G.**
Cow. 17/2-24/3/59.**C/L.**
Cow. 3/5-14/6/60.**C/L.**
Cow. 19/1-20/2/62.**C/L.**

BOILERS:
1904.
1902 *(ex1448)* 20/3/35.
2099 *(ex2697)* 27/4/37.
2710 *(ex1460)* 17/6/39.
2143 *(ex1452)* 23/5/41.
1907 *(ex1473)* 20/4/44.
1918 *(ex1506)* 2/3/46.
2663 *(ex2991)* 5/6/48.
27510 *(ex4934)* 27/2/54.
27555 *(ex64940)* 12/7/58.

SHEDS:
Newport.
Middlesbrough 7/4/30.
Newport 23/1/36.
Darlington 23/3/43.
Blaydon 16/7/43.
Gateshead 18/9/49.
Heaton 7/7/57.
Sunderland 13/12/59.

RENUMBERED:
4701 3/11/46.
64701 2/6/48.

CONDEMNED:
16/11/62.
Cut up at Darlington.

1450

Darlington.

To traffic 14/10/26.

REPAIRS:
Dar. 25/11/29-24/1/30.**G.**
Dar. 19/1-25/2/32.**G.**
Dar. 2/6-11/7/34.**G.**
Dar. 18/3-1/5/36.**G.**
Dar. 20/4-24/5/39.**G.**
Dar. 31/3-2/5/41.**G.**
Dar. 16/3-15/4/42.**L.**
Dar. 23/6-28/7/43.**H.**
Dar. 6-19/11/43.**L.**
Gor. 12/8-20/10/45.**G.**
Gor. 28/4-2/9/47.**L.**
Gor. 11/1-23/2/48.**G.**
Gor. 22/9-6/11/48.**L.**
Gor. 11/2-29/4/50.**G.**
Gor. 31/5-16/6/50.**N/C.**
Str. 4/1-27/4/53.**G.**
Str. 16/6-2/10/54.**C/L.**
Gor. 26/10-8/12/56.**G.**
Str. 15-28/9/59.**N/C.**

BOILERS:
1905.
1922 *(ex2706)* 1/5/36.
8022 *(ex1487)* 24/5/39.
1920 *(ex1471)* 2/5/41.
C7963 *(ex253)* 28/7/43.
2678 *(ex2993)* 20/10/45.
4918 *(ex2997)* 23/2/48.
C2030 *(new)* 29/4/50.
27801 *(ex4957)* 27/4/53.
27682 *(ex4740)* 8/12/56.

SHEDS:
Newport.
Darlington 28/3/43.
Lincoln 15/9/44.
Immingham 17/6/45.
Lincoln 21/10/45.
Stratford 10/11/57.
Sheffield 7/12/58.

RENUMBERED:
4702 3/12/46.
E4702 23/2/48.
64702 6/11/48.

CONDEMNED:
28/9/59.
Cut up at Stratford.

1451

Darlington.

To traffic 15/10/26.

REPAIRS:
Ghd. 5/12/28-30/1/29.**G.**
Ghd. 7/11-23/12/30.**G.**
Ghd. 11-18/8/31.**L.**
Ghd. 13-20/6/32.**L.**
Dar. 13/2-24/3/33.**G.**
Dar. 17/1-26/2/35.**G.**
Dar. 21/4-26/5/37.**G.**
Dar. 22/3-3/5/38.**L.**
Dar. 28/7-4/9/39.**G.**
Dar. 4/2-7/3/41.**G.**
Cow. 23/9-13/10/43.**G.**
Ghd. 8/2-2/3/45.**L.**
Cow. 27/12/46-22/2/47.**G.**
Cow. 6-18/10/47.**L.**
Cow. 7/7-3/9/49.**G.**
Cow. 27/12/51-9/2/52.**H/I.**
Cow. 12/5-22/6/55.**G.**
Cow. 20/3-17/4/59.**H/I.**

BOILERS:
1907.
1909 *(ex1452)* 24/3/33.
2141 *(ex2967)* 26/5/37.
1922 *(ex1450)* 4/9/39.
BP130 *(ex1532)* 7/3/41.
4912 *(ex1922)* 13/10/43.
C1834 *(ex1473)* 3/9/49.
C1834 Reno. 27532 9/2/52.
27503 *(ex64915)* 22/6/55.

SHEDS:
Hull Dairycoates.
Blaydon 25/11/27.
Hull Dairycoates 6/7/52.
Heaton 7/12/52.
Sunderland 13/12/59.

RENUMBERED:
4703 10/2/46.
64703 3/9/49.

CONDEMNED:
29/3/62.
Cut up at Darlington.

1452

Darlington.

To traffic 21/10/26.

REPAIRS:
Ghd. 19/10-5/12/28.**G.**
Ghd. 31/1-7/2/29.**L.**

WORKS CODES:- Cow - Cowlairs. Dar - Darlington. Dby - Derby. Don - Doncaster. Ghd - Gateshead. Gor - Gorton. Imm - Immingham. Inv - Inverurie. Str - Stratford.
REPAIR CODES:- **C/H** - Casual Heavy. **C/L** - Casual Light. **G** - General. **H**- Heavy. **H/I** - Heavy Intermediate. **L** - Light. **L/I** - Light Intermediate. **N/C** - Non-Classified.

After collision.
Ghd. 25/8-9/10/30.**G.**
Dar. 17/1-22/2/33.**G.**
Dar. 25/2-4/4/35.**G.**
Dar. 1/7-28/8/36.**L.**
Dar. 21/4-28/5/37.**G.**
Dar. 6/9-7/10/39.**G.**
Dar. 18/3-18/4/41.**G.**
Cow. 25/10-18/11/44.**G.**
Cow. 5-19/5/45.**L.**
Cow. 12/8-27/9/47.**G.**
Cow. 26/4-20/5/50.**H/I.**
Cow. 27/1-28/2/53.**G.**
Cow. 3/7-11/8/56.**H/I.**
Inv. 18/2-21/4/60.**G.**
Cow. 2-14/10/61.**C/L.**

BOILERS:
1909.
1920 *(ex1481)* 22/2/33.
1904 *(ex1449)* 4/4/35.
1902 *(ex1449)* 28/5/37.
2143 *(ex1481)* 7/10/39.
1922 *(ex1451)* 18/4/41.
1913 *(ex1490)* 18/11/44.
27489 *(ex4818)* 28/2/53.
27550 *(ex64910)* 21/4/60.

SHEDS:
Hull Dairycoates.
Blaydon 25/11/27.
Gateshead 18/9/49.
Sunderland 1/11/59.

RENUMBERED:
4704 27/1/46.
64704 20/5/50.

CONDEMNED:
3/12/62.
Cut up at Darlington.

1454

Darlington.

To traffic 21/10/26.

REPAIRS:
Ghd. 14/9-1/11/28.**G.**
Ghd. 6/6-25/7/30.**G.**
Ghd. 15-24/7/31.**L.**
Ghd. 14-21/10/31.**L.**
Ghd. 7/10-1/12/32.**G.**
Dar. 21/5-1/7/35.**G.**
Dar. 19/1-25/2/37.**G.**
Dar. 4/4-17/5/39.**G.**
Dar. 25/8-26/9/40.*Tender only.*
Dar. 1/4-7/5/41.**G.**
Dar. 30/12/42-23/1/43.**L.**
Cow. 28/8-18/9/43.**G.**
Cow. 22/5-1/7/44.**H.**
Cow. 7/7-4/8/45.**G.**
Cow. 19/10/46-25/1/47.**H.**
Cow. 29/12/47-31/1/48.**L.**
Cow. 29/4-28/5/49.**H/I.**
Cow. 14/9-13/10/51.**G.**
Ghd. 19-26/3/52.**C/L.**
Cow. 23/2-13/3/53.**N/C.**
Cow. 26/1-13/3/54.**H/I.**
Ghd. 17-24/2/55.**C/L.**
Cow. 16/8-27/10/56.**G.**
Ghd. 22/8-11/10/57.**C/L.**
Cow. 1/10-5/11/59.**H/I.**

BOILERS:
1912.
1907 *(ex1458)* 1/7/35.
1926 *(ex1470)* 25/2/37.
BP133 *(ex1536)* 17/5/39.
2940 *(ex1558)* 7/5/41.
822 *(ex2967)* 18/9/43.
RS129 *(ex1467)* 1/7/44.
27536 *(ex4849)* 13/10/51.
27652 *(ex4910)* 27/10/56.

SHEDS:
Hull Dairycoates.
Blaydon 25/11/27.
Hull Dairycoates 4/9/49.
Blaydon 2/10/49.
Alnmouth 16/6/57.
Ardsley 25/1/59.
Wakefield 12/6/60.
Ardsley 26/3/61.

RENUMBERED:
4705 23/6/46.
64705 27/5/49.

CONDEMNED:
29/3/62.
Cut up at Darlington.

1455

Darlington.

To traffic 21/10/26.

REPAIRS:
Dar. 19-31/10/28.**N/C.**
Dar. 16/1-13/3/29.**G.**
Dar. 22/1-18/3/30.**G.**
Dar. 18/7-22/8/30.**L.**
After collision.
Dar. 22/3-4/5/32.**G.**
Dar. 1-31/5/34.**G.**
Dar. 13/3-25/4/36.**G.**
Dar. 25/2-12/4/38.**G.**
Dar. 19/3-18/4/40.**G.**
Dar. 19-28/3/41.**N/C.**
Dar. 12/11-15/12/41.**H.**
Dar. 25/7-9/9/42.**G.**
Cow. 22/7-26/8/44.**G.**
Cow. 14-28/4/45.**L.**
Cow. 12/1-16/2/46.**L.**
Cow. 12/4-12/7/47.**G.**
Cow. 28/11-24/12/49.**H/I.**
Cow. 14/11-8/12/51.**G.**
Cow. 5/2-13/3/54.**H/I.**
Cow. 15/3-21/4/56.**G.**
Cow. 3/10-1/11/58.**H/I.**
Dar. 2-8/7/59.**C/L.**
Dar. 24/10-7/11/60.**C/L.**
Dar. 1-12/8/61.**C/L.**

BOILERS:
1913.
2309 *(ex1429)* 31/5/34.
2129 *(ex1274)* 25/4/36.
1918 *(ex1463)* 18/4/40.
BP142 *(ex1541)* 9/9/42.
4922 *(new)* 12/7/47.
27594 *(new)* 8/12/51.
27725 *(ex4718)* 21/4/56.

SHEDS:
Newport.
Starbeck 26/6/39.
York 13/9/59.
Thornaby 22/11/59.
Sunderland 21/1/62.

RENUMBERED:
4706 16/6/46.
64706 23/12/49.

CONDEMNED:
29/3/62.
Cut up at Darlington.

1456

Darlington.

To traffic 28/10/26.

REPAIRS:
Dar. 8/4-28/5/29.**G.**
Dar. 31/8-13/10/31.**G.**
Dar. 22/8-29/9/33.**G.**
Dar. 18/6-15/8/35.**G.**
Dar. 9/4-7/5/37.**G.**
Dar. 24/3-10/5/39.**G.**
Dar. 26/5-1/7/41.**G.**
Dar. 8/3/43.Weigh.
Dar. 3/6-5/7/43.**H.**
Dar. 6-14/7/43.**N/C.**
Cow. 28/4-26/5/45.**G.**
Cow. 9/11-25/1/47.**L.**
Cow. 4-18/6/47.**L.**
Cow. 9/4-15/5/48.**G.**
Cow. 24/5-23/6/51.**G.**
Ghd. 21-24/8/51.**C/L.**
Cow. 10/9-9/10/53.**L/I.**
Cow. 30/10-1/12/56.**G.**

BOILERS:
1916.
2306 *(ex1418)* 29/9/33.
1907 *(ex1454)* 7/5/37.
2710 *(ex1449)* 1/7/41.
(C1720) 2253 *(ex1896)* 5/7/43.
2713 *(ex1483)* 26/5/45.
27585 *(new)* 23/6/51.
27563 *(ex4710)* 1/12/56.

SHEDS:
Newport.
Darlington 16/7/34.
Blaydon 3/8/43.
Gateshead 18/9/49.
Borough Gardens 4/1/53.
Gateshead 14/6/59.
Sunderland 13/11/60.

RENUMBERED:
4707 23/6/46.
64707 15/5/48.

CONDEMNED:
25/8/61.
Cut up at Inverurie.

1457

Darlington.

To traffic 4/11/26.

REPAIRS:
Dar. 6/2-28/3/30.**G.**
Ghd. 10/12/31-20/1/32.**G.**
Gor. 26/1-17/2/34.**G.**
Dar. 28/10-12/12/35.**G.**
Gor. 11/3-14/5/38.**G.**
Gor. 11/1-22/2/41.**G.**
Str. 22/5-19/6/43.**L.**
Str. 22/1-4/3/44.**G.**
Str. 8/3-13/6/47.**G.**
Dby. 2/8-19/9/51.**G.**
Str. 27/7-4/9/54.**G.**
Str. 15/1-1/3/58.**G.**
Str. 29/12/59-22/1/60.**N/C.**

BOILERS:
1917.
2214 *(ex2726)* 17/2/34.
2121 *(ex2693)* 12/12/35.
2312 *(ex1290)* 14/5/38.
2296 *(ex2970)* 22/2/41.
2184 *(ex2772)* 4/3/44.
2704 *(ex2778)* 13/6/47.
27675 *(ex4955)* 19/9/51.
27891 *(new)* 4/9/54.
27846 *(ex4775)* 1/3/58.

SHEDS:
Newport.
Darlington 16/7/34.
Stratford 12/11/35.
Ipswich 15/10/50.
Stratford 22/10/50.

RENUMBERED:
4708 19/8/46.
64708 11/8/51.

CONDEMNED:
18/8/60.
Cut up at Doncaster.

1458

Darlington.

To traffic 9/11/26.

REPAIRS:
Ghd. 30/1-2/4/29.**G.**
Ghd. 15/12/30-28/1/31.**G.**
Dar. 23/2-5/4/33.**G.**

The original batch of 44 had single red lining on their black paint, but only no.1448 had a standpipe for the front end Westinghouse brake connection. In this opposite sided view to that on page one, we can see the position of the Westinghouse standpipe on the buffer beam clearly. *LNER*

Dar. 11/3-27/4/35.**G.**
Dar. 8/3-9/4/37.**G.**
Gor. 10/8-2/9/39.**G.**
Dar. 10/9-24/10/40.**H.**
Dar. 10/6-11/7/42.**G.**
Cow. 18/9-14/10/44.**G.**
Cow. 21/9-16/11/46.**G.**
Cow. 29/4-28/5/49.**L/I.**
Cow. 26/10-24/11/51.**G.**
Gor. 28/6-28/8/54.**G.**
Gor. 12/10/54-8/1/55.**C/L.**
Cow. 19/12/57-1/2/58.**L/I.**
Cow. 9/7-22/8/59.**G.**

BOILERS:
1918.
1907 *(ex1451)* 5/4/33.
1920 *(ex1452)* 27/4/35.
2623 *(ex1488)* 9/4/37.
2277 *(ex1497)* 2/9/39.
2223 *(ex1453)* 11/7/42.
2719 *(ex1587)* 14/10/44.
3174 *(ex1473)* 16/11/46.
27593 *(new)* 24/11/51.
27710 *(ex4743)* 28/8/54.
25829 *(new)* 22/8/59.

SHEDS:
West Hartlepool.
Haverton Hill 7/11/38.
Blaydon 28/3/43.
Heaton 7/11/48.
Hull Dairycoates 11/2/52.

RENUMBERED:
4709 23/6/46.
64709 16/11/48.

CONDEMNED:
23/11/62.
Cut up at Darlington.

1459

Darlington.

To traffic 12/11/26.

REPAIRS:
Dar. 11/1-6/3/29.**G.**
Ghd. 18/6-12/8/31.**G.**
Dar. 11/11-16/12/32.**L.**
Gor. 26/1-17/2/34.**G.**
Dar. 3/4-9/5/36.**G.**
Dar. 28/7/38.*Weigh.*
Dar. 10/1-16/2/39.**G.**
Dar. 6/10-6/11/41.**G.**
Cow. 21/3-29/4/44.**G.**
Dar. 22/3-4/5/46.**L.**
Cow. 27/12/46-1/3/47.**G.**
Cow. 27/9-29/10/49.**H/I.**
Cow. 11/4-28/6/52.**G.**
Cow. 14/8-4/10/56.**G.**
Cow. 8-16/11/56.**N/C.**

BOILERS:
1919.
2310 *(ex1491)* 17/2/34.
8014 *(ex2717)* 9/5/36.
2571 *(ex1468)* 16/2/39.
2303 *(ex1425)* 6/11/41.
C1719 *(ex1880)* 29/4/44.
27563 *(ex4895)* 28/6/52.
27594 *(ex64706)* 4/10/56.

SHEDS:
West Hartlepool.
Haverton Hill 7/11/38.
Blaydon 28/3/43.
Tweedmouth 8/9/43.
Darlington 23/7/45.
Middlesbrough 13/6/48.
Darlington 25/6/50.
Neville Hill 3/9/50.
Borough Gardens 1/7/51.
Gateshead 14/6/59.
Sunderland 1/11/59.

RENUMBERED:
4710 4/5/46.
64710 28/10/49.

CONDEMNED:
17/4/61.
Cut up at Cowlairs.

1481

Darlington.

To traffic 17/11/26.

REPAIRS:
Dar. 8/3-16/5/28.**G.**
Ghd. 12/12/29-7/2/30.**G.**
Dar. 1/11-9/12/32.**G.**
Dar. 26/10-24/11/34.**G.**
Dar. 3/4-6/5/36.*Tender only.*
Dar. 17/9-29/10/36.**G.**
Dar. 31/5-4/9/39.**G.**
Dar. 21/2-19/3/40.**L.**
Dar. 20/5-2/7/40.**L.**
Dar. 12/10-6/11/42.**G.**
Cow. 1-24/2/45.**G.**
Dar. 21/3-18/4/46.**L.**
Cow. 20/6-23/8/47.**G.**
Cow. 5/10-12/11/49.**L/I.**
Dar. 12-15/9/50.**N/C.**
Cow. 18/4-10/5/52.**G.**
Cow. 12/8-3/9/55.**L/I.**
Cow. 16/4-11/5/57.**G.**

BOILERS:
1920.
2340 *(new)* 9/12/32.
2143 *(ex1270)* 29/10/36.
8014 *(ex1459)* 4/9/39.
2141 *(ex1469)* 6/11/42.
2717 *(ex1418)* 24/2/45.
27523 *(ex spare & 2733)* 10/5/52.
27632 *(new)* 11/5/57.

SHEDS:
West Hartlepool.
Darlington 28/3/43.
Blaydon 3/8/43.

1481 cont.
Tweedmouth 28/2/48.

RENUMBERED:
4711 18/4/46.
64711 10/11/49.

CONDEMNED:
23/5/62.
Cut up at Cowlairs.

1484

Darlington.

To traffic 30/11/26.

REPAIRS:
Don. 1/2-8/3/29.**G.**
Gor. 20/11-31/12/31.**G.**
Gor. 27/5-22/6/35.**G.**
Gor. 30/12/36-23/1/37.**L.**
Don. 27/10-23/11/38.**G.**
Gor. 29/5-22/6/40.**L.**
Don. 19/10/41-24/1/42.**G.**
Gor. 12/12/43-12/2/44.**G.**
Gor. 15/7-26/10/46.**G.**
Gor. 11/10-22/12/48.**G.**
Dby. 25/6-24/8/51.**G.**
Gor. 3/12/53-16/1/54.**G.**
Gor. 19-28/1/54.**N/C.**
Gor. 3-9/2/54.**N/C.**
Gor. 7/10-17/11/56.**G.**
Gor. 28/5-5/7/58.**C/H.**

BOILERS:
1921.
8026 *(ex1298)* 31/12/31.
2291 *(ex2696)* 22/6/35.
1916 *(ex1494)* 12/2/44.
2300 *(ex2780)* 26/10/46.
BP140 *(ex2693)* 22/12/48.
27672 *(ex2698)* 24/8/51.
25807 *(ex4835)* 16/1/54.
27780 *(ex4893)* 17/11/56.

SHEDS:
Immingham.
Stratford 13/10/27.
Bradford 8/8/33.
Doncaster 21/8/33.
Ardsley 17/10/33.
March 12/2/36.
Ardsley 29/2/36.
Doncaster 19/10/41.
Gorton 21/8/43.
Lincoln 13/6/54.
Tuxford 26/9/54.
Lincoln 9/1/55.
Boston 9/11/58.
Colwick 1/3/59.

RENUMBERED:
4712 17/8/46.
64712 22/12/48.

CONDEMNED:
4/2/60.
Cut up at Stratford

1492

Darlington.

To traffic 2/12/26.

REPAIRS:
Imm. 19/5-15/7/27.**L.***New pistons.*
Don. 17/1-2/3/29.**G.**
Gor. 30/5-27/6/31.**G.**
Gor. 2-23/6/34.**G.**
Gor. 11-25/5/35.**L.**
Gor. 6-27/3/37.**G.**
Gor. 6-27/5/39.**G.**
Don. 19/6-12/7/41.**G.**
Cow. 19/5-5/6/43.**G.**
Don. 7/8-25/9/43.**H.**
Gor. 13/10-17/11/45.**G.**
Gor. 31/5-14/6/47.**L.**
Gor. 19/6-7/8/48.**G.**
Dby. 7/3-30/4/51.**G.**
Cow. 1-31/12/53.**L/I.**
Cow. 1/5-7/6/58.**G.**

BOILERS:
822.
8004 *(ex1233)* 27/6/31.
8591 *(ex2973)* 23/6/34.
8011 *(ex1287)* 27/3/37.
8004 *(ex1287)* 27/5/39.
2690 *(ex2996)* 25/9/43.
8583 *(ex1495)* 17/11/45.
825 *(ex2700)* 7/8/48.
27804 *(new)* 30/4/51.
27453 *(ex65911)* 7/6/58.

SHEDS:
Immingham.
Doncaster 28/2/40.
Hull Dairycoates 2/9/51.
Blaydon 30/11/52.
Borough Gardens 4/1/53.
Heaton 16/6/57.
Gateshead 14/6/59.
North Blyth 15/1/61.
Sunderland 11/6/61.

RENUMBERED:
4713 15/6/46.
64713 7/8/48.

CONDEMNED:
18/4/62.
Cut up at Darlington.

1493

Darlington.

To traffic 3/12/26.

REPAIRS:
Don. 28/1-20/2/29.**G.**
Gor. 17/10-15/11/30.**G.**
Gor. 16/6-15/7/33.**G.**
Dar. 29/7-6/9/35.**G.**
Gor. 6-29/1/38.**G.**
Gor. 13/8-5/10/40.**G.**
Gor. 21/8-30/10/43.**G.**
Gor. 25/11/45-16/2/46.**G.**
Gor. 10/12/47-11/2/48.**G.**
Dby. 5/12/50-8/2/51.**L/I.**
Dby. 12-14/2/51.**N/C.**
Dby. 22/2-8/3/51.**N/C.**
Dby. 20/3-13/4/51.**C/L.**
Gor. 17-18/4/52.*Weigh.*
Dby. 25/8-10/10/52.**G.**
Str. 16/5-18/6/55.**G.**

BOILERS:
1922.
8022 *(ex1289)* 15/7/33.
2182 *(ex2694)* 6/9/35.
2123 *(ex1266)* 29/1/38.
2093 *(ex1259)* 5/10/40.
2119 *(ex2706)* 30/10/43.
2766 *(ex2779)* 16/2/46.
2932 *(ex1903)* 11/2/48.
27723 *(ex4719)* 10/10/52.
27696 *(ex4906)* 18/6/55.

SHEDS:
Immingham.
Gorton 13/2/31.
Lincoln 10/6/31.
Ardsley 6/7/39.
Doncaster 19/10/41.
New England 16/4/42.
Gorton 10/6/43.
Liverpool 6/4/47.
Gorton 13/5/48.
Lincoln 13/6/54.
Retford 4/1/59.

RENUMBERED:
4714 22/6/46.
E4714 11/2/48.
64714 8/2/51.

CONDEMNED:
22/5/59.
Cut up at Stratford.

1494

Darlington.

To traffic 10/12/26.

REPAIRS:
Don. 28/1-6/4/29.**G.**
Gor. 27/5-4/7/31.**G.**
Gor. 26/3-5/5/34.**G.**
Gor. 31/8-21/9/34.**L.**
Gor. 20/4-8/5/37.**G.**
Gor. 24/5-1/6/37.**N/C.**
Don. 5-16/6/37.**N/C.**
Gor. 16/8-14/10/39.**G.**
Don. 12/10-27/12/41.**G.**
Gor. 28/10/43-22/1/44.**G.**
Gor. 9/6-28/9/46.**G.**
Gor. 23/1-19/3/49.**G.**
Gor. 25/4-8/5/49.**N/C.**
Dby. 6/9-19/10/51.**H/I.**
Str. 16/3-1/5/54.**G.**
Gor. 14/1-16/2/57.**G.**
Gor. 22/2-2/3/57.**N/C.**
Gor. 28/1-8/3/58.**C/L.**
Str. 5/3/59.*Not repaired.*

BOILERS:
823.
2186 *(ex2785)* 5/5/34.
823 *(ex2964)* 8/5/37.
1916 *(ex1453)* 14/10/39.
2108 *(ex1281)* 22/1/44.
3171 *(ex3090)* 28/9/46.
2690 *(ex3094)* 19/3/49.
27886 *(ex4759)* 1/5/54.
27585 *(ex4707)* 16/2/57.

SHEDS:
Immingham.
Lincoln 16/6/29.
Immingham 29/7/29.
Lincoln 23/1/44.
Immingham 17/6/45.
Lincoln 23/9/45.
Colwick 10/7/55.

RENUMBERED:
4715 23/6/46.
64715 19/3/49.

CONDEMNED:
6/5/59.
Cut up at Stratford.

1495

Darlington.

To traffic 14/12/26.

REPAIRS:
Don. 5/1-16/2/29.**G.**
Don. 12/2-13/3/30.**G.**
Gor. 13-30/1/32.**G.**
Gor. 17/12/34-12/1/35.**G.**
Gor. 2-24/7/36.**G.**
Don. 28/11-31/12/38.**G.**
Gor. 20/4-6/5/39.**L.**
Gor. 16/9-18/11/39.**L.**
Gor. 26/4-27/6/42.**G.**
Gor. 20-25/7/42.**N/C.**
Gor. 31/8-11/9/42.**L.**
Gor. 14/7-6/10/45.**G.**
Gor. 17/4-1/6/46.**G.**
Gor. 12/12/46-8/3/47.**G.**
Gor. 17/4-30/10/47.**C/H.**
Gor. 13/3-20/5/50.**G.**
Gor. 2-3/6/50.**N/C.**
Dby. 1/2-19/3/51.**H/I.**
Dby. 12/12/52-16/1/53.**L/I.**
Dby. 29/1-12/2/53.**N/C.**
Gor. 30/7-28/10/54.**C/L.**
Gor. 2/3-2/4/55.**C/L.**
Gor. 17/8-8/10/55.**G.**
Gor. 21/8-3/10/57.**G.**
Gor. 15-16/10/57.**N/C.**

Nos. 2711 to 2730 were part of an order, but as they were to be used by the Great Eastern Section of Southern Area, they were fitted with Westinghouse air brake for train working. This broadside photograph clearly shows the whistle mounted on a pipe protruding from the front of the cab. Number was on the tender for the first ten but 2721 onwards always had it on the cab sides. *W.H.Whitworth*

The remaining twelve of the order, 2731 to 2742 were allocated to Scottish Area and their tenders were the larger 4200 gallons type. These were the first J39s to be fitted with the safer whistle arrangement, with it placed above an isolating valve and mounted directly on the firebox. 2731 is seen at its home shed, Eastfield in Glasgow. *J.J.Cunningham*

The next order was for twenty-seven, the first sixteen nos.2770-85 allocated to Southern Area, followed by eight nos.1418/25/29, 1466/70/87/89/91 for North Eastern Area, all those having steam and vacuum brakes, and the 3500 gallons tender. The last three 2786, 2787/8, were similar except that their tender was the larger 4200 gallons type. No. 1429 is seen at Carlisle London Road shed, having worked from Blaydon. *J.J.Cunningham*

On the next fifteen, 2962 to 2976, there were three differences of detail to note. They were the first to be fitted with improved drop grate gear (which did not need a semi-circular cover on the running plate), and although the boilers on the first ten had the usual two handholes, 2972 onwards were affected by Gresley's decision to try changing to four plugs for washing out. The third alteration was the move of the upper lamp iron to a more accessible position on the smokebox door. *C.L.Turner*

After the order comprising the last built with four washout plugs, the next order was for twelve, all built from March to December 1934, and for the North Eastern Area. Gresley had decided against washout plugs, so there was reversion to two handholes on each side, and new tenders of 3500 gallons type were built for the first seven nos. 1412/63/7/8/72/88/90. These engines were the last new ones to have circular cover plate to each piston valve on their steam chest. 1467 here in works is, as yet, "No old at all". *J.W.Armstrong*

1495 cont.
BOILERS:
824.
1921 *(ex1484)* 30/1/32.
8582 *(ex2964)* 12/1/35.
8585 *(ex2966)* 24/7/36.
8583 *(ex2771)* 27/6/42.
E1354 *(ex1903)* 6/10/45.
BP143 *(ex1538)* 1/6/46.
8773 *(ex2963)* 30/10/47.
2641 *(ex2721)* 20/5/50.
27741 *(ex4718)* 16/1/53.
27794 *(new)* 8/10/55.
25811 *(ex4736)* 3/10/57.

SHEDS:
Immingham.
Lincoln 16/6/29.
Immingham 30/10/29.
March 3/9/30.
Colwick 5/3/36.
Gorton 11/4/36.
Annesley 30/10/43.
Colwick 30/3/47.
Boston 9/11/58.
Doncaster 1/3/59.

RENUMBERED:
4716 1/6/46.
64716 20/5/50.

CONDEMNED:
5/4/61.
Cut up at Doncaster.

1270

Darlington.

To traffic 11/3/27 (with Bolton superheater).

REPAIRS:

Dar. 21-30/4/27.**L.**
Dar. 27/8-22/11/27.**L.**
Don. 26/4-28/5/29.**G.**
Don. 8/5-20/6/31.**G.**
Bolton superheater removed.
Gor. 19/1-10/2/34.**G.**
Dar. 7/5-3/7/36.**G.**
Gor. 11/4-12/5/38.**G.**
Gor. 13/1-16/3/40.**G.**
Gor. 22/7-12/10/40.**L.**
Gor. 10/1-1/5/43.**G.**
Gor. 23-31/5/43.**N/C.**
Gor. 6/12/44-6/1/45.**G.**
Str. 3/3-1/6/46.**G.**
Gor. 22/1-28/2/48.**L.**
Gor. 19/2-2/4/49.**G.**
Gor. 23/4-7/5/49.**N/C.**
Dby. 23/11/51-17/1/52.**G.**
Gor. 27/2-10/4/54.**G.**
Gor. 15/12/56-12/1/57.**G.**
Gor. 3-31/5/58.**C/H.**
Gor. 30/7/60.*Not repaired.*

BOILERS:
1931.
2143 *(ex2717)* 10/2/34.
118 *(ex1489)* 3/7/36.
2113 *(ex2695)* 12/5/38.
8008 *(ex1290)* 1/5/43.
2945 *(ex3086)* 2/4/49.
27689 *(ex4748)* 17/1/52.
27803 *(ex4840)* 10/4/54.
27577 *(ex4916)* 12/1/57.

SHEDS:
Newport.
New Holland 13/12/27.
Newport 6/2/28.
Immingham 10/2/28.
Sheffield 18/3/39.
Gorton 5/4/41.

RENUMBERED:
4717 6/4/46.
E4717 28/2/48.
64717 5/2/49.

CONDEMNED:
2/8/60.
Cut up at Gorton.

1496

Darlington.

To traffic 12/4/27.

REPAIRS:
Don. 27/7-6/9/29.**G.**
Gor. 7/8-19/9/31.**G.**
Gor. 31/10-3/11/32.**L.**
Gor. 23/11-9/12/33.**G.**
Dar. 16/8-19/9/35.**G.**
Gor. 10-29/1/38.**G.**
Gor. 2/6-6/7/40.**G.**
Gor. 4/10-19/12/42.**G.**
Gor. 29/10-18/11/44.**L.**
Gor. 27/5-11/8/45.**G.**
Gor. 25/1-8/3/48.**G.**
Dby. 26/10-8/12/50.**L/I.**
Dby. 12/9-24/10/52.**G.**
Dby. 30/10-18/11/52.**N/C.**
Gor. 18/6-30/7/55.**G.**
Gor. 29/3-26/4/58.**G.**
Gor. 1-8/8/59.**C/L.** *After collision.*
Gor. 11/3/61.*Weigh.*
Gor. 3/2/62.*Not repaired.*

BOILERS:
826.
2110 *(ex2710)* 19/9/31.
2114 *(ex2704)* 9/12/33.
822 *(ex1269)* 19/9/35.
2216 *(ex2702)* 29/1/38.
2290 *(ex2783)* 6/7/40.
8025 *(ex1275)* 19/12/42.
2666 *(ex2709)* 11/8/45.
4933 *(new)* 8/3/48.
27725 *(ex4799)* 24/10/52.
27841 *(new)* 30/7/55.
25802 *(ex4966)* 26/4/58.

SHEDS:
Gorton.
March 2/7/30.
Ardsley 8/8/30.
Gorton 13/8/30.
Trafford Park 4/2/38.
Gorton 13/1/40.
Barnsley 20/10/46.
Gorton 27/4/47.

RENUMBERED:
4718 9/6/46.
E4718 8/3/48.
64718 8/12/50.

CONDEMNED:
7/2/62.
Cut up at Gorton.

1497

Darlington.

To traffic 14/4/27.

REPAIRS:

Don. 17/9-4/10/29.**G.**
Gor. 16/2-12/3/32.**G.**
Gor. 25/6-14/7/34.**G.**
Gor. 17/8-5/9/36.**G.**
Gor. 29/3-29/4/39.**G.**
Gor. 26/7-19/9/42.**G.**
Gor. 7/3-28/4/45.**G.**
Gor. 10/7-30/11/46.**G.**
Gor. 17/10-19/12/47.**G.**
Gor. 6/2-25/3/50.**G.**
Gor. 31/3-1/4/50.**N/C.**
Dby. 29/10-20/12/51.**G.**
Str. 30/8-9/10/54.**G.**
Gor. 31/10-14/12/57.**G.**
Gor. 21-23/12/57.**N/C.**

BOILERS:
825.
2191 *(new)* 12/3/32.
8020 *(ex1286)* 14/7/34.
2277 *(ex2775)* 5/9/36.
8026 *(ex2727)* 29/4/39.
2772 *(ex2953)* 19/9/42.
2698 *(ex1269)* 28/4/45.
1917 *(ex2705)* 19/12/47.
E1352 *(ex4823)* 25/3/50.
27685 *(ex4712)* 20/12/51.
27675 *(ex4708)* 9/10/54.
27881 *(ex4977)* 14/12/57.

SHEDS:
Gorton.
Liverpool 23/4/27.
Gorton 20/5/29.
Liverpool 29/11/29.
Gorton 30/3/31.
Trafford Park 3/3/37.
Gorton 5/1/38.
Trafford Park 27/10/39.
Gorton 16/11/41.
Annesley 30/10/43.
Colwick 30/3/47.
Peterborough 5/10/52.
Sheffield 7/12/58.
West Auckland 11/9/60.
Ardsley 17/6/62.

RENUMBERED:
4719 1/9/46.
64719 25/3/50.

CONDEMNED:
23/11/62.
Cut up at Darlington.

1498

Darlington.

To traffic 28/4/27.

REPAIRS:
Don. 18/9-17/10/29.**G.**
Gor. 2-31/12/31.**G.**
Gor. 13/11-1/12/33.**G.**
Gor. 7-20/6/35.**G.**
Gor. 18/10-6/11/37.**G.**
Don. 20-29/9/38.**L.**
Gor. 29/10-30/11/40.**G.**
Gor. 23/9/42-23/1/43.**G.**
Gor. 18/7-13/10/45.**G.**
Gor. 10/9-21/11/47.**G.**
Gor. 23/11/49-21/1/50.**G.**
Gor. 19/10-18/12/51.**G.**
Gor. 11/8-29/9/54.**H/I.**
Gor. 23/1-17/3/56.**C/L.**
Gor. 7-30/3/57.**C/L.**
Gor. 26/6-23/8/58.**G.**
Gor. 15/8/61.*Not repaired.*

BOILERS:
1923
*1923 renumbered 8003.**
826 *(ex1496)* 31/12/31.
2184 *(ex1233)* 1/12/33.
1921 *(ex1495)* 20/6/35.
2102 *(ex2704)* 6/11/37.
2123 *(ex1493)* 30/11/40.
8585 *(ex2697)* 13/10/45.
4929 *(new)* 21/11/47.
4984 *(new)* 21/1/50.
27686 *(ex4750)* 18/12/51.
25842 *(new)* 23/8/58.

SHEDS:
Gorton.
March 2/7/30.
Ardsley 6/8/30.
Gorton 19/8/30.
Trafford Park 5/1/38.
Gorton 3/6/38.
Trafford Park 11/10/38.
Gorton 29/8/39.
Annesley 30/10/43.
Colwick 30/3/47.
Ardsley 20/5/51.

RENUMBERED:
4720 28/7/46.

1498 cont.
64720 21/1/50.

CONDEMNED:
8/9/61.
Cut up at Gorton.

** Boilers renumbered to Doncaster series 8003 to 8026 had been built by Darlington and by Armstrong, Whitworth to numbers they had given them.*

1233

Darlington.

To traffic 3/5/27.

REPAIRS:
Don. 28/5-25/6/29.**G.**
Gor. 8/5-6/6/31.**G.**
Gor. 17/7-5/8/33.**G.**
Dar. 28/8-2/10/35.**G.**
Gor. 2-20/6/36.**L.**
Gor. 28/2-19/3/38.**G.**
Gor. 8-25/3/39.**L.**
Gor. 16/12/39-24/2/40.**G.**
Gor. 15/3-6/6/42.**G.**
Gor. 28/6-5/7/42.**N/C.**
Gor. 19/11/44-6/1/45.**G.**
Gor. 15/2-28/9/47.**G.**
Gor. 2/8-18/10/50.**L/I.**
Dby. 17/3-24/5/51.**C/H.**
Str. 29/3-29/5/53.**G.**
Gor. 1/1-3/3/56.**G.**

BOILERS:
827.
827 renumbered 8004.
2184 *(new)* 6/6/31.
8021 *(ex1287)* 5/8/33.
2641 *(new)* 2/10/35.
2302 *(ex1275)* 19/3/38.
2218 *(ex1277)* 24/2/40.
8026 *(ex1275)* 6/1/45.
4925 *(new)* 28/9/47.
27778 *(ex4961)* 29/5/53.
27779 *(ex4967)* 3/3/56.

SHEDS:
Gorton.
Trafford Park 16/10/33.
Gorton 16/8/35.
Trafford Park 3/6/38.
Gorton 27/10/39.
Doncaster 2/5/45.

RENUMBERED:
4721 7/4/46.
64721 18/10/50.

CONDEMNED:
15/2/60.
Cut up at Stratford.

1255

Darlington.

To traffic 10/5/27.

REPAIRS:
Gor. 10/1-23/3/29.**G.**
Gor. 3/7-1/8/31.**G.**
Gor. 11-30/9/33.**G.**
Dar. 4/10-6/11/35.**G.**
Gor. 16/8-4/9/37.**G.**
Don. 24/11-2/12/38.**L.**
Gor. 24/5-22/6/40.**G.**
Gor. 10/1-29/5/43.**G.**
Gor. 20/3-19/5/45.**G.**
Gor. 2/9-29/11/47.**G.**
Dby. 27/6-27/9/50.**L/I.**
Dby. 3/12/52-23/1/53.**G.**
Dby. 1-20/2/53.**N/C.**
Str. 19/3-6/5/55.**G.**
Gor. 3/1-1/3/58.**G.**

BOILERS:
1926.
1926 renumbered 8005.
2132 *(ex2714)* 30/9/33.
2114 *(ex1496)* 6/11/35.
2188 *(ex2721)* 4/9/37.
2114 *(ex1275)* 22/6/40.
2193 *(ex2982)* 29/5/43.
2210 *(ex1267)* 19/5/45
8774 *(ex2704)* 29/11/47.
27740 *(ex4831)* 23/1/53.
27716 *(ex4805)* 6/5/55.
27801 *(ex4702)* 1/3/58.

SHEDS:
Gorton.
Liverpool 20/5/29.
Gorton 29/11/29.
Trafford Park 1/9/36.
Gorton 1/7/37.
Trafford Park 26/2/38.
Gorton 27/9/38.
Lincoln 16/9/45.
Doncaster 4/1/59.

RENUMBERED:
4722 28/4/46.
64722 27/9/50.

CONDEMNED:
15/2/60.
Cut up at Stratford.

1263

Darlington.

To traffic 10/5/27.

REPAIRS:
Don. 16/1-21/2/29.**G.**
Gor. 8/7-16/8/30.**G.**
Gor. 25/7-12/8/32.**G.**
Gor. 11/4-5/5/34.**G.**
Gor. 2-23/5/36.**G.**
Don. 22/9-27/10/38.**G.**
Don. 15-16/11/38.**L.**
Don. 10/7-18/9/41.**G.**
Gor. 17/5-10/6/42.**L.**
Gor. 16-28/8/43.*Tender only.*
Gor. 4/6-29/7/44.**G.**
Gor. 24/3-18/5/46.**G.**
Gor. 27/9/47-22/1/48.**G.**
Gor. 12/2-12/3/49.**C/L.**
Gor. 3/1-25/2/50.**G.**
Gor. 6-22/4/50.**C/L.**
Gor. 10/10-11/11/50.**C/L.**
Str. 27/10-5/12/53.**G.**
Gor. 28/2-6/4/57.**G.**
Gor. 9-10/4/57.**N/C.**

BOILERS:
831.
831 renumbered 8007.
8018 *(ex1281)* 12/8/32.
2218 *(ex2725)* 5/5/34.
2112 *(ex2703)* 23/5/36.
2309 *(ex1272)* 29/7/44.
RS120 *(ex3000)* 22/1/48.
4913 *(ex1539)* 25/2/50.
27878 *(ex4737)* 5/12/53.
25837 *(new)* 6/4/57.

SHEDS:
Gorton.
Trafford Park 16/11/41.
Colwick 11/3/51.
Stockport 5/8/51.
Colwick 12/10/52.
Peterborough 12/10/52.
Lincoln 7/12/58.
Doncaster 1/3/59.

RENUMBERED:
4723 7/4/46.
E4723 22/1/48.
64723 29/1/49.

CONDEMNED:
24/3/61.
Cut up at Doncaster.

1259

Darlington.

To traffic 10/5/27.

REPAIRS:
Don. 4/11/29-18/1/30.**G.**
Gor. 2/7-24/8/32.**G.**
Dar. 10/1-19/3/36.**G.**
Gor. 13/3-14/5/38.**G.**
Gor. 7/7-23/8/40.**G.**
Cow. 29/1-12/9/43.**G.**
Str. 12-29/11/44.**L.**
Str. 28/3-12/6/46.**G.**
Don. 23/5-1/8/48.**G.**
Dby. 14/6-17/8/51.**G.**
Str. 14/2-2/4/54.**G.**
Str. 8/3-28/7/56.**C/L.**
Str. 28/4-7/6/57.**G.**
Str. 20-28/6/56.**C/L.**

BOILERS:
1928.
1928 renumbered 8006.
8010 *(ex1267)* 24/8/32.
2138 *(ex2704)* 19/3/36.
2093 *(ex2709)* 14/5/38.
2220 *(ex2698)* 23/8/40.
27673 *(ex64713)* 17/8/51.
27820 *(new)* 2/4/54.
27685 *(ex4729)* 7/6/57.

SHEDS:
Ardsley.
March 19/3/36.
Carlisle 8/6/38.
March 5/9/38.
Cambridge 12/12/40.
March 9/3/41.
Norwich 29/8/43.
Ipswich 7/11/43.
Norwich 30/4/50.
Lowestoft 18/10/53.
Norwich 24/1/54.
Ipswich 9/10/55.

RENUMBERED:
4724 7/6/46.
64724 31/7/48.

CONDEMNED:
8/2/60.
Cut up at Stratford.

1265

Darlington.

To traffic 13/5/27.

REPAIRS:
Don. 29/6-26/7/29.**G.**
Str. 22/11-31/12/30.**L.**
Gor. 27/1-20/2/32.**G.**
Gor. 22/3-14/4/34.**G.**
Dar. 28/5-9/7/36.*Not repaired. Sent to Gorton.*
Gor. 16/7-7/8/36.**G.**
Gor. 5-28/1/39.**G.**
Don. 8/11-13/12/41.**G.**
Gor. 18/7-12/8/44.**G.**
Gor. 17/2-3/3/45.**L.**
Gor. 24/3-12/4/47.**G.**
Gor. 1-26/2/49.**G.**
Dby. 28/2-30/3/51.**G.**
Cow. 9/10-8/12/53.**H/I.**
Cow. 21/5-12/6/54.**C/L.**
Cow. 24/1-10/3/56.**G.**
Cow. 30/5-24/6/60.**C/L.**

WORKS CODES:- Cow - Cowlairs. Dar - Darlington. Dby - Derby. Don - Doncaster. Ghd - Gateshead. Gor - Gorton. Imm - Immingham. Inv - Inverurie. Str - Stratford.
REPAIR CODES:- **C/H** - Casual Heavy. **C/L** - Casual Light. **G** - General. **H**- Heavy. **H/I** - Heavy Intermediate. **L** - Light. **L/I** - Light Intermediate. **N/C** - Non-Classified.

The other five to that order, 1475 to 1479, began with North Eastern 4125 gallons tenders released by the Raven Pacifics 2400-4 being upgraded to 5000 gallons 8-wheeled tenders. Darlington then changed those five spare tenders from green to black, but did not increase the height of the vertical handrails on them. On the engines, 1475 did begin a change on the steam chest which then became standard. Instead of each piston valve having its own circular cover, a single plate combining the two was now fitted, and on it, the footstep between the valve heads was retained. 1475 shedded at Newport is working one of the cheap day excursion trains from Middlesbrough, and is headed for either Leeds or Bradford. *WBY collection*

BOILERS:
832.
832 renumbered 8008.
8012 *(ex1269)* 20/2/32.
2145 *(ex2730)* 14/4/34.
8589 *(ex2968)* 7/8/36.
2094 *(ex2970)* 28/1/39.
2106 *(ex1295)* 12/8/44.
2674 *(ex1273)* 26/2/49.
27661 *(new)* 30/3/51.
27542 *(ex4897)* 10/3/56.

SHEDS:
Immingham.
Stratford 13/10/27.
Bradford 7/8/33.
Doncaster 1/9/33.
Trafford Park 26/9/33.
Gorton 16/10/33.
Trafford Park 13/12/42.
Gorton 30/9/45.
Sheffield 17/10/47.
Lincoln 25/9/49.
Hull Dairycoates 2/9/51.
Selby 10/10/54.
Neville Hill 15/9/57.
Selby 26/7/59.
York 13/9/59.
Thornaby 13/12/59.

RENUMBERED:
4725 30/3/46.
64725 26/2/49.

CONDEMNED:
22/10/61.
Cut up at Cowlairs.

1266

Darlington.

To traffic 18/5/27.

REPAIRS:
Don. 23/7-5/9/29.**G.**
Gor. 30/1-12/3/32.**G.**
Gor. 17/11-15/12/34.**G.**
Gor. 9/8-4/9/37.**G.**
Gor. 17/2-6/4/40.**G.**
Str. 14/10-5/12/42.**G.**
Str. 18/6-21/7/44.**L.**
Str. 29/7-13/10/45.**G.**
Str. 21/3-24/5/48.**G.**
Gor. 10/2-4/3/50.**C/L.**
Dby. 6/4-16/5/51.**G.**
Str. 20/9-24/10/53.**G.**
Str. 23/7-14/9/56.**G.**

BOILERS:
835.
835 renumbered 8009.
824 *(ex1495)* 12/3/32.
2123 *(ex1267)* 15/12/34.
2273 *(ex2965)* 4/9/37.
2302 *(ex1233)* 6/4/40.
2188 *(ex2951)* 5/12/42.
2689 *(ex2699)* 13/10/45.
2205 *(ex1933)* 24/5/48.
27663 *(ex2732)* 16/5/51.
27876 *(ex4937)* 24/10/53.
27785 *(ex4785)* 14/9/56.

SHEDS:
Immingham.
Stratford 14/10/27.
Southend 15/3/30.
Stratford 26/4/30.
Ipswich 24/10/41.
March 31/12/41.
Norwich 16/7/43.
Ipswich 24/10/43.
Lowestoft 30/4/46.
Norwich 26/3/47.
Ipswich 9/5/54.
Melton Constable 15/6/58.
Lowestoft 19/10/58.
Lincoln 30/11/58.

RENUMBERED:
4726 19/5/46.
64726 24/5/48.

CONDEMNED:
22/11/60.
Cut up at Doncaster.

1267

Darlington.

To traffic 20/5/27.

REPAIRS:
Don. 29/6-3/8/29.**G.**
Don. 13/2-5/3/32.**G.**
Gor. 3-24/11/34.**G.**
Gor. 18/9-9/10/37.**G.**
Gor. 15-29/6/40.**G.**
Gor. 28/7-22/8/42.**G.**
Str. 27/1-18/3/44.**G.**
Cow. 17/3-21/4/45.**G.**
Gor. 2-30/10/48.**G.**
Dby. 22/11-28/12/50.**H/I.**
Cow. 29/10-10/11/51.**L/I.**
Cow. 30/11-19/12/53.**G.**
Cow. 19/8-10/9/55.**H/I.**
Cow. 16-17/9/55.**N/C.**
Cow. 31/7-1/8/56.**N/C.**
Cow. 12/8-4/9/57.**G.**
Gor. 8-29/5/59.**C/H.**
Cow. 14/1-4/3/61.**G.**
Cow. 21-22/2/62.**N/C.**
Cow. 3-19/4/62.*Boiler only.*

BOILERS:
834.
834 renumbered 8010.
2123 *(ex2709)* 5/3/32.
2284 *(ex1268)* 24/11/34.
2103 *(ex2722)* 9/10/37.
2666 *(ex2946)* 29/6/40.
2210 *(ex2780)* 22/8/42.
2103 *(ex2707)* 21/4/45.
4943 *(new)* 30/10/48.
27455 *(ex64884)* 19/12/53.
27558 *(ex4855)* 4/9/57.
27572 *(ex4971)* 4/3/61.
27594 *(ex64710)* 19/4/62.

SHEDS:
Immingham.
Stratford 14/10/27.
March 28/2/40.
Stratford 9/6/43.
Parkeston 19/1/46.
Stratford 8/6/46.
Parkeston 25/9/47.
Gorton 16/10/49.
Trafford Park 18/10/49.
Carlisle 7/1/51.
Gorton 8/11/58.
Woodford 30/7/62.

RENUMBERED:
4727 6/4/46.
64727 30/10/48.

CONDEMNED:
15/10/62.
Cut up at Darlington.

1272

Darlington.

To traffic 25/5/27.

REPAIRS:
Don. 5/6-4/7/29.**G.**
Gor. 7/8-10/10/31.**G.**
Gor. 12/2-8/3/34.**G.**
Dar. 22/4-28/5/36.**G.**
Don. 10/11-7/12/38.**G.**
Don. 24/8-26/10/41.**G.**
Gor. 12/3-29/4/44.**G.**
Gor. 22/2-9/3/46.**G.**
Str. 19/11/46-13/2/47.**G.**
Gor. 8/8-18/9/48.**L.**
Gor. 22/2-9/4/49.**G.**
Dby. 12/1-14/3/51.**H/I.**
Dby. 19-21/3/51.**N/C.**
Str. 14/5-4/7/53.**G.**
Gor. 13/6-18/8/56.**G.**

BOILERS:
829.
829 renumbered 8013.
8015 *(ex1274)* 10/10/31.
1917 *(ex1457)* 8/3/34.
2309 *(ex1455)* 28/5/36.
2318 *(ex2952)* 29/4/44.
4968 *(new)* 9/4/49.
27784 *(ex4967)* 4/7/53.
27760 *(ex4962)* 18/8/56.

SHEDS:
Immingham.
Ardsley 4/7/29.
Immingham 19/8/29.
Lincoln 26/7/30.
Gorton 20/2/35.
Lincoln 16/9/45.
Boston 9/11/58.

RENUMBERED:
4728 7/4/46.
64728 9/4/49.

CONDEMNED:
22/2/60.
Cut up at Gorton.

1273

Darlington.

To traffic 28/5/27.

REPAIRS:
Don. 24/6-10/8/29.**G.**
Gor. 7/2-14/7/31.**G.**
Gor. 6-20/5/33.**G.**
Dar. 12/7-2/9/35.**G.**
Gor. 1-22/1/38.**G.**
Gor. 8-29/6/40.**G.**
Cow. 5-23/6/43.**G.**
Gor. 22/10/45-2/3/46.**G.**
Gor. 2/12/48-5/2/49.**G.**
Dby. 4/1-18/2/52.**L/I.**
Str. 17/10-27/11/54.**G.**
Str. 4-20/12/55.**C/L.**
Str. 24/2-5/3/57.**G.**
Str. 17/2-21/3/58.**C/L.**

BOILERS:
828.
828 renumbered 8014.
2113 *(ex2703)* 20/5/33.
2660 *(new)* 2/9/35.
2665 *(ex2942)* 22/1/38.
2674 *(ex2976)* 29/6/40.
2214 *(ex2975)* 5/2/49.
27685 *(ex4719)* 27/11/54.
27885 *(ex4889)* 5/3/57.

SHEDS:
Immingham.
Lincoln 26/7/30.
Colwick 19/12/38.
Darlington 6/11/43.
Colwick 5/4/45.
New England 18/8/46.
Colwick 19/3/50.
Ardsley 1/4/51.
Tuxford 27/9/53.
Stratford 16/1/55.
Cambridge 15/5/55.
March 28/9/58.
Lincoln 7/12/58.
Boston 25/1/59.
Colwick 8/11/59.

RENUMBERED:
4729 14/4/46.
64729 5/2/49.

CONDEMNED:
14/3/61.
Cut up at Doncaster.

1268

Darlington.

To traffic 28/5/27.

REPAIRS:
Don. 27/7-24/8/29.**G.**
Don. 8-27/2/32.**G.**
Gor. 9-20/10/34.**G.**
Gor. 3-10/12/34.**L.**
Gor. 14-26/1/35.**G.**
Gor. 17/2-12/3/37.**G.**
Gor. 19/8-30/9/39.**G.**
Str. 30/4-21/7/42.**G.**
Str. 1/8-15/9/45.**G.**
Gor. 9/2-10/4/48.**G.**
Gor. 8-15/4/50.**L.**
Dby. 11/12/50-8/2/51.**G.**
Cow. 13/1-20/2/54.**L/I.**
Cow. 19/10-17/11/56.**G.**
Cow. 3-15/12/56.**C/L.**
Cow. 14-30/3/57.**N/C.**
Cow. 24/4-11/5/57.**N/C.**

BOILERS:
839.
839 renumbered 8011.
2284 *(ex2776)* 27/2/32.
8019 *(ex2775)* 20/10/34.
8583 *(ex2965)* 26/1/35.
2097 *(ex1282)* 12/3/37.
2205 *(ex2704)* 30/9/39.
8775 *(ex2715)* 15/9/45.
2122 *(ex2727)* 10/4/48.
27655 *(ex4803)* 8/2/51.
27590 *(ex64946)* 17/11/56.

SHEDS:
Immingham.
Stratford 14/10/27.
Colwick 5/6/43.
Norwich 14/1/46.
Stratford 2/7/47.
Parkeston 16/1/49.
Lincoln 4/6/50.
Hull Dairycoates 2/9/51.
Neville Hill 17/11/51.
Selby 26/9/54.
Neville Hill 15/9/57.
Thornaby 1/11/59.

RENUMBERED:
4730 31/3/46.
64730 10/4/48.

CONDEMNED:
16/11/62.
Cut up at Darlington.

1269

Darlington.

To traffic 30/5/27.

REPAIRS:
Don. 17/9-12/10/29.**G.**
Gor. 10/12/31-16/1/32.**G.**
Gor. 26/11-15/12/34.**G.**
Gor. 21/1-13/2/37.**G.**
Gor. 22/10-16/12/39.**G.**
Str. 8/3-16/6/42.**G.**
Str. 31/12/44-17/3/45.**G.**
Str. 3/12/47-1/3/48.**G.**
Gor. 9/5-7/7/48.**H.**
W.P.U. removed.
Gor. 12-23/7/48.**N/C.**
Dby. 31/1-19/3/51.**G.**
Str. 13/9-10/10/53.**G.**
Str. 17/3-20/5/54.**C/L.**
Str. 9/3-20/4/56.**C/L.**
Str. 2/8-21/9/56.**G.**

BOILERS:
840.
840 renumbered 8012.
822 *(ex1492)* 16/1/32.
8008 *(ex1295)* 15/12/34.
2203 *(ex2772)* 13/2/37.
8774 *(ex1286)* 16/12/39.
2698 *(ex2990)* 16/6/42.
2218 *(ex1233)* 17/3/45.
27660 *(new)* 19/3/51.
27650 *(ex4841)* 10/10/53.
27870 *(ex4802)* 21/9/56.

SHEDS:
Immingham.
Stratford 8/10/27.
March 28/2/40.
Stratford 27/5/43.
Norwich 14/1/46.

RENUMBERED:
4731 31/3/46.
E4731 1/3/48.
64731 3/7/48.

CONDEMNED:
27/7/59.
Cut up at Stratford.

WORKS CODES:- Cow - Cowlairs. Dar - Darlington. Dby - Derby. Don - Doncaster. Ghd - Gateshead. Gor - Gorton. Imm - Immingham. Inv - Inverurie. Str - Stratford.
REPAIR CODES:- **C/H** - Casual Heavy. **C/L** - Casual Light. **G** - General. **H**- Heavy. **H/I** - Heavy Intermediate. **L** - Light. **L/I** - Light Intermediate. **N/C** - Non-Classified.

With trade recovering, in four months from June 1935 Darlington built another twenty-seven nos. 2941-53 and 2981-94 for Southern Area and all with new 4200 gallons tender. Again there was a slight change, but it was not perceptible. They were fitted only with vacuum brake, both for engine and for train working, and that then became standard for the subsequent additions to the class. That same order included twelve for North Eastern Area nos. 1436/60/4/5/73/4/85/6, 1504/5/6 and 1584 which were completed in October to December 1935, and only differed in that their tender was the smaller 3500 gallons type. *W.H.Whitworth*

Darlington then got an order for another thirty-four, but were so busy building B17 and K3 classes that twenty-eight of them were cancelled, and had to be ordered from contractors to get the required delivery dates. The six which Darlington did build, in August 1936, were 2995 to 3000 with 4200 gallons tender and allocated to Southern Area. *WBY collection*

The order on contractors was placed with Beyer, Peacock for nine with 4200 gallons tender numbered between 1803 and 1870, and all for Southern Area; they were delivered in September and October 1936.

Those contractors also supplied North Eastern Area with sixteen numbered from 1532 to 1587, and three nos. 1875/80/94 went to Scottish Area, all these having 3500 gallons tender. They went into traffic from October 1936 to May 1937. *WBY collection*

Before the end of 1936 Darlington were able to accept an order for 38 more J39 class, the first twelve with 3500 gallons tender for North Eastern Area numbered in the 1508 to 1560 range. They were not all exactly alike, although discernible difference was limited. Only the first one, no.1508 had the usual 9" x 5" standard number plate on the centre splasher. Starting with no.1509, out on 25th January 1938 that plate was superseded by a Doncaster style brass plate on the side of the smokebox, but showing the running, and not a works number.

Three of the twelve, nos. 1509/35/37 were fitted with Babcock & Wilcox fusion welded boiler instead of the normal riveted plated type, but there was no external difference to be seen. Although those three boilers continued to be used in normal service until 1961/62, they remained the only ones so constructed. The new tender to be coupled to the last of those twelve, no.1560, was delayed in being completed, so that engine ran in traffic from 7th April to 11th November 1938 with a spare 4200 gallons stepped top type. Built for J38 class no.1419 in 1926, it had since served J39 no.1471, and then V2 class no.4777 before helping out on 1560, after which it went to another new V2 no.4813 where it was used to August 1942. *WBY collection*

The order for 38 was completed by six for Scottish Area nos. 1804/8/35/62/3/96 and then twenty for Southern Area all coupled with 4200 gallons tender. Of the latter, nos. 1898, 1903/22/6/7/8/30 had the hitherto usual low front plate on the tender. *W.H.Whitworth*

Starting with no.1933 out at the end of May 1938 there was a modification to the tender. On the remaining thirteen (to no.1997) the front plate was 1' 8" further forward, and 11" higher in the centre so as to include an access coal gate. Originally slatted with 2" horizontal spacing, during the war it had to be changed to a solid door to hold back the small coal size then having to be used. *WBY collection*

1274

Darlington.

To traffic 30/5/27.

REPAIRS:
Don. 16/2-6/4/29.**G.**
Gor. 21/8-26/9/31.**G.**
Gor. 27/11-16/12/33.**G.**
Dar. 27/1-9/3/36.**G.**
Gor. 18/7-13/8/38.**G.**
Gor. 15/2-5/4/41.**G.**
Gor. 29/12/41-31/1/42.**H.**
Gor. 23/2-28/3/42.**L.**
After collision.
Gor. 11/5-20/6/42.**L.**
After collision.
Don. 31/1-16/8/43.**H.**
Fractured frame.
Gor. 4/6-5/8/44.**G.**
Gor. 31/12/45-24/5/46.**G.**
Gor. 16/10-31/12/47.**L.**
Gor. 28/8-4/11/49.**G.**
Gor. 8-10/11/49.**N/C.**
Dby. 28/9-7/11/51.**H/I.**
Gor. 3/7-4/9/54.**G.**
Gor. 30/11/57-4/1/58.**G.**
Gor. 19/8/61.*Not repaired.*

BOILERS:
830.
830 renumbered 8015.
8013 *(ex1272)* 26/9/31.
2129 *(ex2713)* 16/12/33.
826 *(ex2726)* 9/3/36.
2138 *(ex1259)* 13/8/38.
RS118 *(ex2777)* 5/4/41.
8589 *(ex2706)* 31/1/42.
8009 *(ex1952)* 5/8/44.
3213 *(ex2967)* 24/5/46.
2595 *(ex2985)* 4/11/49.
25813 *(ex4977)* 4/9/54.
27838 *(ex4827)* 4/1/58.

SHEDS:
Immingham.
Gorton 17/2/28.
Trafford Park 27/9/38.
Gorton 17/2/39.
Northwich 5/12/43.
Sheffield 1/1/44.
Barnsley 27/10/46.
Colwick 27/4/47.
Cricklewood 15/12/49.
Stratford 11/3/51.
Cricklewood 1/4/51.
Ardsley 16/3/52.

RENUMBERED:
4732 15/5/46.
64732 4/11/49.

CONDEMNED:
25/8/61.
Cut up at Gorton.

1277

Darlington.

To traffic 8/6/27.

REPAIRS:
Don. 15/6-11/7/29.**G.**
Gor. 25/9-7/11/31.**G.**
Gor. 26/1-24/2/34.**G.**
Dar. 8/6-10/7/36.*Not repaired.*
Sent to Gorton.
Gor. 16/7-8/8/36.**G.**
Gor. 20/7-12/8/39.**G.**
Str. 4/6-29/8/42.**G.**
Gor. 19/5-7/7/45.**G.**
Str. 7/12/46-13/6/47.**G.**
Gor. 20/9-6/11/48.**G.**
Cow. 12/4-2/5/51.**H/I.**
Cow. 18/2-8/3/53.**G.**
Cow. 1/8-1/9/56.**L/I.**
Cow. 20/3-17/4/59.**G.**

BOILERS:
841.
841 renumbered 8017.
2122 *(ex2708)* 7/11/31.
2109 *(ex2702)* 24/2/34.
2218 *(ex1263)* 8/8/36.
2222 *(ex2692)* 12/8/39.
8015 *(ex2951)* 7/7/45.
4916 *(ex2731)* 6/11/48.
27491 *(ex64917)* 8/3/53.
27528 *(ex4847)* 17/4/59.

SHEDS:
Immingham.
Doncaster 5/8/32.
Immingham 9/9/32.
Sheffield 27/11/34.
Retford 6/12/34.
Sheffield 14/4/36.
Retford 1/9/36.
Doncaster 23/8/39.
Stratford 4/7/40.
Parkeston 19/1/46.
Stratford 8/6/46.
Gorton 12/10/49.
Trafford Park 16/10/49.
Stockport 22/5/50.
Carlisle 7/1/51.

RENUMBERED:
4733 6/4/46.
64733 6/11/48.

CONDEMNED:
19/10/61.
Cut up at Cowlairs.

1275

Darlington.

To traffic 9/6/27.

REPAIRS:
Don. 22/6-19/7/29.**G.**
Gor. 28/10-21/11/31.**G.**
Gor. 14/2-16/3/34.**G.**
Gor. 9/4-6/5/36.**G.**
Gor. 20/12/37-15/1/38.**G.**
Gor. 18/2-6/4/40.**G.**
Gor. 30/8-24/10/42.**G.**
Gor. 19/3-7/4/44.**L.**
Gor. 4/10-25/11/44.**G.**
Gor. 11/4-7/6/46.**G.**
Gor. 27/4-13/10/47.**G.**
Gor. 27/10-11/12/48.**L.**
Gor. 26/8-17/9/49.**C/L.**
Dby. 24/11/50-15/1/51.**L/I.**
Dby. 6/7-9/9/52.**G.**
Str. 9-18/9/54.**C/L.**
Gor. 16/6-5/8/55.**G.**
Gor. 9/1-22/2/58.**C/L.**
Str. 14/5/59.*Not repaired.*

BOILERS:
833.
833 renumbered 8016.
8017 *(ex1277)* 21/11/31.
1931 *(ex1270)* 16/3/34.
2302 *(ex2771)* 6/5/36.
2114 *(ex1255)* 15/1/38.
8025 *(ex2702)* 6/4/40.
8026 *(ex1497)* 24/10/42.
2112 *(ex1263)* 25/11/44.
2683 *(ex2775)* 13/10/47.
27717 *(ex4802)* 9/9/52.
27842 *(new)* 5/8/55.

SHEDS:
Immingham.
Lincoln 19/6/29.
Gorton 19/2/35.
Trafford Park 26/5/36.
Gorton 14/6/37.
Trafford Park 26/9/38.
Gorton 30/11/39.
Lincoln 16/9/45.
Immingham 22/12/46.
Lincoln 27/4/47.
Tuxford 6/12/53.
Lincoln 14/2/54.

RENUMBERED:
4734 14/4/46.
64734 11/12/48.

CONDEMNED:
18/5/59.
Cut up at Stratford.

1281

Darlington.

To traffic 10/6/27.

REPAIRS:
Don. 1-26/7/29.**G.**
Gor. 5-28/5/32.**G.**
Gor. 26/9-13/10/34.**G.**
Gor. 19/10-7/11/36.**G.**
Gor. 6-22/12/36.**L.**
Gor. 12/4-6/5/39.**G.**
Gor. 22/5-1/6/39.**N/C.**
Don. 28/8-30/10/41.**G.**
Gor. 28/12/42-8/5/43.**G.**
Gor. 24/9-30/10/43.**L.**
Gor. 25-27/10/44.**N/C.**
Gor. 8-24/3/45.**L.**
Str. 6/1-15/3/46.**G.**
Gor. 6/6-31/7/48.**G.**
Gor. 6-27/8/49.**C/L.**
Gor. 21/2-29/4/50.**C/H.**
Dby. 23/8-10/10/51.**G.**
Dby. 10/11-2/12/52.**C/L.**
Gor. 11/6-17/8/53.**C/L.**
Str. 1/5-18/6/54.**G.**
Gor. 10/12/56-2/2/57.**G.**
Don. 7/9/57.*Weigh.*
Gor. 28/10-14/12/57.**C/L.**
Str. 29/7/59.*Not repaired.*

BOILERS:
836.
836 renumbered 8018.
8009 *(ex1266)* 28/5/32.
8003 *(ex2709)* 13/10/34.
2223 *(ex2776)* 7/11/36.
2108 *(ex1296)* 6/5/39.
2113 *(ex1270)* 8/5/43.
2274 *(ex2723)* 15/3/46.
2689 *(ex1266)* 31/7/48.
27677 *(ex4828)* 10/10/51.
27676 *(ex4789)* 18/6/54.
27756 *(ex4755)* 2/2/57.

SHEDS:
Immingham.
Lincoln 14/12/29.
Colwick 25/9/35.
Gorton 8/2/37.
Trafford Park 29/8/39.
Gorton 30/4/41.
Barnsley 20/10/46.
Colwick 27/4/47.
Tuxford 27/9/53.
Colwick 16/1/55.

RENUMBERED:
4735 14/4/46.
64735 31/7/48.

CONDEMNED:
3/8/59.
Cut up at Stratford.

1282

Darlington.

To traffic 16/6/27.

REPAIRS:
Don. 27/7-21/8/29.**G.**
Gor. 6/10-14/11/31.**G.**
Gor. 23/3-21/4/34.**G.**
Gor. 4/9-3/10/36.**G.**
Don. 24/11-17/12/38.**G.**
Gor. 30/3-28/6/41.**G.**
Cow. 3/2-19/3/44.**G.**
Gor. 21/10-11/11/44.**G.**

Gor. 11/6-28/7/45.**L.**
Str. 1/11/46-22/2/47.**G.**
Gor. 6/5-3/6/48.**L.**
Gor. 21/11/48-5/2/49.**G.**
Dby. 5/10-13/11/51.**G.**
Dby. 27/3-2/5/52.**C/L.**
Str. 5-21/3/53.**N/C.**
Gor. 25/3-15/5/54.**G.**
Gor. 18-25/5/54.**N/C.**
Gor. 29-31/5/54.**N/C.**
Gor. 3-8/6/54.**N/C.**
Gor. 12/4-18/5/57.**G.**

BOILERS:
1933.
1933 renumbered 8019.
2189 *(new)* 14/11/31.
2097 *(ex2700)* 21/4/34.
2145 *(ex1265)* 3/10/36.
8006 *(ex2966)* 17/12/38.
8020 *(ex2969)* 28/6/41.
RS122 *(ex1475)* 19/3/44.
2191 *(ex1984)* 5/2/49.
27680 *(ex1930)* 13/11/51.
25811 *(ex4872)* 15/5/54.
27886 *(ex4715)* 18/5/57.

SHEDS:
Immingham.
Lincoln 22/6/35.
Peterborough 10/7/55.
Sheffield 7/12/58.
Colwick 13/3/60.

RENUMBERED:
4736 31/3/46.
64736 29/5/48.

CONDEMNED:
10/7/61.
Cut up at Doncaster.

1286

Darlington.

To traffic 23/6/27.

REPAIRS:
Don. 24/8-25/9/29.**G.**
Gor. 7/8-19/9/31.**G.**
Gor. 18/5-7/6/34.**G.**
Gor. 30/9-22/10/36.**G.**
Gor. 21/2-8/3/38.**L.**
Gor. 13/9-11/11/39.**G.**
Gor. 24/9-21/11/42.**G.**
Gor. 18/3-9/6/45.**G.**
Gor. 30/9-16/12/47.**G.**
Dby. 3/8-3/10/50.**L/I.**
Dby. 20-25/10/50.**N/C.**
Str. 6/6-15/8/53.**G.**
Gor. 10/6-4/8/56.**G.**
Don. 25/8/59.*Not repaired.*

BOILERS:
838.
838 renumbered 8020.
2108 *(ex2701)* 7/6/34.
8774 *(ex2710)* 22/10/36.
2097 *(ex1268)* 11/11/39.
8588 *(ex2962)* 21/11/42.
8587 *(ex2774)* 9/6/45.
2210 *(ex1255)* 16/12/47.
27872 *(ex4901)* 15/8/53.
27654 *(ex4907)* 4/8/56.

SHEDS:
Copley Hill.
Ardsley 2/12/36.
Grantham 12/7/40.
Gorton 26/3/41.
Liverpool 3/5/43.
Gorton 5/11/43.
Northwich 5/12/43.
Sheffield 1/1/44.
Doncaster 22/9/46.

RENUMBERED:
4737 7/4/46.
64737 3/10/50.

CONDEMNED:
25/8/59.
Cut up at Doncaster.

1287

Darlington.

To traffic 23/6/27.

REPAIRS:
Don. 29/8-3/10/29.**G.**
Gor. 14/3-9/4/32.**G.**
Gor. 15/1-2/2/35.**G.**
Gor. 30/12/36-23/1/37.**G.**
Gor. 22/3-22/4/39.**G.**
Don. 18/6-16/8/41.**G.**
Gor. 26/12/43-26/2/44.**G.**
Str. 6/1-25/5/46.**G.**
Gor. 5/2-3/8/47.**G.**
Gor. 5/3-29/4/50.**G.**
Gor. 3-16/5/50.**N/C.**
Dby. 29/10-9/12/52.**G.**
Dby. 18/12/52-15/1/53.**N/C.**
Gor. 19/12/53.**C/L.**
Gor. 22/10-26/11/55.**G.**
Gor. 18/1-15/2/58.**C/H.**
Gor. 8/10/60.*Not repaired.*

BOILERS:
1929.
1929 renumbered 8021.
825 *(ex1497)* 9/4/32.
8011 *(ex1296)* 2/2/35.
8004 *(ex2781)* 23/1/37.
8582 *(ex2969)* 22/4/39.
4918 *(ex1980)* 26/2/44.
2132 *(ex2981)* 25/5/46.
3193 *(ex3095)* 29/4/50.
27734 *(ex4951)* 9/12/52.
25815 *(ex4732 & spare)* 26/11/55.

SHEDS:
Gorton.
Leicester 22/7/27.
Annesley 14/3/35.
Colwick 9/8/43.
New England 18/8/46.
Lincoln 11/6/50.
Gorton 11/3/51.
Peterborough 21/6/53.
New England 13/9/53.
Gorton 27/9/53.
Sheffield 13/6/54.
Gorton 17/11/57.

RENUMBERED:
4738 25/5/46.
64738 29/4/50.

CONDEMNED:
26/10/60.
Cut up at Gorton.

1289

Darlington.

To traffic 30/6/27.

REPAIRS:
Gor. 26/3-3/5/30.**G.**
Gor. 17/3-13/4/33.**G.**
Dar. 1/11-13/12/35.**G.**
Gor. 8/11-4/12/37.**G.**
Gor. 12-22/12/37.**N/C.**
Gor. 27/12/37-5/1/38.**N/C.**
Gor. 1/11-30/12/39.**G.**
Gor. 26/1-28/2/42.**G.**
Gor. 23/6-2/9/44.**G.**
Gor. 25/6-1/9/45.**L.**
Gor. 17/2-27/9/47.**G.**
Gor. 20/5-25/6/49.**C/L.**
Gor. 1/5-22/7/50.**G.**
Gor. 28-29/7/50.**N/C.**
Gor. 20/5-27/6/53.**G.**
Gor. 30/4-15/5/54.**C/L.**
Gor. 18/3-2/4/55.**C/L.**
Gor. 15/8-8/10/55.**C/L.**
Gor. 11/4-26/5/56.**G.**
Gor. 8-29/6/57.**C/L.**
Gor. 4-26/10/57.**C/L.**
Gor. 2/11-20/12/58.**G.**

BOILERS:
837.
837 renumbered 8022.
8007 *(ex1263)* 13/4/33.
2294 *(ex1290)* 13/12/35.
1921 *(ex1498)* 4/12/37.
8586 *(ex2724)* 30/12/39.
2136 *(ex2770)* 28/2/42.
RS118 *(ex2784)* 2/9/44.
2922 *(ex2785)* 27/9/47.
8583 *(ex4974)* 22/7/50.
27765 *(ex4962)* 27/6/53.
27698 *(ex4878)* 26/5/56.
27843 *(ex4749)* 20/12/58.

SHEDS:
Doncaster.
Ardsley 21/7/27.
Copley Hill 22/8/29.
Ardsley 7/10/29.
Bradford 30/1/31.
Ardsley 10/8/31.
Annesley 15/11/34.
Colwick 9/8/43.
Gorton 3/10/43.
Annesley 30/10/43.
Colwick 30/3/47.
Annesley 3/11/57.

RENUMBERED:
4739 26/5/46.
64739 25/6/49.

CONDEMNED:
31/10/62.
Cut up at Derby.

1290

Darlington.

To traffic 16/7/27.

REPAIRS:
Don. 10/1-8/2/30.**G.**
Don. 14/11-10/12/32.**G.**
Dar. 24/9-30/10/35.**G.**
Gor. 8-26/3/38.**G.**
Gor. 6/4-18/5/40.**G.**
Gor. 18/9-14/11/42.**G.**
Gor. 25/11-12/12/42.**N/C.**
Gor. 24/12/44-3/3/45.**G.**
Gor. 19/5-31/7/46.**G.**
Gor. 25/5-7/9/47.**G.**
Gor. 17/7-3/9/49.**G.**
Dby. 10/10-23/11/51.**G.**
Gor. 22/8-31/10/53.**H/I.**
Gor. 28/8-10/10/56.**G.**
Gor. 4-12/3/59.**C/L.**
Gor. 9/10-10/11/59.**L/I.**
Gor. 18-22/1/60.**N/C.**

BOILERS:
1960.
1960 renumbered 8023.
2294 *(ex2780)* 10/12/32.
2312 *(ex1487)* 30/10/35.
2641 *(ex1233)* 26/3/38.
8008 *(ex2722)* 18/5/40.
E1350 *(ex1898)* 14/11/42.
4908 *(ex1856)* 3/3/45.
3210 *(ex1813)* 7/9/47.
2109 *(ex4878)* 3/9/49.
27682 *(ex4840)* 23/11/51.
27722 *(ex4898)* 10/10/56.

SHEDS:
Ardsley.
Retford 11/2/36.
York 19/6/38.
Retford 23/8/38.
Gorton 19/11/38.
Trafford Park 21/8/40.
Gorton 30/9/45.

The final order for J39 class, placed in January 1940 was for eighteen, and they were intended to have new 4200 gallons tenders built with them. Instead, steel shortage caused second-hand North Eastern tenders (from passenger engines, which had just been, or were about to be withdrawn) having to be found for them. Eight nos. 3081-7/9 were coupled with 3650 gallons tenders which had been built for D17 class in 1893 and 1896. *LNER*

RENUMBERED:
4740 5/5/46.
64740 3/9/49.

CONDEMNED:
11/9/62.
Cut up at Gorton.

1295

Darlington.

To traffic 16/7/27.

REPAIRS:
Gor. 7/4-17/5/30.**G.**
Gor. 6/6-2/7/32.**G.**
Gor. 20/7-4/8/34.**G.**
Gor. 5-21/11/36.**G.**
Gor. 18/1-4/2/39.**G.**
Don. 16/8-16/11/41.**G.**
Gor. 13/5-22/7/44.**G.**
Gor. 26/8-22/2/47.**G.**
Gor. 12-25/4/47.**L.**
Gor. 21/6-20/8/49.**G.**
Gor. 16/9-1/10/49.**N/C.**
Gor. 12-29/10/49.**N/C.**
Dby. 19/3-28/4/52.**G.**
Gor. 5/7-16/9/54.**G.**
Gor. 10/1-2/3/57.**C/L.**
Gor. 2/5-15/6/57.**G.**
Gor. 18-27/6/57.**N/C.**
Str. 19/5/60.*Not repaired.*

BOILERS:
1962.
1962 renumbered 8024.
8008 *(ex1265)* 2/7/32.
8012 *(ex1265)* 4/8/34.
8020 *(ex1497)* 21/11/36.
2106 *(ex2723)* 4/2/39.
2138 *(ex1296)* 22/7/44.
2208 *(ex2781)* 22/2/47.
3203 *(ex1296)* 20/8/49.
27694 *(ex4832)* 28/4/52.
27833 *(new)* 16/9/54.
25801 *(ex4911)* 15/6/57.

SHEDS:
Ardsley.
Stratford 8/10/27.
Colwick 30/5/33.
Trafford Park 10/4/34.
Gorton 30/12/35.
Liverpool 8/2/37.
Gorton 5/11/38.
Trafford Park 17/2/39.
Gorton 21/8/40.
Bidston 3/1/50.
Gorton 10/1/50.
Lincoln 26/9/54.
Colwick 10/7/55.
Boston 9/11/58.
Lincoln 1/3/59.

RENUMBERED:
4741 18/5/46.
64741 20/8/49.
CONDEMNED:
11/7/60.
Cut up at Stratford.

1296

Darlington.

To traffic 31/8/27.

REPAIRS:
Don. 6/3-10/4/30.**G.**
Gor. 31/3-30/4/32.**G.**
Gor. 22/5-14/6/34.**G.**
Gor. 28/10-14/11/36.**G.**
Gor. 15/3-8/4/39.**G.**
Gor. 19/3-24/5/41.**G.**
Gor. 16/4-27/5/44.**G.**
Gor. 2/8-6/10/45.**G.**
Gor. 1/9/46-18/1/47.**G.**
Gor. 9-15/2/47.**N/C.**
Gor. 9/5-1/7/49.**G.**
Dby. 22/11/51-25/1/52.**H/I.**
Gor. 7/5-6/6/53.**C/L.**
Gor. 11-27/2/54.**C/L.**
Gor. 22-24/4/54.**C/L.**
Gor. 18/10-27/11/54.**G.**
Gor. 20/11-21/12/57.**G.**

BOILERS:
1966.
1966 renumbered 8025.
8011 *(ex1268)* 30/4/32.
8016 *(ex1298)* 14/6/34.
2108 *(ex1286)* 14/11/36.
8775 *(ex2728)* 8/4/39.
2138 *(ex1274)* 24/5/41.
3203 *(ex2994)* 27/5/44.
4971 *(new)* 1/7/49.
4971 Reno. 27764 6/6/53.
25814 *(ex4988)* 27/11/54.
27787 *(ex4909)* 21/12/57.

SHEDS:
Ardsley.
Stratford 8/10/27.
Southend 25/1/30.
Stratford 1/2/30.
Colwick 31/5/33.
Trafford Park 28/3/34.
Gorton 27/5/36.
Liverpool 26/7/41.
Gorton 5/11/43.
Woodford 1/6/60.

RENUMBERED:
4742 26/5/46.
64742 1/7/49.

CONDEMNED:
20/7/62.
Cut up at Gorton.

1298

Darlington.

To traffic 2/9/27.

REPAIRS:
Don. 27/2-13/4/29.**G.**
Gor. 23/10-5/12/31.**G.**
Gor. 14/3-7/4/34.**G.**
Dar. 27/3-7/5/36.**G.**
Gor. 1-26/6/37.**G.**
Gor. 11-27/5/38.**L.**
Don. 7/11-2/12/38.**H.**
Gor. 17/11/40-11/1/41.**G.**
Gor. 13/2-13/5/44.**G.**
Gor. 5-29/9/45.**L.**
Gor. 21/3-3/7/47.**G.**
Gor. 9-31/7/47.**L.**
Gor. 16/11-24/12/48.**L.**
Gor. 9/11/49-7/1/50.**G.**
Dby. 2/6-7/8/52. **H/I.**
Gor. 13/3-3/4/54.**G.**
Gor. 18/8-22/9/56.**G.**
Gor. 31/12/60.*Not repaired.*

BOILERS:
1969.
1969 renumbered 8026.
8016 *(ex1275)* 5/12/31.
2122 *(ex1277)* 7/4/34.
2318 *(ex1429)* 7/5/36.
2287 *(ex2691)* 26/6/37.

2284 *(ex2711)* 11/1/41.
2291 *(ex1484)* 13/5/44.
E1351 *(ex2782)* 3/7/47.
4982 *(new)* 7/1/50.
4982 Reno. 27710 7/8/52.
27653 *(ex4979)* 3/4/54.
27784 *(ex4728)* 22/9/56.

SHEDS:
Immingham.
Gorton 20/2/28.

RENUMBERED:
4743 11/5/46.
64743 24/12/48.

CONDEMNED:
13/1/61.
Cut up at Gorton.

2691

Darlington.

To traffic 20/7/28.

REPAIRS:
Gor. 7/11-13/12/30.**G.**
Gor. 17-26/9/31.**L.**
Gor. 29/11-30/12/32.**G.**
Gor. 22/5-7/7/33.**L.**
Gor. 23/11-8/12/34.**G.**
Gor. 2-27/3/37.**G.**
Gor. 11/9-11/11/39.**G.**
Gor. 24/2-26/4/41.**G.**
Gor. 24/1-1/4/44.**G.**
Gor. 9/9-28/10/44.**L.**
Gor. 16/5-18/10/47.**G.**
Dby. 23/4-28/6/51.**H/I.**
Gor. 30/5-27/6/53.**G.**
Gor. 12/11-17/12/55.**G.**
Gor. 25/4-23/5/59.**H/I.**

BOILERS:
2095.
2273 *(ex2772)* 30/12/32.
2287 *(ex2770)* 8/12/34.
8017 *(ex2778)* 27/3/37.
8013 *(ex2780)* 11/11/39.
8582 *(ex1287)* 1/4/44.
4927 *(new)* 18/10/47.
27763 *(ex4798)* 27/6/53.
27516 *(ex4845 & spare)* 17/12/55.

SHEDS:
Gorton.
Liverpool 14/8/35.
Gorton 8/2/37.
Trafford Park 14/6/37.
Gorton 26/9/38.
Trafford Park 13/1/40.
Gorton 13/4/47.
Sheffield 13/6/54.
Gorton 17/11/57.

RENUMBERED:
4744 10/12/46.
64744 2/10/48.

CONDEMNED:
22/3/62.
Cut up at Gorton.

2692

Darlington.

To traffic 18/7/28.

REPAIRS:
Gor. 20/3-25/4/31.**G.**
Gor. 17/3-13/4/33.**G.**
Gor. 12-23/2/35.**G.**
Gor. 25/3-24/4/37.**G.**
Don. 22/9-15/10/38.**G.**
Don. 27/7-21/9/41.**G.**
Don. 6-13/11/43.**L.**
Gor. 13/4-20/5/44.**G.**
Gor. 8/9-2/4/47.**G.**
Gor. 8-11/6/47.**N/C.**
Gor. 12/3-12/5/48.**L.**
Gor. 25/4-4/6/49.**G.**
Gor. 28-30/7/49.**N/C.**
Dby. 15/10-12/12/50.**H/I.**
Dby. 9/10-12/11/52.**G.**
Gor. 15/10-10/12/55.**G.**
Gor. 10-17/3/56.**C/L.**
After collision.
Gor. 22/11-20/12/58.**G.**
Gor. 4/11/61.*Not repaired.*

BOILERS:
2094.
8023 *(ex1290)* 13/4/33.
2205 *(ex2722)* 23/2/35.
2299 *(ex2785)* 24/4/37.
8013 *(ex2691)* 20/5/44.
2601 *(ex2970)* 2/4/47.
8008 *(ex1270)* 4/6/49.
27728 *(ex4736)* 12/11/52.
27799 *(new)* 10/12/55.
27835 *(ex4837)* 20/12/58.

SHEDS:
Gorton.
Trafford Park 16/8/35.
Gorton 3/3/37.
Trafford Park 1/7/37.
Gorton 11/10/38.
Liverpool 5/11/38.
Gorton 26/7/41.

RENUMBERED:
4745 10/1/47.
64745 12/5/48.

CONDEMNED:
8/11/61.
Cut up at Gorton.

2693

Darlington.

To traffic 20/7/28.

REPAIRS:
Gor. 8/5-6/6/31.**G.**
Gor. 7-29/7/33.**G.**
Dar. 24/9-29/10/35.**G.**
Gor. 16/3-9/4/38.**G.**
Gor. 31/5-6/7/40.**G.**
Gor. 14/6-7/8/43.**G.**
Gor. 25/12/45-25/5/46.**G.**
Gor. 20/8-23/10/48.**G.**
Dby. 15/2-24/3/52.**H/I.**
Gor. 22/12/53-6/2/54.**G.**
Gor. 9-13/2/54.**N/C.**
Gor. 7/5-23/6/56.**G.**

BOILERS:
2097
2182 *(new)* 6/6/31.
2121 *(ex2707)* 29/7/33.
2095 *(ex2695)* 29/10/35.
2132 *(ex2971)* 9/4/38.
2675 *(ex2985)* 6/7/40.
2767 *(ex2780)* 7/8/43.
BP140 *(ex2719)* 25/5/46.
2688 *(ex2722)* 23/10/48.
2688 Reno.27705 24/3/52.
25809 *(ex4904)* 6/2/54.
27755 *(ex4798)* 23/6/56

SHEDS:
Gorton.
Trafford Park 30/12/35.
Gorton 26/2/38.
New England 22/9/38.
Boston 28/9/38.
Grantham 16/4/45.
New England 9/2/47.
Sheffield 22/1/50.
Colwick 13/3/60.

RENUMBERED:
4746 31/10/46.
64746 23/10/48.

CONDEMNED:
20/2/61.
Cut up at Doncaster.

2694

Darlington.

To traffic 1/8/28.

REPAIRS:
Gor. 6/3-25/4/31.**G.**
Gor. 24/7-12/8/33.**G.**
Dar. 12/7-22/8/35.**G.**
Gor. 30/4-29/5/37.**G.**
Gor. 3/7-19/8/39.**G.**
Don. 29/9-26/12/41.**G.**
Don. 6/7-30/10/43.**G.**
Gor. 18/11/45-2/2/46.**G.**
Gor. 21/6-21/8/48.**G.**
Gor. 9/9-16/10/48.**N/C.**
Dby. 12/4-24/5/51.**G.**
Dby. 14/1-20/2/52.**C/L.**
Gor. 7/5-20/6/53.**C/L.**
Gor. 30/9-31/10/53.**G.**
Gor. 8/10-6/11/54.**C/L.**
Gor. 3/2-29/3/56.**G.**
Gor. 28/11/58-10/1/59.**G.**

BOILERS:
2093.
2182 *(ex2693)* 12/8/33.
8023 *(ex2692)* 22/8/35.
2300 *(ex2720)* 29/5/37.
8011 *(ex1492)* 19/8/39.
3208 *(new)* 26/12/41.
3209 *(ex1927)* 2/2/46.
4907 *(ex1538)* 21/8/48.
27664 *(ex4903)* 24/5/51.
25803 *(ex4980)* 31/10/53.
27593 *(ex4709)* 29/3/56.
27840 *(ex4820)* 10/1/59.

SHEDS:
Gorton.
Liverpool 5/6/31.
Gorton 21/6/33.
Colwick 4/11/33.
Annesley 2/12/33.
Colwick 30/3/47.
Annesley 3/11/57.
Gorton 28/8/59.
Woodford 1/6/60.

RENUMBERED:
4747 8/12/46.
64747 21/8/48.

CONDEMNED:
5/11/62.
Sold for scrap in December 1964 to T.W.Ward, Killamarsh after being stationary boiler at Woodford 11/62 to 10/64.

2695

Darlington.

To traffic 6/8/28.

REPAIRS:
Gor. 14/11-27/12/30.**G.**
Gor. 18/3-1/4/31.**L.**
Gor. 27/11-19/12/31.**L.**
Gor. 1-24/3/33.**G.**
Dar. 9/9-11/10/35.**G.**
Gor. 13/1-5/2/38.**G.**
Gor. 2/7-17/8/40.**G.**
Gor. 30/9-5/12/42.**G.**
Gor. 15-18/12/42.**N/C.**

WORKS CODES:- Cow - Cowlairs. Dar - Darlington. Dby - Derby. Don - Doncaster. Ghd - Gateshead. Gor - Gorton. Imm - Immingham. Inv - Inverurie. Str - Stratford.
REPAIR CODES:- **C/H** - Casual Heavy. **C/L** - Casual Light. **G** - General. **H**- Heavy. **H/I** - Heavy Intermediate. **L** - Light. **L/I** - Light Intermediate. **N/C** - Non-Classified.

For the other ten, nos. 3088/90-8, D21 class 1237-46 provided 4125 gallons tenders built in 1908/9, but were not the self-trimming type. Their deeper side panels enabled them to be identified. *A.G.Ellis*

Gor. 17/6-25/8/45.**G.**
Gor. 17/1-5/3/49.**G.**
Dby. 19/10-12/12/51.**G.**
Gor. 12/6-10/7/54.**G.**
Gor. 5/1-2/2/57.**G.**
Gor. 30/6/61.*Not repaired.*

BOILERS:
2099.
2095 *(ex2691)* 24/3/33.
2113 *(ex1273)* 11/10/35.
8019 *(ex2712)* 5/2/38.
2132 *(ex2693)* 17/8/40.
8590 *(ex2709)* 5/12/42.
C1711 *(ex1922)* 25/8/45.
4967 *(new)* 5/3/49.
27684 *(ex4891)* 12/12/51.
25812 *(ex4825)* 10/7/54.
27575 *(ex65921)* 2/2/57.

SHEDS:
Gorton.
Liverpool 21/6/33.
Gorton 14/8/35.
New England 23/9/38.
Boston 6/10/38.
New England 16/4/45.
Gorton 11/12/49.

RENUMBERED:
4748 13/1/47.
64748 5/3/49.

CONDEMNED:
1/7/61.
Cut up at Gorton.

2696

Darlington.

To traffic 8/8/28.

REPAIRS:
Gor. 18/6-2/8/30.**G.**
Gor. 16/1-16/2/33.**G.**
Gor. 1-13/4/35.**G.**
Gor. 7/6-3/7/37.**G.**
Gor. 15/5-10/6/39.**G.**
Don. 10/9-10/11/41.**G.**
Don. 11/10-19/12/42.**H.**
Gor. 4/6-12/8/44.**G.**
Gor. 25/10-24/11/45.**L.**
Gor. 18/12/45-16/2/46.**L.**
Gor. 10/6-10/11/47.**G.**
Dby. 29/9-20/11/50.**H/I.**
Dby. 10/11-30/12/52.**G.**
Gor. 24/6-13/8/55.**G.**
Gor. 9/9-18/10/58.**G.**

BOILERS:
2100.
2291 *(ex2779)* 16/2/33.
825 *(ex1287)* 13/4/35.
2210 *(ex2698)* 3/7/37.
2208 *(ex2730)* 10/6/39.
2770 *(ex2969)* 12/8/44.
2112 *(ex1275)* 10/11/47.
27739 *(ex4958)* 30/12/52.
27843 *(new)* 13/8/55.
25844 *(new)* 18/10/58.

SHEDS:
Gorton.
March 2/9/30.
Colwick 29/2/36.
Grantham 17/3/42.
Colwick 13/5/42.
Bradford 18/8/46.
Ardsley 16/11/47.
Copley Hill 30/11/47.
Ardsley 2/5/48.

RENUMBERED:
4749 15/12/46.
64749 20/11/50.

CONDEMNED:
12/11/62.
Cut up at Darlington.

2697

Darlington.

To traffic 9/8/28.

REPAIRS:
Gor. 27/2-11/4/31.**G.**
Gor. 11/7-5/8/33.**G.**
Dar. 22/5-3/7/36.**G.**
Gor. 16/3-8/4/39.**G.**
Gor. 27/6-29/8/42.**G.**
Gor. 25/6-5/8/44.**G.**
Gor. 16/3-23/6/45.**G.**
Gor. 3/1-18/2/48.**G.**
Gor. 30/8-19/11/48.**H.**
Gor. 29/11/48-22/1/49.**C/L.**
Dby. 11/6-17/8/51.**G.**
Str. 26/11/53-8/1/54.**G.**
Str. 10/8-22/9/56.**G.**

BOILERS:
2102.
2099 *(ex2695)* 5/8/33.
2122 *(ex1298)* 3/7/36.
8024 *(ex2720)* 8/4/39.
8585 *(ex1495)* 29/8/42.
2779 *(ex2988)* 23/6/45.
8772 *(ex2952)* 18/2/48.
27671 *(ex64907)* 17/8/51.
27880 *(ex4952)* 8/1/54.
27875 *(ex4834)* 22/9/56.

SHEDS:
Ardsley.
Grantham 12/7/40.
Gorton 25/3/41.
Annesley 30/10/43.
Colwick 30/3/47.
Tuxford 27/9/53.
Stratford 16/1/55.

RENUMBERED:
4750 6/10/46.
E4750 18/2/48.
64750 19/11/48.

CONDEMNED:
13/11/59.
Cut up at Stratford.

2698

Darlington.

To traffic 14/8/28.

REPAIRS:
Gor. 9/1-14/2/31.**G.**
Gor. 26/11-15/12/34.**G.**
Gor. 3-27/5/37.**G.**
Gor. 23/4-18/5/40.**G.**
Don. 1/10-29/11/41.**H.**
Cow. 28/3-6/6/43.**G.**
Cow. 7-11/6/43.**N/C.**
Gor. 2/10-25/11/44.**G.**
Str. 4/3-11/5/46.**G.**
Gor. 10/4-7/10/47.**G.**
Gor. 21/6-28/8/48.**L.**
Dby. 11/1-26/2/51.**G.**
Dby. 16/2-13/3/52.**H/I.**
Str. 24/10-27/11/54.**G.**
Str. 10-14/12/54.**N/C.**
Str. 26/5-25/7/57.**G.**
Str. 11-15/8/57.**N/C.**

BOILERS:
2103.
2210 *(ex2724)* 15/12/34.
2220 *(ex2700)* 27/5/37.
2294 *(ex2709)* 18/5/40.
4903 *(ex2732)* 6/6/43.
1921 *(ex2942)* 11/5/46.
27658 *(new)* 26/2/51.
27692 *(ex4968)* 27/11/54.
27845 *(ex4768)* 25/7/57.

SHEDS:
Ardsley.
Bradford 31/5/33.
Ardsley 31/7/33.
Tuxford 27/9/53.
Stratford 16/1/55.
Cambridge 15/5/55.
March 28/8/58.
Lincoln 7/12/58.

RENUMBERED:
4751 8/9/46.
64751 28/8/48.

CONDEMNED:
7/12/59.
Cut up at Stratford.

2699

Darlington.

To traffic 15/8/28.

REPAIRS:
Gor. 27/3-2/5/31.**G.**
Gor. 23/6-15/7/33.**G.**
Gor. 15/4-6/5/36.**G.**
Gor. 30/6-24/7/37.**G.**
Gor. 22/9-6/10/38.**L.**
Gor. 13/6-13/7/40.**G.**
Gor. 20/3-24/5/41.**L.**
Cow. 1-30/5/43.**G.**
Gor. 16/7-19/8/44.**L.**
Str. 22/7-29/9/45.**G.**
Gor. 13/7-21/9/46.**L.**
Str. 22/7-18/8/47.**L.**
Gor. 1/2-14/3/48.**G.**
Gor. 22/3-6/4/48.**N/C.**
Dby. 14/6-26/7/50.**L/I.**
Dby. 30/3-21/5/52.**G.**
Str. 23/10-26/11/52.**C/L.**
Str. 17/2-19/3/55.**C/L.**
Str. 18/9-22/10/55.**G.**

BOILERS:
2104.
2094 *(ex2692)* 15/7/33.
2128 *(ex2779)* 6/5/36.
2689 *(ex2988)* 13/7/40.
2697 *(ex2728)* 29/9/45.
2273 *(ex2776)* 14/3/48.
27695 *(ex4979 & spare)* 21/5/52.
27723 *(ex4714)* 22/10/55.

SHEDS:
Bradford.
Ardsley 9/2/36.
Ipswich 11/9/43.

RENUMBERED:
4752 21/9/46.
E4752 14/3/48.
64752 6/4/48.

CONDEMNED:
1/6/59.
Cut up at Stratford.

2700

Darlington.

To traffic 17/8/28.

REPAIRS:
Gor. 22/5-20/6/31.**G.**
Gor. 15/3-7/4/34.**G.**
Gor. 25/8-15/9/34.**L.**
Gor. 5-20/3/37.**G.**
Gor. 1/1-10/2/40.**G.**
Gor. 17/11/42-16/1/43.**G.**
Gor. 13/8-27/10/45.**G.**
Gor. 26/11-6/12/45.**L.**
Gor. 18/4-4/6/48.**G.**
Gor. 29/6-28/7/48.**N/C.**
Dby. 24/2-9/5/51.**H/I.**
Gor. 26/12/53-23/1/54.**G.**
Gor. 14/4-12/5/56.**H/I.**

BOILERS:
2106.
2097 *(ex2693)* 20/6/31.
2220 *(ex2728)* 7/4/34.
8590 *(ex2974)* 20/3/37.
8003 *(ex2975)* 10/2/40.
2290 *(ex1496)* 16/1/43.
825 *(ex2702)* 27/10/45.
822 *(ex2740)* 4/6/48.
25808 *(ex4808)* 23/1/54.

SHEDS:
Ardsley.
Bradford 15/1/36.
Ardsley 17/2/36.
Sheffield 4/8/46.
Gorton 27/10/57.

RENUMBERED:
4753 7/4/46.
64753 29/5/48.

CONDEMNED:
21/8/59.
Cut up at Gorton.

2701

Darlington.

To traffic 25/8/28.

REPAIRS:
Gor. 27/5-4/7/31.**G.**
Gor. 4-23/5/34.**G.**
New type fire door.
Dar. 16/9-23/10/35.**G.**
Don. 26/10-24/11/38.**G.**
Don. 8/10-8/12/41.**G.**
Cow. 17/2-4/7/43.**G.**
Gor. 23/10-18/11/44.**G.**
Gor. 16/6-9/11/46.**G.**
Gor. 6/1-4/3/50.**G.**
Gor. 8/3-14/3/50.**N/C.**
Gor. 21/3-6/4/50.**N/C.**
Dby. 20/11-17/12/52.**G.**
Dby. 2-24/1/53.**N/C.**
Gor. 23/10-26/11/55.**G.**
Gor. 30/8-21/9/57.**C/L.**
Gor. 21/7-28/8/59.**G.**
Gor. 24/5-17/6/61.**C/L.**

BOILERS:
2108.
8592 *(ex2974)* 23/5/34.
3215 *(new)* 4/7/43.
2579 *(ex2707)* 9/11/46.
4986 *(new)* 4/3/50.
27736 *(ex4717)* 17/12/52.
27691 *(ex4831)* 26/11/55.
27841 *(ex4718)* 28/8/59.

SHED:
Ardsley.

RENUMBERED:
4754 29/8/46.
64754 4/3/50.

CONDEMNED:
12/11/62.
Cut up at Darlington.

2702

Darlington.

To traffic 27/8/28.

REPAIRS:
Gor. 13/2-28/3/31.**G.**
Gor. 21/11-16/12/33.**G.**
Dar. 31/1-13/3/36.**G.**
Gor. 14/7-7/8/37.**G.**
Gor. 14/12/39-13/1/40.**G.**
Gor. 22/9-21/11/42.**G.**
Gor. 13/2-7/8/43.**L.**
Gor. 1/7-15/9/45.**G.**
Gor. 29/2-10/5/48.**G.**
Gor. 17-18/6/49.**C/L.**
Gor. 23/3-13/5/50.**G.**
Dby. 5/5-23/8/51.**C/L.**
Gor. 30/3-9/5/53.**G.**
Gor. 19-21/5/53.**N/C.**
Gor. 16/12/55-11/2/56.**G.**
Str. 28/7/59.*Not repaired.*

BOILERS:
2109.
2106 *(ex2718)* 16/12/33.
2216 *(ex2709)* 13/3/36.
8025 *(ex2771)* 7/8/37.
2282 *(ex2771)* 13/1/40.
825 *(ex2976)* 21/11/42.
8590 *(ex2695)* 15/9/45.
4936 *(new)* 10/5/48.
4918 *(ex4702)* 13/5/50.
27756 *(ex4983)* 9/5/53.
27704 *(ex4951)* 11/2/56.

SHEDS:
Doncaster.
Mexborough 19/1/29.
Doncaster 24/1/29.
Gorton 2/5/34.
Lincoln 13/6/54.
Boston 7/12/58.
Lincoln 1/3/59.

RENUMBERED:
4755 12/10/46.
64755 8/5/48.

CONDEMNED:
10/8/59.
Cut up at Stratford.

2703

Darlington.

To traffic 31/8/28.

REPAIRS:
Gor. 8/10-22/11/30.**G.**
Gor. 14/2-4/3/33.**G.**
Don. 21-29/3/33.**N/C.**
Gor. 29/5-22/6/35.**G.**
Gor. 10-26/12/36.**G.**
Gor. 14/3-15/4/39.**G.**
Don. 27/9-14/12/41.**G.**
Str. 6/7-18/8/44.**G.**
Dar. 14/7/45.*Weigh.*
Dar. 19/3-18/4/46.**L.**
Cow. 5/4-9/8/47.**G.**
Dar. 19-24/2/48.**L.**
Cow. 23/3-11/6/49.**H/I.**
Cow. 15/12/50-19/1/51.**H/I.**
Cow. 15/5-20/6/53.**G.**
Cow. 26/9-20/10/55.**N/C.**
Cow. 10/5-9/6/56.**H/I.**
Cow. 20/1-5/3/60.**G.**
Cow. 23-24/3/60.**C/L.**

BOILERS:
2113.
2112 *(ex2711)* 4/3/33.
8024 *(ex2781)* 22/6/35.
8588 *(ex2975)* 26/12/36.
1917 *(ex2774)* 15/4/39.
8016 *(ex2720)* 18/8/44.
2253 *(ex1587)* 9/8/47.
2253 Reno.27474 19/1/51.
27479 *(ex4899)* 20/6/53.
27504 *(ex64932)* 5/3/60.

SHEDS:
Doncaster.
Lincoln 6/12/29.
Gorton 14/2/31.
Liverpool 30/3/31.
Gorton 4/6/31.
Lincoln 12/6/31.
Stratford 11/10/35.
Parkeston 21/8/38.
Stratford 26/3/39.
Colchester 25/9/39.
Stratford 3/12/39.
Darlington 7/1/45.
Middlesbrough 27/6/48.
Darlington 25/6/50.
West Auckland 30/7/50.
Middlesbrough 29/8/54.
West Auckland 6/3/55.
Middlesbrough 3/4/55.
West Auckland 26/6/55.
Ardsley 17/6/62.

RENUMBERED:
4756 17/11/46.
E4756 24/2/48.
64756 11/6/49.

CONDEMNED:
3/12/62.
Cut up at Darlington.

One of the 1926 built engines no.1270 was fitted when new with a Cruse-Gray type of superheater made by Bolton's Superheater & Pipe Works. The only visible sign of difference was the pyrometer lead from smokebox side to the cab. Although allocated to Immingham shed in Southern Area, the trials were carried out by Newport shed in the North Eastern Area. *LNER*

2704

Darlington.

To traffic 4/9/28.

REPAIRS:
Gor. 9/7-30/8/30.**G.**
Gor. 16-28/10/33.**G.**
Dar. 14/1-22/2/36.**G.**
Gor. 26/4-21/5/37.**G.**
Gor. 15/5-10/6/39.**G.**
Gor. 15/12/40-18/1/41.**G.**
Gor. 10/4-21/8/43.**G.**
Gor. 10-18/9/43.**N/C.**
Gor. 21/8-16/9/44.**G.**
Gor. 26/8-3/11/45.**G.**
Gor. 27/7-7/11/47.**G.**
Gor. 29/10-3/12/49.**G.**
Dby. 15/8-19/10/50.**C/L.**
Dby. 1/7-18/8/52.**G.**
Gor. 1/6-3/7/54.**C/L.**
Gor. 6-7/7/54.**N/C.**
Gor. 8/4-14/5/55.**G.**
Gor. 25/6-16/8/58.**G.**

BOILERS:
2114.
2138 *(ex2715)* 28/10/33.
2102 *(ex2715)* 22/2/36.
2205 *(ex2692)* 21/5/37.
2145 *(ex1282)* 10/6/39.
2095 *(ex2966)* 18/1/41.
2681 *(ex2971)* 21/8/43.
8774 *(ex1803)* 3/11/45.
8582 *(ex2691)* 7/11/47.
4980 *(new)* 3/12/49.
27712 *(ex4741)* 18/8/52.
27837 *(new)* 14/5/55.
25826 *(new)* 16/8/58.

SHEDS:
Doncaster.
Immingham 10/7/29.
Doncaster 21/9/29.
Colwick 20/9/30.
Annesley 3/10/30.
Leicester 13/3/32.
Annesley 4/4/32.
Colwick 30/3/47.
Ardsley 20/5/51.
Thornaby 16/10/60.

RENUMBERED:
4757 25/8/46.
64757 3/12/49.

CONDEMNED:
26/11/62.
Cut up at Darlington.

2705

Darlington.

To traffic 7/9/28.

REPAIRS:
Gor. 11/7-30/8/30.**G.**
Gor. 11/8-15/9/33.**G.**
Dar. 3/1-12/2/36.**G.**
Gor. 10/2-5/3/38.**G.**
Gor. 11/5-1/6/40.**G.**
Cow. 22/7/43.**G.***
Gor. 21/10/44.**G.***
Gor. 27/7/46.**L.***
Gor. 29/11/47.**G***.
Gor. 7/1/50.**G.***
Cow. 29/1-18/4/53.**H/I.**
Cow. 4/8-5/9/53.**C/L.**
Cow. 24/10/53.**N/C.**
Cow. 27/12/56-7/2/57.**G.**

** These dates signify when loco left the works. Dates of entry not known, as not on History card.*

BOILERS:
2116.
2093 *(ex2694)* 15/9/33.
8007 *(ex1289)* 12/2/36.
2182 *(ex1493)* 5/3/38.
2109 *(ex2974)* 1/6/40.
1917 *(ex2703)* 21/10/44.
8585 *(ex1498)* 29/11/47.
4983 *(new)* 7/1/50.
4983 Reno.27596 18/4/53.
27630 *(new)* 7/2/57.

SHEDS:
Doncaster.
Mexborough 15/12/28.
Doncaster 16/4/29.
Gorton 2/5/34.
Doncaster 4/12/34.
Gorton 1/6/44.
Doncaster 2/5/45.
Darlington 2/9/51.
Neville Hill 6/7/52.
Thornaby 1/11/59.

RENUMBERED:
4758 1/11/46.
64758 7/1/50.

CONDEMNED:
16/11/62.
Cut up at Darlington.

2706

Darlington.

To traffic 12/9/28.

REPAIRS:
Gor. 11/7-16/8/30.**G.**
Gor. 25/2-21/3/31.**L.**
Gor. 21/3-2/4/32.**L.**
Gor. 2-14/10/33.**G.**
Dar. 5/2-14/3/36.**G.**
Gor. 31/1-18/2/39.**G.**
Gor. 24-27/2/39.**N/C.**
Gor. 9-14/3/39.**N/C.**
Gor. 29/11/41-10/1/42.**G.**
Gor. 17/5-2/10/43.**G.**
Str. 27/3-31/8/46.**G.**
Gor. 24/11/48-22/1/49.**G.**
Dby. 14/3-27/4/51.**H/I.**
Str. 30/9-14/11/53.**G.**
Gor. 11/11-22/12/56.**G.**

BOILERS:
2119.
1922 *(ex1493)* 14/10/33.
2194 *(ex2971)* 14/3/36.
8589 *(ex1265)* 18/2/39.
2119 *(ex2715)* 10/1/42.
2095 *(ex2704)* 2/10/43.
2767 *(ex2693)* 31/8/46.
3170 *(ex4807)* 22/1/49.
27877 *(ex4834)* 14/11/53.
27751 *(ex4960)* 22/12/56.

SHEDS:
Doncaster.
Ardsley 15/3/34.
Copley Hill 7/4/34.
Ardsley 27/6/34.
Bradford 26/3/41.

About 100 degrees extra steam temperature was attained on 1270, but that was insufficient to justify further applications being made, and in May 1931 change was made to the standard Robinson type superheater, and the pyrometer lead was removed. *WBY collection*

Doncaster 30/7/45.
Retford 5/10/47.

RENUMBERED:
4759 31/8/46.
64759 22/1/49.

CONDEMNED:
15/3/60.
Cut up at Gorton.

2707

Darlington.

To traffic 17/9/28.

REPAIRS:
Gor. 20/6-9/8/30.**G.**
Gor. 13-31/3/33.**G.**
Dar. 25/6-19/7/35.**G.**
Gor. 7/2-3/3/38.**G.**
Gor. 18/9-26/10/40.**G.**
Cow. 7/5-24/6/43.**G.**
Gor. 22/9-11/11/44.**G.**
Gor. 12/6-19/10/46.**G.**
Gor. 23/5-31/7/48.**L.**
Gor. 17/8-24/9/49.**G.**
Gor. 10-22/10/49.**N/C.**
Dby. 22/1-13/3/51.**L/I.**
Gor. 17/8-3/10/53.**G.**
Gor. 6-13/10/53.**N/C.**
Gor. 7/4-19/5/56.**G.**
Gor. 17/2-26/3/59.**G.**
Gor. 17/1-16/2/61.**C/L.**

BOILERS:
2121.
2100 *(ex2696)* 31/3/33.
1912 *(ex1454)* 19/7/35.
822 *(ex1496)* 3/3/38.
2103 *(ex1267)* 26/10/40.
2579 *(ex2781)* 11/11/44.
2108 *(ex1494)* 19/10/46.
2695 *(ex2941)* 24/9/49.
27659 *(ex4907)* 3/10/53.
27741 *(ex4716)* 19/5/56.
27593 *(ex4747)* 26/3/59.

SHEDS:
Doncaster.
Gorton 2/5/34.
Doncaster 2/12/34.
Ardsley 1/7/39.
Bradford 26/3/41.
Ardsley 11/7/41.

RENUMBERED:
4760 3/5/46.
64760 31/7/48.

CONDEMNED:
30/11/62.
Cut up at Darlington.

2708

Darlington.

To traffic 19/9/28.

REPAIRS:
Don. 30/10-7/12/29.**H.**
New cylinders.
Gor. 19/9-21/10/31.**G.**
Gor. 13-28/7/34.**G.**
Gor. 28/9-24/10/36.**G.**
Gor. 2-31/8/38.**G.**
Gor. 8/9-26/10/40.**G.**
Str. 10/1-8/5/43.**G.**
Gor. 1/3-19/5/45.**G.**
Gor. 15/9-26/10/46.**L.**
Str. 14/5-14/8/47.**G.**
Gor. 27/1-4/3/50.**G.**
Gor. 8-23/3/50.**N/C.**
Dby. 24/10-12/12/52.**H/I.**
Str. 14/11/54-8/1/55.**G.**
Str. 25/8-28/9/57.**G.**

BOILERS:
2122.
2188 *(new)* 21/10/31.
2191 *(ex1497)* 28/7/34.
2274 *(ex2780)* 24/10/36.
826 *(ex1274)* 31/8/38.
824 *(ex2784)* 26/10/40.
2672 *(ex2949)* 8/5/43.
8593 *(ex2726)* 19/5/45.
RS120 *(ex4723)* 4/3/50.
RS120 Reno.27730 12/12/52.
27824 *(new)* 8/1/55.
27692 *(ex4751)* 28/9/57.

SHEDS:
Doncaster.
March 28/7/34.
Cambridge 12/12/40.
March 9/3/41.
Norwich 16/9/43.

RENUMBERED:
4761 25/8/46.
64761 4/3/50.

CONDEMNED:
6/11/59.
Cut up at Stratford.

2709

Darlington.

To traffic 28/9/28.

REPAIRS:
Gor. 15/1-6/2/32.**G.**
Gor. 13/4-5/5/34.**G.**
Dar. 23/1-26/2/36.**G.**
Gor. 7/2-5/3/38.**G.**
Gor. 30/3-4/5/40.**G.**
Gor. 9/7-12/9/42.**G.**
Gor. 30/12/43-15/1/44.**G.**
Gor. 30/12/44-10/3/45.**G.**

For comparison with 1270's special superheater, no.1452 was fitted with this recording pyrometer to establish what temperature was given by the superheater which was in normal use. The recorder was removed when the trials were terminated in December 1927. *WBY collection*

Gor. 5/7-19/10/46.**G.**
Gor. 24/11/47-18/2/48.**G.**
Gor. 24/8-19/11/48.**L.**
Dby. 15/5-20/8/50.**G.**
Gor. 4/3-25/4/53.**G.**
Gor. 30/4-23/5/53.**N/C.**
Gor. 30/7-9/10/54.**C/L.**
Gor. 16/8-29/10/55.**G.**
Gor. 5-30/11/55.**N/C.**
Gor. 14/10-30/11/57.**G.**
Gor. 9-26/4/58.**C/L.**

BOILERS:
2123.
8003 *(ex1498)* 6/2/32.
2216 *(ex2710)* 5/5/34.
2093 *(ex2705)* 26/2/36.
2294 *(ex1289)* 5/3/38.
8590 *(ex2700)* 4/5/40.
2666 *(ex1267)* 12/9/42.
2769 *(ex2963)* 10/3/45.
2309 *(ex1263)* 18/2/48.
4917 *(ex4904)* 20/8/50.
27754 *(ex4749)* 25/4/53.
27795 *(new)* 29/10/55.
27888 *(ex4908)* 30/11/57.

SHEDS:
Gorton.
Annesley 31/10/28.
Lincoln 24/6/29.
Ardsley 7/8/29.
Annesley 20/8/29.
Lincoln 20/6/30.
Ardsley 5/8/30.
Annesley 21/8/30.
Colwick 30/3/47.

RENUMBERED:
4762 29/8/46.
E4762 18/2/48.
64762 19/11/48.

CONDEMNED:
29/6/59.
Cut up at Stratford.

2710

Darlington.

To traffic 28/9/28.

REPAIRS:
Gor. 17/7-29/8/31.**G.**
Gor. 26/3-21/4/34.**G.**
Gor. 15/9-10/10/36.**G.**
Gor. 3/7-26/8/39.**G.**
Gor. 4-12/9/39.**N/C.**
Gor. 6/12/43-1/4/44.**G.**
Gor. 12/9-21/12/46.**G.**
Gor. 7/1-19/2/49.**G.**
Dby. 4/3-4/4/52.**H/I.**
Str. 15/8-24/9/54.**G.**
Gor. 24/2-7/4/56.**C/L.**
Gor. 7/6-28/7/56.**C/L.**
Gor. 22/5-29/6/57.**G.**

BOILERS:
2110.
2216 *(ex2725)* 29/8/31.
8774 *(new)* 21/4/34.
8015 *(ex2773)* 10/10/36.
2189 *(ex2778)* 26/8/39.
3168 *(ex1854)* 19/2/49.
3168 Reno.27706 4/4/52.
27807 *(ex4976)* 24/9/54.
27684 *(ex4878)* 29/6/57.

SHEDS:
Gorton.
Annesley 10/11/28.
Lincoln 24/6/29.
Ardsley 14/8/29.
Annesley 19/8/29.
Leicester 23/8/29.
Colwick 14/8/43.
Ardsley 20/5/51.
Tuxford 27/9/53.
Colwick 16/1/55.

RENUMBERED:
4763 9/11/46.
64763 19/2/49.

CONDEMNED:
29/6/59.
Cut up at Stratford.

Access to each end of the superheater header was provided by a removable circular plate, fitted flush with the smokebox wrapper plate on each side. Normal fixing was by six screws. *WBY collection*

During the last year of the LNER, Stratford introduced variants to the normal access plates on the engines which they maintained. 4774 ex works at the end of May had a rectangular overlapping plate fastened by eight screws. 4761 out in August had a similar plate but only six screws, whilst E4767 ex works on 5th February 1948 had a square plate which overlapped but with eight screws. *WBY collection*

By May 1948 when Stratford turned out 64726 they had reverted to the normal flush fitting plate with its six screws. This view also shows the extra handhole low down on the firebox which was put in from August 1931 to help washing out scale more effectively. *L&GRP*

2711

Darlington.

To traffic 9/10/28.

REPAIRS:
Gor. 19/9-25/10/30.**G.**
Gor. 30/12/32-27/1/33.**G.**
Gor. 15/4-4/5/35.**G.**
Gor. 7/2-3/3/38.**G.**
Gor. 3/10-15/12/40.**G.**
Gor. 13/11/41-10/1/42.**L.**
Str. 11/12/43-22/1/44.**G.**
Str. 17/11/46-10/1/47.**G.**
Str. 23/3-7/5/47.**L.**
Gor. 31/8-29/10/49.**G.**
Gor. 4-7/11/49.**N/C.**
Dby. 6/10-28/11/52.**G.**
Dby. 12-29/12/52.**N/C.**
Str. 22/5-18/8/56.**G.**
Str. 24/6-26/7/57.**C/L.**
After collision.

BOILERS:
2112.
2296 *(ex2781)* 27/1/33.
824 *(ex1266)* 4/5/35.
2284 *(ex1267)* 3/3/38.
2186 *(ex2721)* 15/12/40.
8007 *(ex2972)* 22/1/44.
2128 *(ex2712)* 10/1/47.
8023 *(ex4804)* 29/10/49.
27733 *(ex4830)* 28/11/52.
27738 *(ex4890)* 18/8/56.

SHEDS:
York.
Stratford 3/12/28.
Parkeston 28/10/56.
Stratford 13/4/58.
March 25/5/58.

RENUMBERED:
4764 19/8/46.
64764 29/10/49.

CONDEMNED:
19/10/60.
Cut up at Stratford.

2712

Darlington.

To traffic 12/10/28.

REPAIRS:
Gor. 19/9-25/10/30.**G.**
Gor. 28/10-25/11/32.**G.**
Gor. 11/1-16/2/33.**L.**
Gor. 23/4-18/5/35.**G.**
Gor. 27/9-23/10/37.**G.**
Gor. 21/7-3/8/40.**G.**
Str. 29/5-10/6/42.**L.**
Don. 11/7-29/9/43.**G.**
Str. 27/8-19/11/46.**G.**
Gor. 26/5-13/8/49.**G.**
Dby. 16/6-7/9/50.**L/I.**
Dby. 10/9-3/10/50.**L/I.**
Dby. 17/3-9/5/52.**G.**
Str. 7/2-25/3/55.**G.**
Str. 30/9-9/11/57.**G.**

BOILERS:
2128.
8006 *(ex1259)* 25/11/32.
8019 *(ex1268)* 18/5/35.
8773 *(ex2717)* 23/10/37.
2128 *(ex2699)* 3/8/40.
8020 *(ex2976)* 19/11/46.
2296 *(ex2773)* 13/8/49.
27806 *(new)* 9/5/52.
27683 *(ex4777)* 25/3/55.
27806 *(ex4873)* 9/11/57.

SHEDS:
York.
Stratford 22/11/28.
Parkeston 25/9/47.
Stratford 16/1/49.
Peterborough 21/6/53.
Stratford 30/8/53.

RENUMBERED:
4765 9/11/46.
64765 13/8/49.

CONDEMNED:
17/8/60.
Cut up at Doncaster.

2713

Darlington.

To traffic 22/11/28.

REPAIRS:
Gor. 17/10-29/11/30.**G.**
Gor. 27/10-2/12/33.**G.**
Dar. 23/1-2/3/36.**G.**
Gor. 25/7-20/8/38.**G.**
Gor. 22/2-10/5/41.**G.**
Gor. 29/8-14/10/44.**G.**
Str. 26/11/47-10/4/48.**G.**
Dby. 4/2-28/3/52.**H/I.**
Str. 20/12/54-29/1/55.**G.**
Str. 25/6-16/8/57.**C/L.**
Str. 9-21/9/57.**C/L.**
Str. 30/12/57-1/2/58.**G.**
Str. 28/4-8/5/58.**C/L.**
Str. 24/9/59.*Not repaired.*

BOILERS:
2129.
8594 *(ex2976)* 2/12/33.
2119 *(ex2718)* 2/3/36.
2214 *(ex2783)* 20/8/38.
2701 *(ex2992)* 10/5/41.
2194 *(ex2778)* 14/10/44.
2186 *(ex2720)* 10/4/48.
2186 Reno.27707 28/3/52.
27711 *(ex4874)* 29/1/55.
27678 *(ex4958)* 1/2/58.

SHEDS:
York.
Stratford 3/12/28.
Ardsley 15/5/49.
Stratford 18/9/49.

RENUMBERED:
4766 24/8/46.
64766 3/4/48.

CONDEMNED:
28/9/59.
Cut up at Stratford.

2714

Darlington.

To traffic 22/11/28.

REPAIRS:
Gor. 2/3-4/4/31.**G.**
Gor. 1-26/8/33.**G.**
Dar. 18/10-27/11/35.**G.**
Gor. 10/5-4/6/38.**G.**
Gor. 27/10-15/12/40.**G.**
Str. 3/3-7/4/44.**G.**
Str. 21/10/47-5/2/48.**G.**
Str. 15/5-31/7/48.**L.**
Dby. 10/1-25/2/52.**G.**
Str. 31/1-11/3/55.**G.**
Str. 3/2-3/4/58.**G.**

BOILERS:
2132.
2104 *(ex2699)* 26/8/33.
RS120 *(ex1471)* 27/11/35.
1912 *(ex2707)* 4/6/38.
8023 *(ex2968)* 15/12/40.
826 *(ex2721)* 7/4/44.
27809 *(new)* 25/2/52.
27707 *(ex4766)* 11/3/55.
27724 *(ex4829)* 3/4/58.

SHEDS:
York.
Stratford 3/12/28.
Colchester 25/9/39.
Stratford 3/12/39.
Parkeston 2/11/41.
Stratford 16/11/41.
Ardsley 15/5/49.
Stratford 28/9/49.
Ipswich 15/10/50.
Stratford 14/1/51.

RENUMBERED:
4767 13/11/46.
E4767 5/2/48.
64767 31/7/48.

CONDEMNED:
13/1/61.
Cut up at Stratford.

2715

Darlington.

To traffic 26/11/28.

REPAIRS:
Gor. 30/1-7/3/31.**G.**
Gor. 11-29/9/33.**G.**
Dar. 10/1-21/2/36.**G.**
Dar. 22-28/2/36.**N/C.**
Gor. 7/10-6/11/36.*Tender only.*
Gor. 15/8-17/9/38.**G.**
Gor. 26/4-14/6/41.**G.**
Str. 21/5-1/7/44.**G.**
Str. 11/8-19/9/45.**L.**
Str. 7/5-8/11/47.**G.**
Dby. 27/6-30/8/51.**H/I.**
Str. 30/12/52-24/1/53.**C/L.**
Str. 23/6-7/8/54.**G.**
Str. 15/4-24/5/57.**G.**
Str. 12-28/3/58.**C/L.**

BOILERS:
2138.
2102 *(ex2697)* 29/9/33.
8584 *(ex2784)* 21/2/36.
2119 *(ex2713)* 17/9/38.
8775 *(ex1296)* 14/6/41.
2920 *(ex1971)* 1/7/44.
2920 Reno.27770 24/1/53.
27845 *(new)* 7/8/54.
27706 *(ex4968)* 24/5/57.

SHEDS:
York.
Stratford 5/12/28.
Ardsley 15/5/49.
Stratford 18/9/49.

RENUMBERED:
4768 10/11/46.
64768 30/8/51.

CONDEMNED:
18/5/59.
Cut up at Stratford.

2716

Darlington.

To traffic 27/11/28.

REPAIRS:
Gor. 16/1-21/2/31.**G.**
Gor. 27/10-25/11/33.**G.**
Dar. 19/2-26/3/36.**G.**
Gor. 21/9-14/10/38.**G.**
Don. 24/8-12/10/41.**G.**
Gor. 30/7-9/9/44.**G.**
Str. 7/12/46-10/3/47.**G.**
Gor. 24/11/48-23/1/49.**G.**
Gor. 17/11/49-4/2/50.**C/H.**
Gor. 11/2-12/2/50.**N/C.**
Dby. 27/6-29/8/52.**L/I.**
Gor. 24-26/11/53.**C/L.**
Str. 16/6-13/8/55.**G.**

BOILERS:
2141.
8773 *(new)* 25/11/33.
8594 *(ex2713)* 26/3/36.
2110 *(ex3000)* 9/9/44.
2300 *(ex1484)* 23/1/49.
2300 Reno.27713 29/8/52.
27554 *(ex4864)* 13/8/55.

SHEDS:
York.
Stratford 7/12/28.
Colchester 20/7/41.
Stratford 3/8/41.
March 23/3/58.

RENUMBERED:
4769 3/10/46.
64769 23/1/49.

CONDEMNED:
21/1/60.
Cut up at Stratford.

2717

Darlington.

To traffic 29/11/28.

REPAIRS:
Gor. 30/1-7/3/31.**G.**
Gor. 24/10-18/11/33.**G.**
Dar. 5/3-4/4/36.**G.**
Gor. 18/8-18/9/37.**G.**
Gor. 22/6-20/7/40.**G.**
Str. 19/11-30/12/41.**L.**
Str. 28/8-16/10/43.**G.**
Str. 14/12/44-23/2/45.**L.**
Str. 15/9-8/12/45.**G.**
Gor. 10/8-16/10/48.**G.**
Gor. 31/12/49-15/4/50.**C/H.**
Gor. 19/4-25/5/50.**N/C.**
Dby. 26/3-1/6/51.**H/I.**
Str. 2/2-17/3/53.**N/C.**
Str. 21/10-28/11/53.**G.**
Str. 10/5-23/6/56.**G.**

BOILERS:
2143.
8014 *(ex1273)* 18/11/33.
8773 *(ex2716)* 4/4/36.
2193 *(ex2770)* 18/9/37.
8591 *(ex2964)* 20/7/40.
3175 *(ex3087)* 16/10/43.
824 *(ex2722)* 8/12/45.
2188 *(ex3084)* 16/10/48.
2188 Reno.27773 17/3/53.
27802 *(ex4965)* 28/11/53.
27873 *(ex4841)* 23/6/56.

SHEDS:
York.
Stratford 18/1/29.
Parkeston 18/6/50.
Stratford 24/6/51.
Parkeston 8/7/51.
March 23/3/58.

RENUMBERED:
4770 25/10/46.
64770 16/10/48.

CONDEMNED:
19/10/60.
Cut up at Stratford.

2718

Darlington.

To traffic 30/11/28.

REPAIRS:
Gor. 5/6-4/7/31.**G.**
Gor. 25/10-18/11/33.**G.**
Dar. 20/11-27/12/35.**G.**
Gor. 7/6-2/7/38.**G.**
Gor. 16/3-24/5/41.**G.**
Gor. 12/11-22/12/44.**G.**
Str. 23/3-12/7/47.**G.**
Str. 16-31/10/47.**L.**
Gor. 29/7-23/10/48.**G.**
Gor. 28/4-10/6/50.**G.**
Gor. 14/6-3/7/50.**N/C.**
Str. 1/1-2/4/53.**G.**
Str. 10-18/9/53.**C/L.**
Str. 7/4-6/5/55.**C/L.**
Str. 14/11-23/12/55.**G.**
Str. 17-20/9/56.**C/L.**
March. 27/4/58-28/1/60.*In store.*

BOILERS:
2145.
2106 *(ex2700)* 4/7/31.
2119 *(ex2706)* 18/11/33.
8772 *(ex2976)* 27/12/35.
RS120 *(ex2714)* 2/7/38.
2214 *(ex2713)* 24/5/41.
2671 *(ex1870)* 22/12/44.
2184 *(ex1457)* 12/7/47.
4936 *(ex4755)* 10/6/50.
27748 *(ex4754)* 2/4/53.
27719 *(ex4807)* 23/12/55.

SHEDS:
York.
Stratford 7/12/28.
Parkeston 13/4/41.
Stratford 19/1/46.
Ipswich 15/10/50.
Norwich 14/1/51.
Stratford 15/4/51.
Parkeston 28/10/56.
March 20/4/58.

RENUMBERED:
4771 22/11/46.
64771 23/10/48.

CONDEMNED:
1/2/60.
Cut up at Stratford.

2719

Darlington.

To traffic 4/12/28.

REPAIRS:
Gor. 31/10-13/12/30.**G.**
Gor. 16/3-7/4/34.**G.**
Gor. 25/11-12/12/36.**G.**
Str. 9-24/12/37.**L.**
Gor. 29/6-14/10/39.**G.**
Str. 20/6-18/8/42.**G.**
Str. 21/10/45-26/1/46.**G.**
Str. 28/6-17/8/46.**L.**
Str. 6/6-3/9/47.**L.**
Gor. 23/8-8/10/49.**G.**
Str. 17/12/52-16/3/53.**G.**
Str. 24/10-3/12/55.**G.**
Mar. 30/3/58-13/6/60.*In store.*

BOILERS:
2146.
8586 *(ex2968)* 7/4/34.
8012 *(ex1295)* 12/12/36.
8015 *(ex2710)* 14/10/39.
BP140 *(ex1803)* 18/8/42.
2114 *(ex2952)* 26/1/46.
BP143 *(ex4981)* 8/10/49.
BP143 Reno.27772 16/3/53.
27713 *(ex4769)* 3/12/55.

SHEDS:
York.
Stratford 11/12/28.
Parkeston 26/1/29.
Colchester 30/7/36.
Stratford 25/9/39.
Colchester 3/12/39.
Stratford 2/11/41.
March 23/3/58.

RENUMBERED:
4772 17/8/46.
64772 8/10/49.

CONDEMNED:
3/7/61.
Cut up at Doncaster.

2720

Darlington.

To traffic 6/12/28.

REPAIRS:
Gor. 11/2-14/3/31.**G.**
Gor. 5-24/3/34.**G.**
Gor. 13/4-1/5/37.**G.**
Gor. 7-11/12/37.**L.**
Gor. 3-25/2/39.**G.**
Don. 21/6-18/8/41.**G.**
Str. 20/9-3/10/42.**L.**
Str. 26/3-6/5/44.**G.**
Str. 11/5/47-3/3/48.**G.**
Dby. 13/6-20/7/51.**H/I.**
Dby. 9/10-1/11/51.**N/C.**
Str. 29/12/53-6/2/54.**G.**
Str. 22/10-15/12/56.**G.**
Str. 27/2-30/5/58.**G.**
Str. 21/8/59.*Not repaired.*

BOILERS:
2136.
2300 *(ex2783)* 24/3/34.
8024 *(ex2703)* 1/5/37.
8016 *(ex2772)* 25/2/39.
2186 *(ex2711)* 6/5/44.
2303 *(ex2734)* 3/3/48.
27821 *(new)* 6/2/54.
27874 *(ex4905)* 15/12/56.

SHEDS:
York.
Stratford 14/12/28.
Parkeston 25/1/29.
Colchester 5/11/35.
Stratford 25/9/39.
Colchester 3/12/39.
Stratford 20/7/41.
Colchester 3/8/41.
Stratford 19/1/46.
Ipswich 22/10/50.
Stratford 19/1/51.
Parkeston 12/8/51.
Stratford 13/4/58.

RENUMBERED:
4773 22/11/46.
E4773 3/3/48.
64773 20/7/51.

CONDEMNED:
25/8/59.
Cut up at Stratford.

2721

Darlington.

To traffic 26/3/29.

REPAIRS:
Gor. 15/5-13/6/31.**G.**
Gor. 25/8-22/9/34.**G.**
Gor. 17/7-12/8/37.**G.**
Gor. 13/10-16/11/40.**G.**
Str. 27/11/43-15/1/44.**G.**
Str. 12/12/46-28/5/47.**G.**
Gor. 23/10-24/12/49.**G.**
Gor. 31/12/49-5/1/50.**N/C.**
Dby. 13/10-26/11/52.**H/I.**
Str. 8/3-25/4/53.**C/L.**
Str. 28/9-18/11/55.**G.**
March. 30/3/58-3/3/60.*In store.*

BOILERS:
2203.
2188 *(ex2708)* 22/9/34.
2186 *(ex1494)* 12/8/37.
826 *(ex2708)* 16/11/40.
2641 *(ex2985)* 15/1/44.
2128 *(ex4764)* 24/12/49.
2128 Reno.27731 26/11/52.
27747 *(ex4957)* 18/11/55.

SHEDS:
York.
Parkeston 9/4/29.
Stratford 25/9/39.
Parkeston 24/6/44.
Stratford 23/6/45.
March 23/3/58.

RENUMBERED:
4774 5/12/46.
64774 24/12/49.

CONDEMNED:
15/3/60.
Cut up at Stratford.

2722

Darlington.

To traffic 8/4/29.

REPAIRS:
Gor. 22/9-31/10/31.**G.**
Gor. 12/1-2/2/35.**G.**
Gor. 9/6-3/7/37.**G.**
Gor. 28/11/39-3/2/40.**G.**
Str. 23/1-4/6/43.**G.**
Str. 16/1-7/4/44.**L.**
Str. 6/9-27/10/45.**G.**
Str. 17/3-10/6/47.**G.**
Gor. 19/3-28/5/48.**G.**
Str. 5-8/6/48.**N/C.**
Gor. 7/12/48-23/1/49.**L.**
Dby. 16/11/51-8/2/52.**G.**
Str. 30/12/54-29/1/55.**G.**
Str. 10/12/57-18/1/58.**G.**

BOILERS:
2205.
2103 *(ex2698)* 2/2/35.
8008 *(ex1269)* 3/7/37.
1921 *(ex1289)* 3/2/40.
824 *(ex2708)* 4/6/43.
2688 *(ex2724)* 27/10/45.
2282 *(ex2771)* 28/5/48.
27808 *(new)* 8/2/52.
27846 *(new)* 29/1/55.
27674 *(ex4777)* 18/1/58.

SHEDS:
York.
Ipswich 18/4/29.
Parkeston 25/4/29.
Colchester 3/4/34.
Stratford 25/9/39.

RENUMBERED:
4775 25/8/46.
64775 28/5/48.

CONDEMNED:
26/8/60.
Cut up at Doncaster.

2723

Darlington.

To traffic 10/4/29.

REPAIRS:
Gor. 30/1-28/2/31.**G.**
Gor. 25/10-15/11/33.**G.**
Dar. 30/3-5/5/36.**G.**
Gor. 29/8-8/10/38.**G.**
Str. 27/12/41-30/5/42.**G.**
Str. 5-19/6/42.**L.**
Str. 22/3-13/7/43.**G.**
Str. 29/11/44-13/1/45.**L.**
Str. 9/9-1/12/45.**G.**
Gor. 4/12/49-4/2/50.**G.**
Gor. 11-23/2/50.**N/C.**
Str. 23/3-21/5/53.**G.**
Str. 20/11/55-13/1/56.**G.**
Str. 28/4-16/5/58.**C/L.**

BOILERS:
2208.
2116 *(ex2705)* 15/11/33.
2106 *(ex2702)* 5/5/36.
2274 *(ex2708)* 8/10/38.
2102 *(ex1933)* 1/12/45.
2681 *(ex4901)* 4/2/50.
27777 *(ex4702)* 21/5/53.
27746 *(ex4913)* 13/1/56.

SHEDS:
York.
Ipswich 18/4/29.
Parkeston 31/5/29.
Colchester 26/1/35.
Parkeston 2/3/35.
Stratford 25/9/39.
Parkeston 8/9/40.
Stratford 19/1/46.
Parkeston 28/10/56.

RENUMBERED:
4776 26/10/46.
64776 4/2/50.

CONDEMNED:
17/8/59.
Cut up at Stratford.

2724

Darlington.

To traffic 15/4/29.

REPAIRS:
Gor. 27/5-4/7/31.**G.**
Gor. 27/7-16/8/34.**G.**
Gor. 17/2-6/3/37.**G.**
Gor. 2-18/6/37.**L.**
Gor. 20/8-4/11/39.**G.**
Str. 28/1-10/2/40.**L.**
Str. 13/1-15/5/43.**G.**
Str. 10/8-29/9/45.**G.**
Gor. 24/2-2/4/49.**G.**
Gor. 18-23/4/49.**N/C.**
Dby. 13/10-12/12/51.**G.**
Str. 10/5-20/6/53.**C/L.**
Str. 22/10-24/12/53.**C/L.**
Str. 30/11/54-15/1/55.**G.**
Str. 13/10/55-7/2/56.**C/L.**
Str. 23/9-19/10/57.**G.**

BOILERS:
2210.
2282 *(ex2777)* 16/8/34.
8586 *(ex2719)* 6/3/37.
8012 *(ex2719)* 4/11/39.
2688 *(ex2968)* 15/5/43.
8012 *(ex2972)* 29/9/45.
2106 *(ex1265)* 2/4/49.
27683 *(ex1269)* 12/12/51.
27674 *(ex4891)* 15/1/55.
27890 *(ex4826)* 19/10/57.

SHEDS:
York.
Ipswich 20/4/29.
Parkeston 30/5/29.
Colchester 26/3/34.
Stratford 3/12/39.
Parkeston 18/6/50.
Stratford 8/11/59.

RENUMBERED:
4777 12/12/46.
64777 2/4/49.

CONDEMNED:
4/1/60.
Cut up at Stratford.

2725

Darlington.

To traffic 22/4/29.

REPAIRS:
Gor. 3/7-8/8/31.**G.**
Gor. 22/3-14/4/34.**G.**
Dar. 29/8-7/10/35.**G.**
Dar. 29/10/36.*Weigh.*
Dar. 22/2-25/3/37.**G.**
Dar. 25/1-14/3/38.**H.**
Dar. 6/3-18/4/39.**G.**
Dar. 4/2-21/3/41.**G.**
Dar. 10/6-16/7/43.**G.**
Cow. 27/10-10/11/45.**G.**
Dar. 19/12/45.*Weigh.*
Cow. 22/3-26/4/47.**G.**
Ghd. 15/11-8/12/48.**L.**
Cow. 28/1-5/2/49.**C/L.**
Cow. 20/8-16/9/50.**L/I.**
Cow. 28/4-24/5/52.**G.**
Cow. 24/4-14/5/53.**C/L.**
Cow. 8/7-8/8/53.**C/L.**
Cow. 6/1-4/2/56.**H/I.**
Dar. 13-17/3/58.**N/C.**
Cow. 14/8-13/9/58.**G.**
Cow. 28/7/60.*Not repaired.*

BOILERS:
2216.
2218 *(ex2727)* 8/8/31.
2136 *(ex2720)* 14/4/34.
2100 *(ex2707)* 7/10/35.
2116 *(ex1491)* 18/4/39.
2708 *(ex1436)* 21/3/41.
BP136 *(ex1460)* 16/7/43.
2946 *(ex1577)* 10/11/45.
1909 *(ex1863)* 26/4/47.
27476 *(ex4856)* 24/5/52.
27510 *(ex4701)* 13/9/58.

SHEDS:
York.
Stratford 2/5/29.
Southend 2/8/30.
Stratford 9/8/30.
Darlington 14/12/35.
West Auckland 4/1/48.
Sheffield 11/9/60.

RENUMBERED:
4778 1/12/46.
64778 8/12/48.

CONDEMNED:
12/9/60.
Engine and tender cut up at Cowlairs. Boiler to J38 class.

2726

Darlington.

To traffic 24/4/29.

REPAIRS:
Gor. 12/6-18/7/31.**G.**
Gor. 8-27/1/34.**G.**
Dar. 11/11-27/12/35.**G.**
Don. 6-28/10/38.**G.**
Don. 29/6-16/10/41.**G.**
Gor. 14/12/41-14/2/42.**L.**
Gor. 9/8-28/9/44.**G.**
Str. 29/5-8/8/46.**G.**
Str. 17/3-7/6/47.**H.**
Gor. 17/7-27/8/49.**G.**
Str. 14/1-16/4/53.**G.**
Str. 16/1-25/2/56.**G.**
March 1/6/58-1/2/59.*In store.*
March 15/2/59-13/6/60.*In store.*

BOILERS:
2214.
826 *(ex1498)* 27/1/34.
2104 *(ex2714)* 27/12/35.
8593 *(ex2780)* 28/10/38.
8006 *(ex2999)* 28/9/44.
2145 *(ex2945)* 8/8/46.
4976 *(new)* 27/8/49.

WORKS CODES:- Cow - Cowlairs. Dar - Darlington. Dby - Derby. Don - Doncaster. Ghd - Gateshead. Gor - Gorton. Imm - Immingham. Inv - Inverurie. Str - Stratford.
REPAIR CODES:- **C/H** - Casual Heavy. **C/L** - Casual Light. **G** - General. **H** - Heavy. **H/I** - Heavy Intermediate. **L** - Light. **L/I** - Light Intermediate. **N/C** - Non-Classified.

27771 *(ex4954)* 16/4/53.
27748 *(ex4771)* 25/2/56.

SHEDS:
York.
Stratford 1/5/29.
Parkeston 8/9/40.
Stratford 13/4/41.
Parkeston 4/6/50.
Stratford 8/7/51.
March 25/5/58.

RENUMBERED:
4779 1/11/46.
64779 27/8/49.

CONDEMNED:
20/9/61.
Cut up at Doncaster.

2727

Darlington.

To traffic 30/4/29.

REPAIRS:
Gor. 26/6-25/7/31.**G.**
Gor. 12/1-3/2/34.**G.**
Gor. 20/4-16/5/36.**G.**
Gor. 22/3-22/4/39.**G.**
Str. 8/2-1/5/42.**G.**
Str. 14/12/42-16/1/43.**L.**
Gor. 15/11-9/12/44.**L.**
Str. 29/9-15/12/45.**G.**
Gor. 31/1-25/3/48.**G.**
Dby. 13/8-23/10/51.**G.**
Str. 16/9-30/10/54.**G.**
Str. 6-26/7/56.**C/L.**
Str. 2/4-10/5/57.**G.**

BOILERS:
2218.
2223 *(ex2730)* 25/7/31.
2208 *(ex2723)* 3/2/34.
8026 *(ex1484)* 16/5/36.
2122 *(ex2697)* 22/4/39.
2193 *(ex2777)* 25/3/48.
27678 *(ex4838)* 23/10/51.
27497 *(ex4931)* 30/10/54.
27709 *(ex4826)* 10/5/57.

SHEDS:
York.
Stratford 10/5/29.
Parkeston 4/6/50.
Stratford 18/6/50.

RENUMBERED:
4780 5/10/46.
64780 25/3/48.

CONDEMNED:
4/1/60.
Cut up at Stratford.

2728

Darlington.

To traffic 10/5/29.

REPAIRS:
Gor. 4/9-17/10/31.**G.**
Gor. 5-22/3/34.**G.**
Dar. 29/5-8/8/36.**G.**
Dar. 10-14/8/36.**N/C.**
Gor. 17/2-18/3/39.**G.**
Str. 1/3-5/6/42.**G.**
Str. 22/7-15/9/45.**G.**
Str. 6/6-13/8/48.**G.**
Dby. 27/1-22/3/51.**L/I.**
Str. 17/11/53-2/1/54.**G.**
Str. 10-24/9/54.**C/L.**
Str. 5/11-8/12/56.**G.**

BOILERS:
2220.
1919 *(ex1459)* 22/3/34.
8775 *(ex2963)* 8/8/36.
8581 *(ex2775)* 18/3/39.
2697 *(ex2999)* 5/6/42.
8586 *(ex2953)* 15/9/45.
4941 *(new)* 13/8/48.
27663 *(ex4726)* 2/1/54.
27880 *(ex4750)* 8/12/56.

SHEDS:
York.
Stratford 15/6/29.
Southend 14/12/29.
Stratford 12/4/30.
Southend 19/4/30.
Stratford 9/8/30.
Parkeston 8/9/40.
Stratford 23/6/45.
Parkeston 20/5/51.
Stratford 24/6/51.

RENUMBERED:
4781 22/3/46.
64781 13/8/48.

CONDEMNED:
7/3/60.
Cut up at Stratford.

2729

Darlington.

To traffic 10/5/29.

REPAIRS:
Gor. 25/9-7/11/31.**G.**
Gor. 29/12/33-27/1/34.**G.**
Dar. 7/4-21/5/36.**G.**
Don. 20/10-11/11/38.**G.**
Don. 3/8-26/9/41.**G.**
Gor. 8/8-7/10/44.**G.**
Str. 6/6-14/11/47.**G.**
Dby. 5/10-27/11/50.**L/I.**
Dby. 7-13/12/50.**N/C.**
Dby. 17/7-29/8/52.**G.**
Str. 14/3-23/4/55.**G.**
Str. 27/7-25/8/56.**C/L.**
March 18/5/58-11/3/60.*In store.*

BOILERS:
2222.
2110 *(ex1496)* 27/1/34.
2310 *(ex1459)* 21/5/36.
2136 *(ex1289)* 7/10/44.
27715 *(ex4837)* 29/8/52.
27892 *(ex4881)* 23/4/55.

SHEDS:
York.
Stratford 24/5/29.
March 20/4/58.

RENUMBERED:
4782 4/5/46.
64782 27/11/50.

CONDEMNED:
15/3/60.
Cut up at Stratford.

2730

Darlington.

To traffic 17/5/29.

REPAIRS:
Gor. 12/6-18/7/31.**G.**
Gor. 20/2-10/3/34.**G.**
Gor. 30/6-18/7/36.**G.**
Gor. 17/2-18/3/39.**G.**
Gor. 25/3-6/4/39.**N/C.**
Gor. 16/12/40-29/3/41.**G.**
Str. 17/3-22/4/44.**G.**
Str. 28/1-14/6/47.**G.**
Dby. 18/12/50-22/2/51.**G.**
Dby. 3-16/3/51.**N/C.**
Str. 4/1-12/2/54.**G.**
Str. 15/11-29/12/56.**G.**

BOILERS:
2223.
2145 *(ex2718)* 18/7/31.
2316 *(ex1470)* 10/3/34.
2208 *(ex2727)* 18/7/36.
2636 *(new)* 18/3/39.
2191 *(ex2779)* 29/3/41.
2706 *(ex2996)* 22/4/44.
27657 *(new)* 22/2/51.
27882 *(ex4804)* 12/2/54.
27871 *(ex4900)* 29/12/56.

SHEDS:
York.
Stratford 24/5/29.
Southend 12/4/30.
Stratford 19/4/30.
Parkeston 8/2/48.
Stratford 16/1/49.
Parkeston 4/6/50.
Stratford 18/6/50.
Peterborough 24/7/55.
Stratford 4/9/55.

RENUMBERED:
4783 26/5/46.
64783 22/2/51.

CONDEMNED:
2/11/60.
Cut up at Stratford.

2731

Darlington.

To traffic 30/5/29.

REPAIRS:
Cow. 1-6/6/29.**N/C.**
Cow. 28/1-6/3/31.**G.**
Cow. 27/9-18/11/32.**G.**
Cow. 28/2-2/3/35.**G.**
Cow. 12-13/3/35.**N/C.**
Cow. 22/9-31/10/36.**G.**
Cow. 23/8-16/9/38.**G.**
Cow. 18/6-15/7/40.**L.**
Cow. 22-23/9/41.**L.**
Cow. 3/3-11/4/42.**G.**
Cow. 17/11-8/12/43.**G.**
Cow. 21/2-8/3/44.**L.**
Cow. 21/11-15/12/45.**G.**
Str. 4-21/11/47.**L.**
Gor. 8/8-25/9/48.**G.**
Water scoop off.
Dby. 31/5-30/8/50.**H/I.**
Dby. 25/4-20/6/52.**G.**
Str. 10/6-30/7/55.**G.**
Str. 13/2-22/3/57.**G.**
Str. 30/4-30/5/58.**G.**
Str. 3-13/6/58.**N/C.**
Str. 5-25/1/60.**N/C.**

BOILERS:
2230
*2230 renumbered C1709.**
C1711 *(ex2733)* 2/3/35.
C1710 *(ex2736)* 16/9/38.
4916 *(ex1857)* 8/12/43.
E1350 *(ex1828)* 25/9/48.
27434 *(new)* 20/6/52.
27431 *(ex4876)* 30/7/55.
27891 *(ex4708)* 30/5/58.

SHEDS:
York.
Eastfield 31/5/29.
St Margarets 17/4/43.
Carlisle 5/3/45.
Thornton Junction 15/7/46.
Dundee 4/11/46.
Norwich 21/9/47.
Stratford 14/10/51.

RENUMBERED:
4784 26/5/46.
64784 25/9/48.

CONDEMNED:
20/8/60.
Cut up at Doncaster.

** Boiler numbers with C prefix are those which Cowlairs used.*

2732

Darlington.

To traffic 29/5/29.

REPAIRS:
Ghd. 13/4-21/5/31.**G.**
Ghd. 20/11/31-26/1/32.**L.**
Cow. 31/10-5/12/33.**G.**
Cow. 3/4-13/5/35.**G.**
Cow. 29/6-6/8/37.**G.**
Cow. 20/12/38-20/1/39.**G.**
Cow. 20/8-25/9/40.**G.**
Cow. 29/3-16/4/41.**L.**
Cow. 3-5/3/42.**L.**
Cow. 13/1-9/2/43.**G.**
Cow. 1-13/3/44.**L.**
Cow. 4-23/3/45.**G.**
Cow. 23/6-18/7/46.**H.**
Str. 10/7-31/10/47.**G.**
Dby. 16/8-31/10/50.**G.**
Str. 22/5-25/7/53.**G.**
Str. 11/1-5/3/54.**C/L.**
Str. 5/4-18/5/56.**G.**

BOILERS:
2231. (C1710).
C1720 *(ex2742)* 5/12/33.
C1719 *(ex2742)* 13/5/35.
4903 *(ex1835)* 25/9/40.
C1796 *(ex2979)* 9/2/43.
BP133 *(ex1425)* 18/7/46.
2579 *(ex2701)* 31/10/50.
27785 *(ex4893)* 25/7/53.
27782 *(ex4793)* 18/5/56.

SHEDS:
York.
Eastfield 30/5/29.
St Margarets 17/4/43.
Carlisle 20/8/45.
Ipswich 28/3/47.

RENUMBERED:
4785 31/3/46.
64785 31/10/50.

CONDEMNED:
12/6/59.
Cut up at Stratford.

2733

Darlington.

To traffic 6/6/29.

REPAIRS:
Dar. 14/12/31-1/2/32.**G.**
Cow. 3/11/34.**G.**
Cow. 8/8/35.**L.**
Cow. 16/6/37.**G.**
Cow. 15/4/38.**L.**
Cow. 21/1-25/2/39.**G.**
Cow. 28/12/39.**L.**
Cow. 21/9/40.**G.**
Cow. 29/3/41.**L.**
Cow. 27/6/41.**L.**
Cow. 9/2/42.**G.**
Cow. 5/8/42.**L.**
Cow. 10/2/43.**L.**
Cow. 10/7-14/8/43.**H.**
Cow. 20/9-13/10/45.**G.**
Cow. 17/11/45.**L.**
Cow. 22/2-8/3/47.**L.**
Cow. 25/11-13/12/47.**G.**
Cow. 9/1-4/2/50.**G.**
Cow. 19/8-3/10/50.**L/I.**
Cow. 5/10-14/11/53.**H/I.**
Dee. 26/5-1/7/55.**C/L.**
Cow. 13/3-21/4/56.**G.**
Cow. 3-28/6/58.**H/I.**
Cow. 3/4-6/5/59.**C/L.**
Inv. 30/8-24/11/61.**G.**

BOILERS:
2234. (C1711).
C1715 *(ex2737)* 3/11/34.
C1711 *(ex2731)* 25/2/39.
BP139 *(ex1869)* 14/8/43.
3172 *(ex4792)* 4/2/50.
3172 Reno.27550 14/11/53.
27562 *(ex4914)* 21/4/56.
27552 *(ex4947)* 24/11/61.

SHEDS:
Parkhead.
Eastfield 30/10/31.
St Margarets 17/4/43.
Carlisle 20/8/45.
Dundee 18/6/47.

RENUMBERED:
4786 1/12/46.
64786 4/2/50.

CONDEMNED:
29/12/62.
Cut up at Inverurie.

2734

Darlington.

To traffic 11/6/29.

REPAIRS:
Dar. 23/2-7/4/32.**G.**
Cow. 11-15/7/32.**L.**
Cow. 2/5-2/6/33.**L.**
Cow. 10/4-21/5/34.**G.**
Cow. 19/11-23/12/35.**G.**
Cow. 9/4-18/5/37.**G.**
Cow. 15/12/38-5/1/39.**G.**
Cow. 19/10-16/11/39.**G.**
Cow. 24/3-15/5/41.**G.**
Cow. 15/12/42-16/1/43.**G.**
Cow. 25-28/8/43.**H.**
Cow. 22/4-18/5/44.**H.**
Cow. 5/7-4/8/45.**H.**
Inv. 21/3-1/5/46.**L.**
Str. 15/4-28/10/47.**G.**
Gor. 10/8-16/10/48.**L.**
Gor. 26/10-2/11/48.**N/C.**
Dby. 9/10/50-4/1/51.**H/I.**
Str. 19/12/51-18/1/52.**C/L.**
Str. 4/3-4/5/53.**G.**
Str. 26/9-19/11/55.**G.**

BOILERS:
2236.(C1712).
C1718 *(ex2740)* 23/12/35.
C1799 *(ex2978)* 16/1/43.
2303 *(ex1459)* 18/5/44.
2671 *(ex2718)* 28/10/47.
27745 *(ex4765)* 4/5/53.
27783 *(ex4894)* 19/11/55.

SHEDS:
Parkhead.
Eastfield 30/10/31.
Dundee 7/11/33.
Carlisle 15/7/46.
Parkeston 20/3/47.
Stratford 10/5/47.
Parkeston 16/1/49.
Ardsley 20/5/51.
Parkeston 24/6/51.
Stratford 9/3/58.

RENUMBERED:
4787 10/11/46.
64787 16/10/48.

CONDEMNED:
1/6/59.
Cut up at Stratford.

2735

Darlington.

To traffic 14/6/29.

REPAIRS:
Cow. 5/2-7/3/31.**G.**
Cow. 13-16/4/31.**L.**
Cow. 12-23/10/31.**L.**
Cow. 23/1-10/3/33.**G.**
Cow. 9-20/6/33.**L.**
Cow. 26/9-5/11/34.**G.**
Cow. 11/2-12/3/36.**G.**
Cow. 3-17/3/37.**L.**
Cow. 15/2-14/3/38.**G.**
Dar. 7/6-4/8/39.**H.**
Dar. 15/7-16/9/40.**L.**
Cow. 23/10-20/11/40.**G.**

Late shoppings at Gorton show the access hole to have been dispensed with entirely, probably due to the wrapper plate having had to be replaced. 64739 ex works on 20th December 1958 also acquired the flat top dome cover peculiar to Gorton production. Disappearance of firebox access hole was also noted on 64798 out 22nd November 1958 and 64747 ex Gorton on 10th January 1959. *A.R.Goult*

Cow. 13-24/10/42.**L.**
Cow. 3-31/12/42.**H.**
Inv. 18-22/1/43.**N/C.**
Inv. 6-18/2/43.**N/C.**
Cow. 12-15/9/44.**L.**
Cow. 26/10-15/11/44.**G.**
Cow. 1-5/4/45.**L.**
Cow. 6-27/10/45.**L.**
Cow. 10-25/1/47.**H.**
Gor. 14/4-17/6/48.**L.**
Gor. 4/11/49-14/1/50.**G.**
Gor. 20-21/1/50.**N/C.**
Dby. 8/3-11/6/51.**G.**
Dby. 30/7-15/9/51.**C/L.**
Str. 5/1-20/2/54.**G.**
Str. 25/6-7/9/56.**G.**
Str. 30/4-3/5/57.**C/L.**

BOILERS:
2240.(C1713).
7946 *(new)* 10/3/33.
2568 *(ex1467)* 4/8/39.
4901 *(ex1804)* 15/11/44.
C1710 *(ex4954)* 14/1/50.
27666 *(ex4883)* 11/6/51.
27657 *(ex4783)* 20/2/54.
27802 *(ex4770)* 7/9/56.

SHEDS:
St Margarets.
Tweedmouth 19/3/39.
Malton 1/7/39.
Starbeck 29/9/39.
York 22/11/39.
Selby 29/2/40.
Carlisle 1/10/40.
Stratford 17/3/47.
Parkeston 10/5/47.
Stratford 9/3/58.

RENUMBERED:
4788 10/11/46.
64788 12/6/48.

CONDEMNED:
22/6/59.
Cut up at Stratford.

2736

Darlington.

To traffic 20/6/29.

REPAIRS:
Ghd. 26/2-29/4/31.**G.**
Ghd. 16/10-10/12/31.**L.**
Cow. 27/9-3/11/32.**G.**
Cow. 5/2-14/3/34.**G.**
Cow. 3-5/5/34.**L.**
Cow. 28/5-11/7/35.**G.**
Cow. 1/9-6/10/36.**G.**
Cow. 15/2-23/3/38.**G.**
Dar. 7/9-11/10/40.**G.**
Cow. 30/4-10/5/41.**L.**
Cow. 11/6-10/7/43.**H.**
Cow. 15-22/7/43.**N/C.**
Cow. 23/10-9/11/45.**H.**
Cow. 17/10-1/11/46.**L.**
Str. 4/7-20/10/47.**H.**
Gor. 1/8-18/9/48.**G.**
Dby. 9/8-11/10/51.**G.**
Str. 13/3-23/4/54.**G.**
Gor. 1/4-11/5/57.**G.**
Str. 28/6/60.*Not repaired.*

BOILERS:
2242.(C1714).
C1710 *(ex2732)* 14/3/34.
C1797 *(ex2978)* 23/3/38.
2595 *(ex1477)* 11/10/40.
3221 *(new)* 10/7/43.
3177 *(ex4808)* 18/9/48.
27676 *(ex4796)* 11/10/51.
27884 *(ex4773)* 23/4/54.
25841 *(new)* 11/5/57.

SHEDS:
St Margarets.
Tweedmouth 19/3/39.
Consett 8/7/39.
Carlisle 19/10/40.
Stratford 22/4/47.
Parkeston 8/2/48.
Lincoln 4/6/50.
Peterborough 12/10/52.
March 31/1/60.

RENUMBERED:
4789 7/4/46.
64789 18/9/48.

CONDEMNED:
11/7/60.
Cut up at Stratford.

2737

Darlington.

To traffic 26/6/29.

REPAIRS:
Ghd. 27/2-1/5/31.**G.**
Cow. 1/34-19/5/34.**G.**
Cow. 28/11/35.**G.**
Cow. 12/7/37.**G.**
Cow. 16/3/39.**G.**
Cow. 13/3/39.**L.**
Cow. 11/1/41.**G.**
Cow. 9/8/41.**L.**
Cow. 11/8/42.**L.**
Cow. 23/7/43.**G.**
Cow. 28/9/44.**L.**
Cow. 2/12/44.**G.**
Cow. 13-27/10/45.**L.**
Cow. 4-23/11/46.**H.**
Cow. 29/11-13/12/47.**L.**
Cow. 28/6-8/7/48.**L.**
Cow. 6/6-9/7/49.**G.**
Cow. 15/8-7/9/51.**H/I.**
Cow. 8/6-3/7/54.**G.**
Cow. 14/7/54.**N/C.**
Cow. 2-24/10/57.**H/I.**
W.P.U. gear removed.
Cow. 24/2-25/3/61.**G.**
A.W.S. fitted.

BOILERS:
2244.(C1715).
C1717 *(ex2739)* 1/5/31.
C1738 *(ex2786)* 19/5/34.
C1715 *(ex2733)* 16/3/39.
BP137 *(ex1558)* 2/12/44.
2601 *(ex Gorton)* 9/7/49.
2601 Reno. 27494 7/9/51.
27521 *(ex64700)* 3/7/54.
27527 *(ex4935)* 25/3/61.

SHEDS:
St Margarets.
Carlisle 20/8/45.
Dundee 28/9/47.
Thornton Junction 17/8/59.

RENUMBERED:
4790 7/4/46.
64790 10/7/48.

CONDEMNED:
29/12/62.
Cut up at Cowlairs.

2738

Darlington.

To traffic 3/7/29.

REPAIRS:
Cow. 11/30.**G.**
Cow. 5/32.**G.**
Cow. 20/4-15/5/34.**G.**
Cow. 21-22/3/35.**L.**
Cow. 1-2/8/35.**L.**
Cow. 3-24/6/36.**G.**
Cow. 20/1-12/2/38.**G.**
Cow. 21-29/12/38.**L.**
Cow. 3-22/8/39.**L.**
Cow. 27/4-17/5/40.**G.**
Cow. 2-4/7/40.**L.**
Cow. 22-25/10/40.**L.**
Cow. 30/6-28/8/42.**G.**
Cow. 16/7-9/8/43.**L.**
Dar. 22/2-13/3/44.*Tender only.*
Cow. 3/11-29/12/45.**G.**
Dar. 15/12/45-12/1/46.**L.**
Cow. 26/9-20/12/47.**G.**
Cow. 11/6-3/7/48.**L.**
Cow. 16/10-10/11/51.**G.**
Cow. 15/11-8/12/51.**N/C.**
Cow. 2-26/12/53.**H/I.**
Cow. 2/7-10/8/57.**G.**
Gor. 26/2-25/3/61.**L/I.**

BOILERS:
2246.(C1716).
C1740 *(ex2788)* 24/6/36.
3212 *(new ex Dar)* 28/8/42.
C1716 *(ex1875)* 20/12/47.
27591 *(new)* 10/11/51.
27743 *(ex65928)* 10/8/57.

SHEDS:
Eastfield.
Darlington 18/8/43.
Saltburn 30/12/46.
Darlington 10/1/47.
Neville Hill 29/1/50.
Bradford 15/9/57.
Low Moor 12/1/58.

RENUMBERED:
4791 5/5/46.
64791 3/7/48.

CONDEMNED:
26/11/62.
Cut up at Crewe.

2739

Darlington.

To traffic 3/7/29.

REPAIRS:
Ghd. 25/2-30/4/31.**G.**
Cow. 21/6-15/7/33.**G.**
Cow. 8/9/34.**G.**
Cow. 6/2/36.**G.**
Cow. 10/10/37.**G.**
Cow. 8/9/38.**L.**
Cow. 2/12/39.**G.**
Cow. 6/4/40.**L.**
Cow. 1/2/41.**L.**
Cow. 18/4/42.**G.**
Cow. 4-18/12/43.**G.**
Inv. 19/4-26/5/45.**L.**
Cow. 20/10-3/11/45.**L.**
Cow. 4-18/4/47.**H.**
Cow. 18/10-24/11/49.**G.**
Inv. 10/10-1/11/51.**L/I.**
Cow. 25/3-9/4/55.**G.**
Cow. 13-14/4/55.**N/C.**
Cow. 18/2-15/3/58.**H/I.**
Cow. 2-4/10/58.**C/L.**
Cow. 28-30/4/59.**C/L.**
Cow. 14-26/3/60.**C/H.**
Cow. 11-19/5/60.**C/L.**
Cow. 24/10/60-6/1/61.**C/L.**

BOILERS:
2249.(C1717).
C1715 *(ex2737)* 30/4/31.
C1713 *(ex2735)* 15/7/33.
C1714 *(ex2736)* 8/9/34.
C1713 *(ex2742)* 2/12/39.
3172 *(ex3085)* 18/12/43.
2843 *(ex4700)* 24/11/49.

WORKS CODES:- Cow - Cowlairs. Dar - Darlington. Dby - Derby. Don - Doncaster. Ghd - Gateshead. Gor - Gorton. Inv - Inverurie. Str - Stratford.
REPAIR CODES:- **C/H** - Casual Heavy. **C/L** - Casual Light. **G** - General. **H**- Heavy. **H/I** - Heavy Intermediate. **L** - Light. **L/I** - Light Intermediate. **N/C** - Non-Classified.

All were equipped to enable the front part of the grate to be dropped for easier cleaning out of ash and clinker. The first 123, to no.2788 built in February 1930, had a system of bell cranks and rods which needed a semi-circular casing on the running plate to protect the screwed end of the operating rod. *Real Photos*

2843 Reno.27534 1/11/51.
27544 *(ex64939)* 9/4/55.
27556 *(ex64975)* 26/3/60.

SHEDS:
Carlisle.
St Margarets 1/35.
Polmont 8/40.
Dundee 18/8/43.
Thornton Junction 17/8/59.

RENUMBERED:
4792 24/3/46.
64792 24/11/49.

CONDEMNED:
4/1/62.
Cut up at Cowlairs.

2740

Darlington.

To traffic 9/7/29.

REPAIRS:
Cow. 2/9-11/10/30.**G.**
Cow. 16/3-22/4/32.**G.**
Cow. 19/1-28/2/34.**G.**
Cow. 31/8-4/9/34.**L.**
Cow. 6-15/11/34.**L.**
Cow. 8/10-18/11/35.**G.**
Cow. 17/8-8/9/37.**G.**
Cow. 2/2-16/3/40.**G.**
Cow. 11-14/6/40.**L.**
Cow. 14-15/8/40.**L.**
Cow. 5/7-2/8/41.**L.**
Cow. 17/2-18/3/43.**G.**
Cow. 5-11/7/44.**L.**
Cow. 20/6-10/7/45.**G.**
Cow. 21-27/8/45.**L.**
Cow. 3-23/10/46.**L.**
Cow. 23/1/47.**N/C.**
Spark arrestor fitted.
Cow. 19-22/3/47.**L.**
Gor. 14/3-17/5/48.**G.**
Gor. 21/10-27/11/48.**L.**
Gor. 28/1-18/2/49.**L.**
Dby. 20/11/50-24/1/51.**H/I.**
Str. 10/3-25/6/53.**G.**
Str. 22/4-30/6/54.**C/L.**
Str. 8/1-15/2/56.**G.**
Str. 15-28/5/57.**C/L.**
Str. 17-23/10/58.**C/L.**

BOILERS:
2250.(C1718).
C1720 *(ex2732)* 18/11/35.
C1714 *(ex2739)* 16/3/40.
822 *(ex1454)* 10/7/45.
4914 *(ex3091)* 17/5/48.
27782 *(ex4776)* 25/6/53.
27772 *(ex4772)* 15/2/56.

SHEDS:
Carlisle.
Eastfield 11/11/31.
Carlisle 1/2/33.
Ipswich 1/5/47.

RENUMBERED:
4793 7/4/46.
64793 15/5/48.

CONDEMNED:
26/11/59.
Cut up at Stratford.

2741

Darlington.

To traffic 12/7/29.

REPAIRS:
Cow. 2/31.**G.**
Cow. 2/33-17/3/33.**G.**
Cow. 19/9/34.**G.**
Cow. 21/3/36.**G.**
Cow. 4/6/37.**G.**
Cow. 16/4/39.**G.**
Cow. 28/9/40.**G.**
Cow. 29/11/41.**G.**
Cow. 19/8/42.**L.**
Cow. 20/3/43.**H.**
Cow. 28/10/44.**G.**
Inv. 31/3-31/5/45.**L.**
Cow. 25/3-12/4/47.**H.**
Cow. 23/4-15/5/48.**L.**
Cow. 24/11-24/12/49.**G.**
Cow. 4-6/1/50.**N/C.**
Cow. 17/11-5/12/52.**L/I.**
Cow. 1/7-13/8/55.**G.**
W.P.U. gear removed.
Cow. 22-25/8/55.**N/C.**
Cow. 31/8-3/9/55.**N/C.**
Cow. 2/5-7/6/57.**L/I.**
Inv. 25/8-28/9/60.**L/I.**
A.W.S. fitted.

BOILERS:
2251.(C1719).
C1801 *(new)* 17/3/33.
C1739 *(ex2787)* 21/3/36.
C1738 *(ex2737)* 16/4/39.
2143 *(ex1449)* 28/10/44.
C2019 *(new)* 24/12/49.
C2019 Reno.27568 5/12/52.
27534 *(ex64792)* 13/8/55.

SHEDS:
Dundee.
Aberdeen 1/8/29.
St Margarets 18/12/49.
Bathgate 10/5/53.
St Margarets 31/1/54.
Dalry Road 11/8/58.
Thornton Junction 18/12/61.

RENUMBERED:
4794 9/6/46.
64794 15/5/48.

CONDEMNED:
13/8/62.
Cut up at Inverurie.

2742

Darlington.

To traffic 31/7/29.

REPAIRS:
Cow. 17/6/33.**G.**
Cow. 1/12/34.**G.**
Cow. 11/6/36.**G.**
Cow. 4/12/36.**L.**
Cow. 27/8/37.**G.**
Cow. 17/6/39.**G.**
Cow. 1/7/39.**L.**
Cow. 7/12/40.**G.**
Cow. 26/2/43.**L.**
Cow. 20/8/43.**H.**
Cow. 11/12/43.**L.**
Inv. 7/4-5/5/45.**L.**
Cow. 27/4-28/5/46.**H.**
Cow. 21/4-25/6/47.**G.**
Inv. 2-4/3/48.**L.**
Cow. 13/10-4/11/50.**H/I.**
Cow. 2-27/3/54.**G.**
Cow. 5/3-6/4/57.**G.**
Inv. 4-6/11/57.**N/C.**
Cow. 26/2/59.**N/C.**
Cow. 25-30/6/59.**C/L.**
Inv. 23/1-17/3/61.**H/I.**
A.W.S. fitted.

BOILERS:
2253.(C1720).
C1719 *(ex2741)* 17/6/33.
C1713 *(ex2739)* 1/12/34.
C1739 *(ex2741)* 17/6/39.
2636 *(ex4858)* 25/6/47.
27546 *(ex4848)* 27/3/54.
27543 *(ex4842)* 6/4/57.

SHEDS:
Aberdeen.
St Margarets 10/3/59.
Dunfermline 22/1/62.

RENUMBERED:
4795 11/8/46.
64795 4/11/50.

CONDEMNED:
29/12/62.
Cut up at Inverurie.

Beginning with 2962 new in September 1931, a simpler gear was fitted, with operating rod going through the running plate, on which the casing was no longer needed. Many, but not all, had the casing removed, but 2699 (64752 later) survived general repairs by Gorton, Cowlairs, Stratford, and Derby and still kept the casing. *WBY collection*

2770

Darlington.

To traffic 28/8/29.

REPAIRS:
Gor. 20/11-26/12/31.**G.**
Gor. 30/10-17/11/34.**G.**
Gor. 1-26/6/37.**G.**
Gor. 13-28/1/38.**L.**
Gor. 1-13/8/38.**G.**
Gor. 10/1-21/2/42.**G.**
Gor. 14/4-17/6/44.**G.**
Str. 31/3-3/8/46.**G.**
Str. 26/8-14/9/46.**L.**
Gor. 13/6-21/8/48.**L.**
Gor. 22/9-26/11/49.**G.**
Gor. 8-21/12/49.**N/C.**
Gor. 24/2-22/4/50.**C/L.**
Dby. 7/4-6/7/51.**G.**
Gor. 27/11-31/12/53.**G.**
Gor. 3-9/1/54.**N/C.**
Gor. 25/10-1/12/56.**G.**
Gor. 18/9-22/11/58.**C/L.**
Gor. 13/9-29/10/60.**G.**
Gor. 15-22/11/60.**N/C.**
Gor. 20-29/9/61.**N/C.**

BOILERS:
2194.
2287 *(ex2777)* 26/12/31.
2193 *(ex2772)* 17/11/34.
8023 *(ex2694)* 26/6/37.
2136 *(ex2976)* 13/8/38.
RS120 *(ex2718)* 21/2/42.
2667 *(ex1943)* 17/6/44.
2291 *(ex4811)* 26/11/49.
27669 *(ex4725)* 6/7/51.
25806 *(ex4966)* 31/12/53.
27832 *(ex4823)* 1/12/56.
27844 *(ex4974)* 29/10/60.

SHEDS:
York.
Ipswich 7/9/29.
Parkeston 21/9/29.
Ipswich 7/1/35.
Parkeston 9/2/35.
Ardsley 1/2/36.
Bradford 16/6/57.
Low Moor 12/1/58.
Ardsley 14/6/59.

RENUMBERED:
4796 14/9/46.
64796 25/12/48.

CONDEMNED:
13/12/62.
Cut up at Darlington.

2771

Darlington.

To traffic 4/9/29.

REPAIRS:
Gor. 29/2-26/3/32.**G.**
Gor. 1-18/4/35.**G.**
Gor. 3-24/7/37.**G.**
Gor. 24/9-18/11/39.**G.**
Gor. 4/1-19/2/42.**G.**
Str. 29/4-3/6/44.**G.**
Str. 9/12/45-6/2/46.**G.**
Gor. 15/2-25/3/48.**G.**
Dby. 28/5-24/8/50.**G.**
Dby. 28/8-4/9/50.**N/C.**
Str. 31/5-1/8/53.**G.**
Str. 4/5-1/6/54.**C/L.**
Str. 21/7-6/8/55.**C/L.**
Str. 15/1-18/2/56.**G.**
Str. 22/9/59.*Not repaired.*

BOILERS:
2193.
2302 *(ex2785)* 26/3/32.
8025 *(ex2780)* 18/4/35.
2282 *(ex2724)* 24/7/37.
8583 *(ex2973)* 18/11/39.
8584 *(ex2776)* 19/2/42.
8591 *(ex2717)* 3/6/44.
2282 *(ex2944)* 6/2/46.
2666 *(ex1496)* 25/3/48.
27786 *(ex4728)* 1/8/53.
27775 *(ex4803)* 18/2/56.

SHEDS:
York.
Ipswich 7/9/29.
Parkeston 26/1/35.
March 2/3/36.
Stratford 25/5/43.
Parkeston 24/6/44.
Stratford 23/6/45.
Ipswich 7/4/46.
Norwich 19/5/46.
Lowestoft 21/10/51.
Norwich 10/2/52.
Lowestoft 28/9/52.
Norwich 28/12/52.
Lowestoft 29/9/57.

RENUMBERED:
4797 5/1/47.
64797 25/3/48.

CONDEMNED:
28/9/59.
Cut up at Stratford.

2772

Darlington.

To traffic 11/9/29.

REPAIRS:
Gor. 14/3-9/4/32.**G.**
Gor. 3-18/10/34.**G.**
Gor. 26/11-19/12/36.**G.**
Gor. 13/1-11/2/39.**G.**
Gor. 7/1-16/3/40.**G.**
Don. 8/6-14/8/41.**G.**
Str. 5/12/43-22/1/44.**G.**
Str. 13/7-20/8/45.**L.**
Str. 21/4-28/8/46.**G.**
Str. 1/6-29/7/47.**L.**
Gor. 3/10-4/12/48.**G.**
Gor. 4/2-23/4/49.**C/H.**
Dby. 29/8-10/11/50.**G.**
Gor. 7/4-16/5/53.**G.**
Gor. 15/2-24/3/56.**G.**
Gor. 20/10-22/11/58.**G.**

BOILERS:
2273.
2193 *(ex2771)* 9/4/32.
2203 *(ex2721)* 18/10/34.
8016 *(ex1296)* 19/12/36.
2184 *(ex2972)* 11/2/39.
E1355 *(ex1933)* 22/1/44.
2317 *(ex1940)* 28/8/46.
8592 *(ex3093)* 4/12/48.
2309 *(ex4762)* 10/11/50.
27755 *(ex4960)* 16/5/53.
27727 *(ex64820)* 24/3/56.
27837 *(ex4757)* 22/11/58.

SHEDS:
York.
Ipswich 18/9/29.
Stratford 9/5/32.
Parkeston 21/8/38.
Stratford 26/3/39.
March 20/10/39.
Stratford 28/5/43.
Norwich 13/9/44.
Yarmouth 9/10/46.
Norwich 10/12/46.
Yarmouth 12/10/47.
Norwich 12/11/47.
Woodford 16/4/50.
Colwick 8/10/50.
Annesley 3/11/57.

RENUMBERED:
4798 31/10/46.
64798 4/12/48.

CONDEMNED:
11/9/62.
Cut up at Gorton.

2773

Darlington.

To traffic 30/9/29.

REPAIRS:
Gor. 3/9-17/10/31.**G.**
Gor. 30/4-19/5/34.**G.**
Gor. 17/8-19/9/36.**G.**
Don. 25/11-23/12/38.**G.**

Gor. 23/5-6/7/40.**L.**
Don. 25/10-13/12/41.**G.**
Str. 10/3-29/4/44.**G.**
Str. 22/4-18/6/46.**L.**
Str. 12/6-9/10/47.**G.**
Str. 30/12/47-20/1/48.**L.**
Gor. 13/5-1/7/49.**G.**
Dby. 23/3-2/5/52.**G.**
Str. 25/1-24/2/55.**G.**
Str. 10/4-9/5/58.**G.**
Str. 20/7/59.*Not repaired.*

BOILERS:
2274.
8015 *(ex1272)* 19/5/34.
1931 *(ex1275)* 19/9/36.
2296 *(ex1457)* 29/4/44.
4972 *(new)* 1/7/49.
27432 *(new)* 2/5/52.
27847 *(new)* 24/2/55.
27711 *(ex4766)* 9/5/58.

SHEDS:
York.
Stratford 9/10/29.
Norwich 15/4/46.
Yarmouth 12/11/47.
Norwich 4/1/48.
Ardsley 30/4/50.
Tuxford 27/9/53.
Stratford 16/1/55.
New England 28/10/56.
Stratford 17/3/57.

RENUMBERED:
4799 25/10/46.
64799 1/7/49.

CONDEMNED:
27/7/59.
Cut up at Stratford.

2774

Darlington.

To traffic 20/9/29.

REPAIRS:
Gor. 7/10-21/11/31.**G.**
Gor. 18-31/5/34.**G.**
Dar. 29/5-11/7/36.**G.**
Gor. 6-25/3/39.**G.**
Str. 23/11/41-19/3/42.**G.**
Str. 19/8-4/9/42.**L.**
Gor. 11/8-7/10/44.**G.**
Str. 16/3-14/4/45.**L.**
Gor. 21/7-23/11/46.**G.**
Str. 21-28/8/47.**L.**
Gor. 30/12/49-25/2/50.**G.**
Dby. 11/1-28/2/52.**L/I.**
Dby. 9/10-24/11/52.**C/L.**
Str. 6-16/9/53.**C/L.**
Str. 23-24/9/53.**N/C.**
Str. 4/10-13/11/54.**G.**
Str. 10/3-18/4/57.**G.**

BOILERS:
2277.
8580 *(ex2962)* 31/5/34.
1917 *(ex1272)* 11/7/36.
8587 *(ex2963)* 25/3/39.
2094 *(ex1265)* 7/10/44.
3215 *(ex2701)* 23/11/46.
2102 *(ex2723)* 25/2/50.
2102 Reno.27708 24/11/52.
27688 *(ex4981)* 13/11/54.
27882 *(ex4783)* 18/4/57.

SHEDS:
York.
Stratford 28/9/29.
March 16/10/39.
Norwich 12/9/43.
Ipswich 7/11/43.
March 25/10/59.

RENUMBERED:
4800 7/9/46.
64800 25/2/50.

CONDEMNED:
21/1/60.
Cut up at Stratford.

2775

Darlington.

To traffic 30/9/29.

REPAIRS:
Gor. 4/11-5/12/31.**G.**
Gor. 2-23/6/34.**G.**
Gor. 16/7-1/8/36.**G.**
Gor. 3-25/2/39.**G.**
Don. 15/6-18/8/41.**G.**
Gor. 18/1-4/3/44.**G.**
Gor. 26/1-30/8/47.**G.**
Dby. 22/4-29/6/51.**G.**
Gor. 18/3-28/4/54.**G.**
Gor. 1-6/5/54.**N/C.**
Gor. 3/2-12/3/55.**C/H.**
Gor. 20/3-5/4/55.**N/C.**
Gor. 4/10-24/11/56.**C/L.**
Gor. 31/7-21/9/57.**G.**
Gor. 15-28/4/59.**C/L.**
Gor. 21/5-4/6/59.**C/L.**
Gor. 30/5-5/7/60.**C/L.**

BOILERS:
2282.
8019 *(ex1282)* 5/12/31.
2277 *(ex2774)* 23/6/34.
8581 *(ex2777)* 1/8/36.
2146 *(ex2776)* 25/2/39.
2683 *(ex2782)* 4/3/44.
2771 *(ex2784)* 30/8/47.
27670 *(ex4910)* 29/6/51.
25810 *(ex4753)* 28/4/54.
27791 *(ex4955)* 21/9/57.

SHEDS:
York.
Stratford 11/10/29.
March 16/10/39.
Stratford 3/6/43.
Ardsley 30/9/43.
Bradford 27/5/56.
Low Moor 12/1/58.

RENUMBERED:
4801 17/11/46.
64801 29/6/51.

CONDEMNED:
26/11/62.
Cut up at Crewe.

2776

Darlington.

To traffic 7/10/29.

REPAIRS:
Gor. 31/12/31-23/1/32.**G.**
Gor. 2-24/2/34.**G.**
Dar. 27/5-9/7/36. *Not repaired.*
Sent to Gorton.
Gor. 14/7-6/8/36.**G.**
Gor. 17/1-11/2/39.**G.**
Gor. 13/4-14/6/41.**G.**
Cow. 15/5-25/7/43.**G.**
Gor. 14/4-21/7/45.**G.**
Str. 14/12/47-8/3/48.**G.**
Dby. 2/12/50-9/2/51.**G.**
Str. 9/8-12/9/53.**G.**
Str. 22-28/9/53.**N/C.**
Str. 2/5-16/6/56.**G.**
Str. 18/7/60.*Not repaired.*

BOILERS:
2284.
2194 *(ex2770)* 23/1/32.
2223 *(ex2727)* 24/2/34.
2146 *(ex2972)* 6/8/36.
8584 *(ex2715)* 11/2/39.
8772 *(ex2782)* 14/6/41.
2273 *(ex2984)* 21/7/45.
2776 *(ex2988)* 8/3/48.
27656 *(ex2965)* 9/2/51.
27870 *(ex4797)* 12/9/53.
27771 *(ex4779)* 16/6/56.

SHEDS:
York.
Stratford 15/10/29.
Norwich 29/9/44.
Yarmouth Beach 24/6/56.
Norwich 26/8/56.
Melton Constable 6/1/57.
Norwich 13/10/57.
Lincoln 30/11/58.
Colwick 4/1/59.

RENUMBERED:
4802 8/12/46.
E4802 8/3/48.
64802 9/2/51.

CONDEMNED:
25/7/60.
Cut up at Stratford.

2777

Darlington.

To traffic 16/10/29.

REPAIRS:
Gor. 10/11-12/12/31.**G.**
Gor. 13-28/7/34.**G.**
Gor. 28/4-16/5/36.**G.**
Gor. 2-30/8/38.**G.**
Gor. 27/11/40-18/1/41.**G.**
Str. 8/8-28/9/43.**G.**
Gor. 14/4-16/6/45.**G.**
Gor. 16/12/47-29/2/48.**G.**
Gor. 26/3-3/6/50.**G.**
Gor. 9-15/6/50.**N/C.**
Gor. 20/6-31/7/50.**N/C.**
Str. 24/3-16/5/53.**G.**
Str. 16/10-1/12/55.**G.**
Str. 1/5-1/6/56.**C/L.**
Str. 15/9/59.*Not repaired.*

BOILERS:
2287.
2282 *(ex2775)* 12/12/31.
8581 *(ex2963)* 28/7/34.
8009 *(ex1281)* 16/5/36.
RS118 *(ex1270)* 30/8/38.
2216 *(ex1496)* 18/1/41.
2665 *(ex2942)* 28/9/43.
2193 *(ex1255)* 16/6/45.
2678 *(ex1450)* 29/2/48.
4987 *(new)* 3/6/50.
27775 *(ex4913)* 16/5/53.
27666 *(ex4788)* 1/12/55.

SHEDS:
York.
Stratford 21/10/29.
Southend 18/1/30.
Stratford 25/1/30.
Southend 1/2/30.
Stratford 8/2/30.
Colchester 25/9/39.
Stratford 3/12/39.
Norwich 22/9/44.
Ipswich 29/7/46.
Stratford 14/10/51.
Cambridge 15/5/55.

RENUMBERED:
4803 1/12/46.
E4803 29/2/48.
64803 3/6/50.

CONDEMNED:
28/9/59.
Cut up at Stratford.

2778

Darlington.

To traffic 18/10/29.

REPAIRS:
Gor. 10/11-12/12/31.**G.**
Gor. 9-30/6/34.**G.**
Str. 31/7-1/8/34.**L.**
Gor. 4/9-3/10/36.**G.**
Gor. 10/2-4/3/39.**G.**
Don. 28/6-16/8/41.**G.**
Str. 18/3-23/7/42.**L.**
Str. 8/9-19/10/43.**L.**
Str. 27/6-25/8/44.**G.**
Str. 2/3-4/6/47.**G.**
Gor. 30/4-25/6/49.**G.**
Dby. 29/9-30/10/51.**H/I.**
Str. 8/12/53-5/2/54.**G.**
Gor. 5/11-15/12/56.**G.**

BOILERS:
2290.
8017 *(ex1275)* 30/6/34.
2189 *(ex2970)* 3/10/36.
2194 *(ex2706)* 4/3/39.
2704 *(ex2991)* 25/8/44.
8023 *(ex1965)* 4/6/47.
4920 *(ex2976)* 25/6/49.
27671 *(ex4750)* 5/2/54.
27887 *(ex4830)* 15/12/56.

SHEDS:
York.
Stratford 28/10/29.
Parkeston 13/11/43.
Lincoln 4/6/50.
Stratford 10/11/57.
March 26/11/58.
Sheffield 7/12/58.
Colwick 13/3/60.

RENUMBERED:
4804 15/6/46.
64804 25/6/49.

CONDEMNED:
19/4/61.
Cut up at Doncaster.

2779

Darlington.

To traffic 25/10/29.

REPAIRS:
Gor. 4-28/1/33.**G.**
Gor. 8-22/3/35.**G.**
Gor. 10-28/11/36.**G.**
Don. 11/11-9/12/38.**G.**
Gor. 23/11/40-11/1/41.**G.**
Don. 26/7-15/10/43.**G.**
Gor. 26/8-24/11/45.**G.**
Gor. 20/10-30/12/47.**G.**
Dby. 23/11/50-15/1/51.**H/I.**
Dby. 7-19/3/51.**N/C.**
Dby. 14/7-1/9/52.**G.**
Gor. 2/11-24/12/53.**C/L.**
Str. 31/1-19/3/55.**G.**

BOILERS:
2291.
2128 *(ex2712)* 28/1/33.
2290 *(ex2778)* 22/3/35.
2191 *(ex2708)* 28/11/36.
2766 *(ex1952)* 11/1/41.
2123 *(ex1498)* 24/11/45.
8587 *(ex1286)* 30/12/47.
27716 *(ex4987)* 1/9/52.
27809 *(ex4767)* 19/3/55.

SHEDS:
York.
Annesley 31/10/29.
Colwick 4/11/33.
Annesley 2/12/33.
Colwick 30/3/47.
Gorton 11/12/49.
Bidston 25/12/49.
Gorton 1/1/50.
Colwick 14/5/50.
Tuxford 27/9/53.
Stratford 16/1/55.
New England 28/10/56.
Stratford 17/3/57.

RENUMBERED:
4805 29/9/46.
64805 15/1/51.

CONDEMNED:
5/10/59.
Cut up at Stratford.

2780

Darlington.

To traffic 4/11/29.

REPAIRS:
Gor. 3-29/10/32.**G.**
Gor. 12/11-1/12/34.**G.**
Gor. 24/8-24/9/36.**G.**
Gor. 19/7-6/8/38.**G.**
Gor. 4/8-7/10/39.**G.**
Gor. 15/5-2/8/41.**G.**
Gor. 3/1-26/4/43.**G.**
Str. 8/2-1/6/46.**G.**
Gor. 5/8-18/9/48.**G.**
Dby. 31/8-22/10/51.**H/I.**
Dby. 29/10-14/11/51.**N/C.**
Gor. 16/4-2/5/53.**C/L.**
Gor. 1/5-5/6/54.**G.**
Gor. 8-19/6/54.**N/C.**
Gor. 9/1-18/2/56.**C/L.**
Gor. 12/9-2/11/57.**G.**
Gor. 7/3-28/4/61.**H/I.**

BOILERS:
2294.
8025 *(ex1296)* 29/10/32.
2274 *(ex2773)* 1/12/34.
8593 *(ex2969)* 24/9/36.
8013 *(ex2782)* 6/8/38.
2210 *(ex2696)* 7/10/39.
2767 *(ex1943)* 2/8/41.
2300 *(ex2973)* 26/4/43.
8580 *(ex1488)* 1/6/46.
2290 *(ex1857)* 18/9/48.
2290 Reno.27758 2/5/53.
27689 *(ex4717)* 5/6/54.
27730 *(ex4885)* 2/11/57.

SHEDS:
York.
Colwick 8/11/29.
Annesley 15/11/29.
Lincoln 20/6/30.
Ardsley 4/8/30.
Annesley 19/8/30.
Colwick 9/8/43.
Darlington 26/10/43.
Colwick 16/2/45.
Ardsley 18/8/46.
Heaton 13/12/59.
Sunderland 14/1/62.

RENUMBERED:
4806 1/12/46.
64806 18/9/48.

CONDEMNED:
17/5/62.
Cut up at Gorton.

2781

Darlington.

To traffic 7/11/29.

REPAIRS:
Gor. 17/10-11/11/32.**G.**
Gor. 21/1-8/2/35.**G.**
Gor. 7-26/12/36.**G.**
Gor. 1-26/3/38.**G.**
Gor. 12/8-28/10/39.**G.**
Str. 17/12/41-29/3/42.**G.**
Gor. 1/12/42-17/4/43.**G.**
Gor. 6/8-7/10/44.**G.**
Gor. 19/8/46-8/2/47.**G.**
Gor. 10-15/3/47.**L.**
Gor. 30/9-11/12/48.**G.**
Gor. 12/7-19/8/49.**C/L.**
Dby. 18/9-23/11/50.**H/I.**
Dby. 30/7-19/9/52.**G.**
Str. 20/7-27/8/54.**C/L.**
Str. 29/9-4/11/55.**G.**
Str. 4/11/57-10/1/58.**C/L.**

BOILERS:
2296.
8024 *(ex1295)* 11/11/32.
8004 *(ex1492)* 8/2/35.
2290 *(ex2779)* 26/12/36.
2301 *(ex2784)* 26/3/38.
2579 *(ex1488)* 28/10/39.
2208 *(ex2696)* 7/10/44.
3170 *(ex3083)* 8/2/47.
2103 *(ex1267)* 11/12/48.
27719 *(ex4971 & spare)* 19/9/52.
27848 *(new)* 4/11/55.

SHEDS:
York.
Colwick 15/11/29.
Annesley 19/11/29.
Colwick 9/8/43.
Gorton 3/10/43.
Colwick 14/5/50.
Tuxford 27/9/53.
Stratford 16/1/55.
Sheffield 7/12/58.

RENUMBERED:
4807 24/10/46.
64807 11/12/48.

CONDEMNED:
5/4/60.
Cut up at Stratford.

2782

Darlington.

To traffic 12/11/29.

REPAIRS:
Gor. 8/2-5/3/32.**G.**
Gor. 29/3-21/4/34.**G.**
Dar. 7/4-16/5/36.**G.**
Gor. 28/6-23/7/38.**G.**
Gor. 6/12/40-18/1/41.**G.**
Gor. 1/12/43-5/2/44.**G.**
Gor. 25/3-16/6/45.**G.**
Gor. 7/10/46-7/4/47.**G.**
Gor. 8-21/8/48.**G.**
Gor. 5/9-2/10/48.**N/C.**
Dby. 28/6-23/8/51.**H/I.**
Gor. 6/11-12/12/53.**G.**
Gor. 15-19/12/53.**N/C.**
Gor. 1/7-1/9/56.**G.**

BOILERS:
2299.
8013 *(ex1274)* 21/4/34.
8772 *(ex2718)* 23/7/38.
2683 *(ex2952)* 18/1/41.
E1351 *(ex1997)* 5/2/44.
3177 *(ex1926)* 7/4/47.
4942 *(new)* 21/8/48.
27665 *(ex4955)* 12/12/53.
25809 *(ex4746)* 1/9/56.

SHEDS:
York.
Sheffield 16/11/29.
Staveley 16/12/37.
Sheffield 29/7/38.

RENUMBERED:
4808 9/6/46.
64808 21/8/48.

CONDEMNED:
21/2/61.
Cut up at Doncaster.

Stratford in particular left the useless casing in place on the J39s that it repaired, as 64780 shows in this 12th May 1957 photograph, after its final repair two days earlier. When withdrawn on 4th January 1960 the casing was still there, and this was one J39 which did *not* change from emblem to crest on its tender. *A.R.Goult*

Only the 44 built in 1926/7 had their reversing gear operated by the N.E.R. design of two-handle steam control, the linkage and piping for which can be clearly seen on no.1275. The 245 built from 2691 in July 1928 had screw operated reversing gear, and in April 1935 to May 1937, the twelve in North Eastern Area were changed from steam to screw. Conversion of the 32 in Southern Area took from September 1935 until April 1948! *T.G.Hepburn*

Until February 1930, the upper lamp iron was fitted in the customary Darlington position, which put the lamp above the top of the smokebox. It was rare to see it being used for one of the Great Eastern discs as here on no.1269. *LPC*

On the East Coast main line from York to as far north as Morpeth, Vincent Raven's system of fog signalling apparatus was in mandatory operation until October 1933. Those J39s allocated to North Eastern Area thus needed to be fitted for it, and on no.1458 the striker for it can be seen between the rear coupled wheel and the cab footstep.

After the Raven system went out of use at the end of October 1933, the engines which had been fitted to use it had their equipment removed at their next works visit, no.1491 being so denuded in February 1934. *W.L.Good*

The late introduction by British Railways of their Automatic Warning System led to only sparse fitting of it on J39 class, mainly on N.E. Region allocated engines. One of them, 64904 of Hull Dairycoates shed, was so equipped by Cowlairs, evidence of it being the receiver under the front end, and the brake cylinder on running plate. All the class were fitted at the front end with Group Standard buffers from new, and they showed remarkable consistency in retaining that type to withdrawal. *WBY collection*

2783

Darlington.

To traffic 18/11/29.

REPAIRS:
Gor. 29/10-5/12/31.**G.**
Gor. 20/2-15/3/34.**G.**
Dar. 17/12/35-25/1/36.**G.**
Gor. 29/3-26/4/38.**G.**
Gor. 22/3-4/5/40.**G.**
Gor. 8/11/43-15/1/44.**G.**
Gor. 2-9/2/44.**L.**
Gor. 7/10/46-16/4/47.**G.**
Gor. 28/4-16/5/47.**N/C.**
Gor. 28/10-24/12/49.**G.**
Gor. 29-30/12/49.**N/C.**
Gor. 2-21/1/50.**N/C.**
Dby. 24/10-27/11/52.**H/I.**
Gor. 18/12/54-22/1/55.**G.**
Gor. 28/9-26/10/57.**G.**
Gor. 20/1/62.*Not repaired.*

BOILERS:
2300.
2301 *(ex2784)* 15/3/34.
2214 *(ex1457)* 25/1/36.
2290 *(ex2781)* 26/4/38.
2301 *(ex2781)* 4/5/40.
2203 *(ex2974)* 15/1/44.
2287 *(ex2998)* 16/4/47.
4981 *(new)* 24/12/49.
4981 Reno.27702 27/11/52.
27764 *(ex4742)* 22/1/55.
27839 *(ex4980)* 26/10/57.

SHEDS:
York.
Sheffield 21/11/29.
Retford 14/4/36.
Sheffield 6/7/36.
York 19/6/38.
Sheffield 12/8/38.
Gorton 27/10/57.
Woodford 1/6/60.

RENUMBERED:
4809 6/10/46.
64809 24/12/49.

CONDEMNED:
26/1/62.
Cut up at Gorton.

2784

Darlington.

To traffic 26/11/29.

REPAIRS:
Gor. 19/2-12/3/32.**G.**
Gor. 12/2-3/3/34.**G.**
Dar. 13/1-15/2/36.**G.**
Gor. 11/2-12/3/38.**G.**
Gor. 11/7-31/8/40.**G.**
Gor. 2/2-18/4/42.**G.**
Gor. 10-15/5/42.**N/C.**
Gor. 6/6-29/7/44.**G.**
Gor. 7/1-2/3/46.**L.**
Gor. 13/12/46-28/5/47.**G.**
Dby. 10/10-20/11/51.**G.**
Dby. 28/2-22/3/52.**N/C.**
Gor. 4-6/7/53.**N/C.**
Gor. 28/6-21/8/54.**G.**
Gor. 25-28/8/54.**N/C.**
Gor. 30/5-4/8/56.**C/L.**
Gor. 23/10-7/12/57.**G.**
Str. 24/2-10/3/59.**N/C.**
Tender change.

BOILERS:
2301.
8584 *(ex2966)* 3/3/34.
2301 *(ex2783)* 15/2/36.
824 *(ex2711)* 12/3/38.
8773 *(ex2712)* 31/8/40.
RS118 *(ex1274)* 18/4/42.
2771 *(ex2998)* 29/7/44.
3176 *(ex3098)* 28/5/47.
27681 *(ex4965)* 20/11/51.
27670 *(ex4801)* 21/8/54.
25810 *(ex4801)* 7/12/57.

SHEDS:
York.
Sheffield 5/12/29.
Retford 17/6/36.
Sheffield 1/9/36.
Barnsley 24/10/46.
Gorton 28/5/47.
Sheffield 29/8/54.
Stratford 17/10/54.
Parkeston 20/3/55.
Doncaster 27/11/55.
Retford 25/9/60.

RENUMBERED:
4810 24/11/46.
64810 20/11/51.

CONDEMNED:
26/6/61.
Cut up at Doncaster.

2785

Darlington.

To traffic 29/11/29.

REPAIRS:
Gor. 23/2-19/3/32.**G.**
Gor. 3-21/4/34.**G.**
Gor. 19/8-19/9/36.**G.**
Don. 13/10-17/11/38.**G.**
Gor. 24/2-19/4/41.**G.**
Gor. 21/7-22/8/43.**G.**
Cow. 22/2-9/4/44.**G.**
Gor. 28/8-28/10/44.**L.**
Gor. 9/1-9/7/47.**G.**
Gor. 15/9-12/11/49.**G.**
Gor. 16-17/11/49.**N/C.**
Dby. 27/7-10/9/52.**H/I.**
Dby. 13-27/9/52.**N/C.**
Gor. 5-21/11/53.**C/L.**
Gor. 24-28/11/53.**N/C.**
Gor. 11/8-1/10/55.**G.**
Gor. 4-13/10/55.**N/C.**
Gor. 17-19/10/55.**N/C.**
Gor. 27-31/10/55.**N/C.**
Gor. 3/2-13/3/59.**H/I.**
Gor. 21/3/62.*Not repaired.*

BOILERS:
2302.
2186 *(new)* 19/3/32.
2299 *(ex2782)* 21/4/34.
2316 *(ex2730)* 19/9/36.
2636 *(ex2730)* 19/4/41.
2922 *(ex1486)* 9/4/44.
2291 *(ex1298)* 9/7/47.
2108 *(ex2707)* 12/11/49.
2108 Reno.27720 10/9/52.
27793 *(new)* 1/10/55.

SHEDS:
York.
Sheffield 10/12/29.
Ardsley 14/3/34.
Colwick 12/2/36.
Ardsley 18/8/46.

RENUMBERED:
4811 5/11/46.
64811 12/11/49.

CONDEMNED:
30/3/62.
Cut up at Gorton.

1418

Darlington.

To traffic 11/12/29.

REPAIRS:
Dar. 25/8-5/10/31.**G.**
Dar. 13/7-22/8/33.**G.**
Dar. 7/3-17/4/35.**L.**
Dar. 10/10-15/11/35.**G.**
Dar. 16/3-30/4/37.**G.**
Dar. 11/5-17/6/39.**G.**
Dar. 6/1-11/2/41.**G.**
Dar. 4/7-20/8/42.**H.**
Dar. 29/3-3/5/43.**H.**
Cow. 6/12/44-6/1/45.**G.**
Cow. 15/12/45-12/1/46.**L.**
Cow. 23/3-26/4/47.**G.**
Cow. 29/4-28/5/49.**H/I.**
Dar. 5-18/10/50.**C/L.**
Cow. 21/6-4/8/51.**G.**
Cow. 12/6-8/8/52.**C/H.**
Cow. 4/3-3/4/54.**H/I.**
Cow. 14/2-16/3/57.**G.**
Cow. 20/2-21/3/58.**C/L.**
Inv. 4/4-2/6/61.**G.**
Inv. 22/8-24/11/61.**N/C.**
Dar. 10/4-10/5/62.**C/L.**

BOILERS:
2306.
1918 *(ex1458)* 22/8/33.
1919 *(ex2728)* 30/4/37.
2601 *(ex375)* 17/6/39.
BP132 *(ex1534)* 11/2/41.
2717 *(ex1506)* 3/5/43.
1922 *(ex1452)* 6/1/45.
C1832 *(ex1808)* 26/4/47.
27586 *(new)* 4/8/51.
27465 *(ex4849)* 16/3/57.
27493 *(ex4844)* 2/6/61.

SHEDS:
Blaydon.
Darlington 23/7/45.
Blaydon 29/8/48.
Hull Dairycoates 4/9/49.
Blaydon 2/10/49.
Alston 4/1/53.
Blaydon 7/6/53.
Gateshead 14/6/59.
Tyne Dock 26/2/61.
Sunderland 20/8/61.

RENUMBERED:
4812 17/11/46.
64812 28/5/49.

CONDEMNED:
3/12/62.
Cut up at Darlington.

1425

Darlington.

To traffic 19/12/29.

REPAIRS:
Ghd. 11-21/8/31.**L.**
Ghd. 17/9-23/10/31.**G.**
Ghd. 13-21/6/32.**L.**
Dar. 19/6-2/8/34.**G.**
Dar. 26/10-7/12/37.**G.**
Dar. 21/11-22/12/39.**G.**
Dar. 8/9-7/10/41.**G.**
Cow. 21/2-18/3/44.**G.**
Cow. 25/5-29/6/46.**G.**
Ghd. 19/1-19/2/48.**L.**
Cow. 18/3-16/4/49.**L/I.**
Cow. 16/8-15/9/51.**G.**
Cow. 16/10-13/11/51.**N/C.**
Ghd. 12-26/11/52.**C/L.**
Cow. 31/7-7/8/53.**L.**
Ghd. 26/8-16/9/53.**C/L.**
Cow. 19/9-22/10/55.**G.**
Cow. 5/11-12/12/59.**G.**

BOILERS:
2303.
2317 *(ex1489)* 2/8/34.
RS129 *(ex1412)* 7/12/37.
2303 *(ex1470)* 22/12/39.
2617 *(ex1448)* 7/10/41.
BP133 *(ex1533)* 18/3/44.
BP136 *(ex2725)* 29/6/46.
27451 *(ex4815)* 15/9/51.
27568 *(ex64794)* 22/10/55.
25834 *(new)* 12/12/59.

SHEDS:
Blaydon.
Tweedmouth 28/2/48.

RENUMBERED:
4813 8/12/46.
64813 16/4/49.

CONDEMNED:
3/12/62.
Cut up at Cowlairs.

1466

Darlington.

To traffic 3/1/30.

REPAIRS:
Ghd. 2-12/6/31.**L.**
Ghd. 14/9-20/10/31.**G.**
Ghd. 19-28/7/32.**L.**
Dar. 26/9-4/11/33.**G.**
Dar. 11-19/7/35.**L.**
Dar. 10/6-5/8/36.**G.**
Dar. 4/1-2/2/40.**G.**
Dar. 27/10-26/11/41.**G.**
Cow. 6/12/44-6/1/45.**G.**
Cow. 8/1-22/3/47.**G.**
Cow. 18/11-25/12/48.**G.**
Cow. 4/7-11/8/51.**H/I.**
Cow. 22/4-29/5/54.**G.**
Ghd. 1/12/54-14/1/55.**C/L.**
Cow. 17/4-19/5/56.**H/I.**
Cow. 12/6-5/7/58.**G.**
Dar. 2/7-17/8/59.**C/L.**
Dar. 24/11-9/12/59.**C/L.**
Cow. 16-30/6/60.**C/L.**
Dar. 15/5-2/6/61.**C/L.**
Cow. 23/11/62.*Not repaired.*

BOILERS:
2312.
1916 *(ex1456)* 4/11/33.
8580 *(ex2774)* 5/8/36.
1904 *(ex1480)* 2/2/40.
2625 *(ex1474)* 26/11/41.
2124 *(ex234)* 6/1/45.
BP130 *(ex1533)* 22/3/47.
8022 *(ex1486)* 25/12/48.
8022 Reno.27460 11/8/51.
27501 *(ex4701)* 29/5/54.
27551 *(ex4856)* 5/7/58.

SHEDS:
Blaydon.
Gateshead 14/6/59.
North Blyth 15/1/61.
Heaton 30/7/61.
North Blyth 8/10/61.
Alnmouth 8/4/62.

RENUMBERED:
4814 23/6/46.
64814 25/12/48.

CONDEMNED:
23/11/62.
Cut up at Cowlairs.

1429

Darlington.

To traffic 8/1/30.

REPAIRS:
Ghd. 7/10-9/11/31.**G.**
Ghd. 8-16/3/32.**L.**
Ghd. 19-29/7/32.**L.**
Dar. 28/12/33-26/1/34.**G.**
Dar. 3/3-6/4/36.**G.**
Dar. 26/4-7/6/38.**G.**
Dar. 3/4-6/5/40.**G.**
Dar. 1/10-1/11/41.**G.**
Cow. 18/1-19/2/44.**G.**
Cow. 12/10-23/11/46.**G.**
Ghd. 4-11/7/47.**L.**
Ghd. 9-28/9/48.**L.**
Cow. 16/12/49-14/1/50.**L/I.**
Cow. 30/12/50-27/1/51.**G.**
Cow. 9/7-21/8/54.**H/I.**
Cow. 28/6-17/8/57.**G.**
Inv. 2/8/61.*Not repaired.*

BOILERS:
2309.
2318 *(ex1487)* 26/1/34.
8010 *(ex1259)* 6/4/36.
1909 *(ex1469)* 6/5/40.
8005 *(ex1473)* 1/11/41.
1905 *(ex1448)* 19/2/44.
27581 *(new)* 27/1/51.
27513 *(ex4928)* 17/8/57.

SHEDS:
Blaydon.
Alnmouth 22/3/45.
Blaydon 29/9/46.
Alnmouth 13/4/47.
Blaydon 11/11/56.
West Hartlepool 9/10/60.

RENUMBERED:
4815 11/8/46.
64815 14/1/50.

CONDEMNED:
12/8/61.
Cut up at Inverurie.

1470

Darlington.

To traffic 13/1/30.

REPAIRS:
Dar. 6/4-13/5/32.**G.**
Gor. 30/1-17/2/34.**G.**
Dar. 4/10-12/12/34.**L.**
Dar. 10/12/36-29/1/37.**G.**
Dar. 1-9/2/37.**L.**
Dar. 25/10/39-13/1/40.**G.**
Dar. 15/2-9/4/40.**H.**
Dar. 14/11-19/12/42.**G.**
Dar. 2-5/4/43.**N/C.** *Tender only.*
Cow. 15/2-17/3/45.**G.**
Cow. 19/9-29/11/47.**G.**
Cow. 12/10-19/11/49.**H/I.**
Cow. 20/11-15/12/51.**G.**
Cow. 19/3-24/4/54.**H/I.**
Cow. 12/4-17/5/57.**G.**

BOILERS:
2316.
8005 *(ex1255)* 17/2/34.
2303 *(ex1448)* 29/1/37.
7946 *(ex2735)* 13/1/40.
2622 *(ex1504)* 19/12/42.
2846 *(ex1469)* 17/3/45.
3196 *(ex1536)* 29/11/47.
27538 *(ex4942)* 15/12/51.
27633 *(new)* 17/5/57.

SHEDS:
York.
Hull Dairycoates 28/10/37.
Darlington 20/11/40.
Stockton 30/12/40.
Blaydon 23/6/43.
Heaton 15/1/61.

RENUMBERED:
4816 10/11/46.
64816 19/11/49.

CONDEMNED:
10/12/61.
Cut up at Cowlairs.

1487

Darlington.

To traffic 18/1/30.

REPAIRS:
Dar. 28/5-31/7/31.**G.**
Dar. 23/10-28/11/33.**G.**
Dar. 2/9-10/10/35.**G.**
Dar. 3/5-11/6/38.**G.**
Dar. 12/9-23/10/40.**G.**
Dar. 5/2-6/3/43.**G.**
Dar. 1-31/12/43.**L.**
Dar. 15/6-1/7/44.**N/C.** *Tender only.*
Cow. 10-31/3/45.**G.**
Cow. 19/1-9/3/46.**L.**
Cow. 11/6-8/11/47.**G.**
Cow. 23/2-18/3/50.**L/I.**
Dar. 26-28/2/51.**C/L.**
Cow. 10/5-20/6/51.**L/I.**
Gor. 19/11/53-9/1/54.**G.**
Cow. 20/9-26/10/57.**H/I.**
Dar. 7-16/1/58.**C/L.**
Cow. 12/11-1/12/58.**N/C.**
Dar. 22/5-7/8/59.**C/L.**
Cow. 9/1-18/2/61.**G.**
Cow. 15/2/62.*Not repaired.*

BOILERS:
2318.
2312 *(ex1466)* 28/11/33.
8022 *(ex1493)* 10/10/35.
2714 *(ex1474)* 11/6/38.
8010 *(ex1429)* 23/10/40.
8014 *(ex1481)* 6/3/43.
C1833 *(ex1894)* 8/11/47.
C1833 Reno.27531 20/6/51.
27525 *(ex4947)* 9/1/54.
27769 *(ex4933)* 18/2/61.

SHEDS:
York.
Hull Dairycoates 22/10/37.
Stockton 28/3/43.
Blaydon 21/6/43.
Heaton 7/11/48.
Darlington 19/11/50.
Middlesbrough 7/1/51.
West Hartlepool 14/9/52.
Northallerton 19/9/54.
West Auckland 6/3/55.
Sunderland 25/9/55.
Low Moor 25/1/59.

RENUMBERED:
4817 5/1/47.
64817 18/3/50.

CONDEMNED:
29/3/62.
Cut up at Cowlairs.

1489

Darlington.

To traffic 30/1/30.

REPAIRS:
Dar. 9-16/4/31.**L.**
Exp'l Fog S.A. fitted.
Dar. 29/3-6/5/32.**G.**
Dar. 5-27/9/32.**L.**
Dar. 24/7-28/8/33.**L.**
Dar. 4/6-13/7/34.**G.**
Dar. 4/5-13/6/36.**G.**
Dar. 7/9/36.*Weigh.*
Dar. 30/6-3/9/37.**H.**
Don. 26/8-30/9/38.**G.**
Dar. 25/6-24/7/40.**G.**
Dar. 24/7-4/9/42.**G.**
Dar. 20/2-2/3/43.**L.**
Cow. 16/11-23/12/44.**G.**
Cow. 24/5-16/8/47.**G.**
Cow. 6/5-4/6/49.**L/I.**
Cow. 17/3-14/4/51.**H/I.**
Cow. 17/9-24/10/52.**G.**
Cow. 6-30/4/55.**L/I.**
Cow. 13-29/12/56.**C/L.**

WORKS CODES:- Cow - Cowlairs. Dar - Darlington. Dby - Derby. Don - Doncaster. Ghd - Gateshead. Gor - Gorton. Inv - Inverurie. Str - Stratford.
REPAIR CODES:- **C/H** - Casual Heavy. **C/L** - Casual Light. **G** - General. **H**- Heavy. **H/I** - Heavy Intermediate. **L** - Light. **L/I** - Light Intermediate. **N/C** - Non-Classified.

Cow. 31/1-8/3/58.**G.**
Cow. 22/4-4/6/60.**H/I.**
Cow. 13/10-3/11/60.**N/C.**

BOILERS:
2317.
RS118 *(ex1453)* 13/7/34.
1905 *(ex1450)* 13/6/36.
RS121 *(ex1504)* 24/7/40.
2306 *(ex1479)* 4/9/42.
2564 *(ex1547)* 16/8/47.
2564 Reno.27489 14/4/51.
27472 *(ex4710)* 24/10/52.
27455 *(ex4727)* 8/3/58.

SHEDS:
Newport.
Darlington 28/3/43.
Starbeck 14/7/43.
Selby 14/6/59.
York 13/9/59.
Thornaby 22/11/59.
West Auckland 24/12/61.
Ardsley 17/6/62.

RENUMBERED:
4818 12/1/47.
64818 3/6/49.

CONDEMNED:
3/12/62.
Cut up at Darlington.

1491

Darlington.

To traffic 31/1/30.

REPAIRS:
Dar. 1/12/31-21/1/32.**G.**
Gor. 22/1-9/2/34.**G.**
Dar. 28/4-28/5/36.**G.**
Dar. 20/5-22/7/38.**G.**
Dar. 13/5-7/6/40.**G.**
Dar. 24/7-5/9/42.**G.**
Dar. 12/7-7/8/43.**L.**
Cow. 14/4-12/5/45.**G.**
Cow. 17/11/47-10/1/48.**G.**
Cow. 20/12/50-13/1/51.**H/I.**
Dar. 30/3-4/4/51.**C/L.**
Cow. 27/11-21/12/51.**C/L.**
Cow. 13/10-20/11/52.**C/L.**
Cow. 24/12/53-29/1/54.**G.**
Cow. 20/9-20/10/56.**L/I.**
Cow. 2/10-1/11/58.**G.**
Cow. 30/7-21/8/59.**N/C.**
Cow. 15-18/9/59.**C/L.**
Cow. 24/5-24/6/60.**C/L.**

BOILERS:
2310.
2222 *(ex2729)* 9/2/34.
2116 *(ex2723)* 28/5/36.
2717 *(ex1504)* 22/7/38.
8021 *(ex1468)* 7/6/40.
2935 *(ex1551)* 12/5/45.
2715 *(ex1472)* 10/1/48.
27567 *(ex4945)* 29/1/54.
27456 *(ex4861)* 1/11/58.

SHEDS:
Newport.
Darlington 28/3/43.
Middlesbrough 13/6/48.
Darlington 25/6/50.
Neville Hill 27/8/50.
Hull Dairycoates 13/6/54.

RENUMBERED:
4819 22/12/46.
64819 13/1/51.

CONDEMNED:
12/9/62.
Cut up at Cowlairs.

2786

Darlington.

To traffic 13/2/30.

REPAIRS:
Cow. 17/8-12/9/31.**G.**
Cow. 19/10-29/11/32.**G.**
Cow. 23/1-22/2/34.**G.**
Cow. 6-24/9/34.**L.**
Cow. 5-11/2/35.**L.**
Cow. 4-13/4/35.**L.**
Cow. 1/1-1/2/36.**G.**
Cow. 2-28/10/37.**G.**
Cow. 8-9/3/38.**N/C.**
Cow. 30/5-2/6/39.**L.**
Cow. 22/2-22/3/40.**G.**
Cow. 21-22/8/40.**N/C.**
Cow. 26/6-8/8/42.**G.**
Cow. 3-25/8/44.**H.**
Inv. 26/1-21/2/45.**L.**
Cow. 21/6-18/7/46.**G.**
Cow. 18-19/9/46.**L.**
Str. 12/8-9/10/47.**G.**
Str. 21/11/47-10/1/48.**H.**
New cylinders.
Gor. 12/4-17/6/50.**G.**
Gor. 23-24/6/50.**N/C.**
Dby. 17/9-4/11/52.**H/I.**
Gor. 22/5-7/7/55.**G.**
Gor. 11/7-6/8/55.**N/C.**
Gor. 9/10-15/11/58.**G.**
Gor. 24/5/62. *Not repaired.*

BOILERS:
2307. (C1738)
C1717 *(ex2739)* 22/2/34.
C1712 *(ex2734)* 1/2/36.
C1801 *(ex2788)* 8/8/42.
4988 *(new)* 17/6/50.
4988 Reno.27727 4/11/52.
27840 *(new)* 7/7/55.
25845 *(new)* 15/11/58.

SHEDS:
Heaton.
Dundee 17/2/30.
Ipswich 15/6/47.
Ardsley 21/1/51.

RENUMBERED:
4820 20/10/46.
64820 17/6/50.

CONDEMNED:
24/5/62.
Cut up at Gorton.

2787

Darlington.

To traffic 17/2/30.

REPAIRS:
Cow. 18/5-10/6/32.**G.**
Cow. 12/6-1/7/32.**N/C.**
Cow. 16-23/9/33.**L.**
Cow. 24/11-2/12/33.**L.**
Cow. 25/10-29/11/34.**G.**
Cow. 21/1-26/2/36.**H.**
Cow. 23/11-20/12/37.**G.**
Cow. 28/12/37-4/1/38.**N/C.**
Cow. 31/1-29/2/40.**G.**
Cow. 29/10-12/12/41.**G.**
Cow. 13/7-3/9/43.**G.**
Dar. 15/5/45.*Weigh.*
Cow. 1/2-23/3/46.**G.**
Cow. 29/4-3/7/48.**G.**
Cow. 13/6-12/7/50.**H/I.**
Cow. 26/9-18/10/52.**G.**
Cow. 11/2-12/3/53.**N/C.**
Cow. 15/12/55-21/1/56.**L/I.**
Cow. 20/2-12/4/58.**G.**
Dar. 20/4-5/5/61.**C/L.**

BOILERS:
2315.*(C1739).*
C1717 *(ex2786)* 26/2/36.
C1714 *(ex2740)* 23/3/46.
BP131 *(ex1535)* 3/7/48.
27473 *(ex4925)* 18/10/52.
27480 *(ex65901)* 12/4/58.

SHEDS:
Heaton.
Eastfield 27/2/30.
Darlington 23/9/43.
Middlesbrough 15/1/50.
Starbeck 27/9/53.
York 13/9/59.
Thornaby 13/12/59.

RENUMBERED:
4821 23/3/46.
64821 3/7/48.

CONDEMNED:
16/11/62.
Cut up at Darlington.

2788

Darlington.

To traffic 24/2/30.

REPAIRS:
Dar. 18/12/31-1/2/32.**G.**
Cow. 30/11/33.**G.**
Cow. 21/3/36.**G.**
Cow. 16/4/38.**G.**
Cow. 10/8/38.**L.**
Cow. 5/1/40.**G.**
Cow. 8/2/40.**L.**
Cow. 11/10/40.**L.**
Cow. 27/6/42.**G.**
Cow. 9/10/42.**H.**
Cow. 10/8/44.**H.**
Cow. 11-25/8/45.**L.**
Cow. 17/11-15/12/45.**L.**
Cow. 3/1-12/3/47.**H.**
Cow. 16-23/8/47.**L.**
Cow. 20/4-21/5/49.**H/I.**
Cow. 3/3-5/4/52.**G.**
Cow. 19/3-1/5/54.**H/I.**
Cow. 30/7-1/9/56.**G.**
Inv. 9/11-11/12/59.**H/I.**

BOILERS:
2304.(C1740).
C1801 *(ex2741)* 21/3/36.
4902 *(ex1808)* 27/6/42.
27565 *(ex4855)* 5/4/52.
27570 *(ex4942)* 1/9/56.

SHEDS:
Eastfield.
Darlington 11/7/43.
St Margarets 25/11/43.
Dundee 30/4/47.

RENUMBERED:
4822 3/11/46.
64822 21/5/49.

CONDEMNED:
29/12/62.
Cut up at Inverurie.

2962

Darlington.

To traffic 18/9/31.

REPAIRS:
Gor. 1-19/5/34.**G.**
Dar. 9/5-22/6/36.**G.**
Gor. 5/4-12/5/39.**G.**
Gor. 30/6-30/9/39.**L.**
Gor. 7/6-1/8/42.**G.**
Gor. 5/11-16/12/44.**G.**
Gor. 21/9-17/12/47.**G.**
Gor. 15/9-29/10/49.**G.**
Dby. 20/2-27/3/52.**L/I.**
Gor. 3/7-4/9/54.**G.**
Gor. 6-8/9/54.**N/C.**
Gor. 7/9-3/11/56.**C/H.**
Gor. 9/10-9/11/57.**H/I.**
Str. 25/2-17/4/59.**N/C.**

BOILERS:
8580.
8587 *(ex2969)* 19/5/34.

Only one deviation from Group Standard buffers was either noted or photographed, so far as known. By the end of 1935, Parkeston's 2964 had been changed to buffers which had parallel case instead of stepped type. That seems to have been done at the shed rather than at a works repair. *S.J.Rhodes*

2222 *(ex1491)* 22/6/36.
8588 *(ex2703)* 12/5/39.
8773 *(ex2784)* 1/8/42.
2316 *(ex1824)* 16/12/44.
E1352 *(ex2964)* 17/12/47.
4977 *(new)* 29/10/49.
4977 Reno.27699 27/3/52.
27832 *(new)* 4/9/54.
27766 *(ex4918)* 3/11/56.

SHEDS:
Gorton.
Trafford Park 2/9/36.
Gorton 24/2/39.
Trafford Park 30/11/39.
Colwick 11/3/51.
Boston 9/11/58.
Colwick 8/11/59.

RENUMBERED:
4823 19/12/46.
64823 26/3/49.

CONDEMNED:
5/1/61.
Cut up at Doncaster.

2963

Darlington.

To traffic 16/9/31.

REPAIRS:
Gor. 9-23/6/34.**G.**
Dar. 13/5-6/7/36.**G.**
Dar. 30/7-14/9/36.**L.**
Gor. 3-7/3/38.**L.**
Gor. 20/1-18/2/39.**G.**
Don. 28/9/41-5/1/42.**G.**
Gor. 14/3-27/7/43.**L.**
Gor. 5/12/43-8/1/44.**L.**
Gor. 3/12/44-16/2/45.**G.**
Gor. 8/3-10/4/45.**L.**
Gor. 8/8-14/12/46.**G.**
Gor. 22/6-21/10/47.**G.**
Gor. 10-16/11/47.**N/C.**
Dby. 29/3-5/6/51.**H/I.**
Gor. 28/3-18/4/53.**G.**
Gor. 17/9-22/10/55.**G.**
Gor. 26/3/60. *Not repaired.*

BOILERS:
8581.
8775 *(new)* 23/6/34.
8587 *(ex2962)* 6/7/36.
2769 *(ex3000)* 18/2/39.
8773 *(ex2962)* 16/2/45.
2312 *(ex2999)* 21/10/47.
27753 *(ex4716)* 18/4/53.
27796 *(new)* 22/10/55.

SHEDS:
Gorton.
Trafford Park 15/9/36.
Gorton 4/2/38.
Trafford Park 24/2/39.
Gorton 13/4/47.
Sheffield 8/4/51.
Gorton 27/10/57.

RENUMBERED:
4824 27/10/46.
64824 5/6/51.

CONDEMNED:
29/3/60.
Cut up at Gorton. Boiler retained and used on 64918.

2964

Darlington.

To traffic 29/9/31.

REPAIRS:
Gor. 26/11-15/12/34.**G.**
Gor. 31/3-24/4/37.**G.**
Gor. 29/2-15/6/40.**G.**
Gor. 6/10-28/11/42.**G.**
Gor. 11/12/44-9/2/45.**G.**
Gor. 7/10-18/12/47.**G.**
Gor. 6/2-9/4/49.**C/H.**
Dby. 17/8-9/10/51.**L/I.**
Gor. 25/3-24/4/54.**G.**
Gor. 30/11-28/12/57.**G.**
Gor. 28/10/61.*Not repaired.*

BOILERS:
8582.
823 *(ex1494)* 15/12/34.
8591 *(ex1492)* 24/4/37.
2182 *(ex2705)* 15/6/40.
3201 *(new)* 28/11/42.
E1352 *(ex2990)* 9/2/45.
3211 *(ex3081)* 18/12/47.
27831 *(new)* 24/4/54.
27764 *(ex4809)* 28/12/57.

SHEDS:
Parkeston.
Ardsley 7/2/36.
Sunderland 13/12/59.

RENUMBERED:
4825 25/11/46.
64825 9/4/49.

CONDEMNED:
2/11/61.
Cut up at Gorton.

2965

Darlington.

To traffic 13/10/31.

REPAIRS:
Gor. 12/12/34-2/1/35.**G.**
Gor. 15/6-10/7/37.**G.**
Gor. 9/10-2/12/39.**G.**
Str. 8/11/42-9/1/43.**G.**
Gor. 9/1-30/3/45.**G.**
Gor. 12/7-12/9/46.**L.**
Str. 1/11-20/12/47.**G.**
Gor. 7/2-1/4/50.**G.**
Gor. 5-10/4/50.**N/C.**
Gor. 21-23/4/50.**N/C.**
Dby. 25/1-6/3/52.**H/I.**
Str. 19/7-28/8/54.**G.**
Str. 18-30/10/54.**C/L.**
Str. 9/6-15/8/57.**G.**

BOILERS:
8583.
2273 *(ex2691)* 2/1/35.
825 *(ex2696)* 10/7/37.
823 *(ex1494)* 2/12/39.
2302 *(ex1266)* 9/1/43.
8594 *(ex2716)* 30/3/45.
2669 *(ex4830)* 1/4/50.
2669 Reno.27709 6/3/52.
27890 *(ex4908)* 28/8/54.
27820 *(ex4724)* 15/8/57.

SHEDS:
Parkeston.
Stratford 18/1/35.
Ipswich 24/10/41.
March 25/10/42.
Norwich 16/7/43.
Ipswich 26/4/46.
March 25/10/59.

RENUMBERED:
4826 5/1/47.
64826 1/4/50.

CONDEMNED:
8/2/60.
Cut up at Stratford.

2966

Darlington.

To traffic 9/12/31.

REPAIRS:
Dar. 11-18/12/31.**N/C.**
Gor. 19-31/12/31.**L.**
Gor. 19/1-9/2/34.**G.**
Gor. 4-23/5/36.**G.**
Gor. 25/7-27/8/38.**G.**
Gor. 24/11-28/12/40.**G.**
Don. 5/8-6/10/43.**G.**
Gor. 2-29/4/44.**G.**
Gor. 9/9-8/12/45.**G.**
Gor. 23/10/47-3/1/48.**G.**
Dby. 17/5-18/7/50.**G.**
Gor. 7/1-28/3/53.**G.**
Gor. 18/4-28/5/55.**G.**
Gor. 26/9-5/11/55.**C/L.**
Gor. 6/10-16/11/57.**G.**
Str. 28/1/60. *Not repaired.*

BOILERS:
8584.
8585 *(ex2967)* 9/2/34.
8006 *(ex2712)* 23/5/36.
2095 *(ex2693)* 27/8/38.
1912 *(ex2714)* 28/12/40.
2681 *(ex2704)* 8/12/45.
2316 *(ex2962)* 3/1/48.
2672 *(ex4829)* 18/7/50.
27750 *(ex4885)* 28/3/53.
27838 *(new)* 28/5/55.
27794 *(ex4716)* 16/11/57.

SHEDS:
Lincoln.
Immingham 17/6/45.
Lincoln 9/12/45.
Immingham 22/12/46.
Colwick 27/4/47.
Doncaster 1/3/59.

RENUMBERED:
4827 15/12/46.
64827 18/7/50.

CONDEMNED:
1/2/60.
Cut up at Stratford.

When second-hand ex North Eastern tenders were coupled with J39 engines, it was usual to change their buffers to Group Standard type, but in contrast to what was done on Group Standard tenders, their short vertical handrails were never made taller. *M.Mitchell*

(below) **A Darlington feature which applied only to the 44 engines built in 1926/7 was the circular cover fitted around the base of the safety valves. The first one no.1448, which became 4700 and then 64700, certainly carried that cover when it was ex Cowlairs in June 1951, although on what was that engine's eighth different boiler.** *A.G.Ellis*

2967

Darlington.

To traffic 29/10/31.

REPAIRS:
Gor. 18/12/33-13/1/34.**G.**
Dar. 25/5-29/7/36.**G.**
Gor. 8/8-2/9/38.**G.**
Gor. 13/10-30/11/40.**G.**
Gor. 7-17/12/40.**N/C.**
Cow. 14/4-6/6/43.**G.**
Gor. 5/6-8/7/44.**G.**
Gor. 23-29/9/45.**L.**
Str. 17/2-6/4/46.**G.**
Gor. 16/6-21/8/48.**G.**
Dby. 2/3-24/4/51.**G.**
Dby. 4-14/5/51.**N/C.**
Gor. 19/5-4/7/53.**C/L.**
Gor. 7-16/7/53.**N/C.**
Str. 29/11/53-9/1/54.**G.**
Gor. 10/9-27/10/56.**G.**

BOILERS:
8585.
2141 *(ex2716)* 13/1/34.
2110 *(ex2729)* 29/7/36.
8009 *(ex2777)* 2/9/38.
822 *(ex2707)* 30/11/40.
3213 *(new)* 6/6/43.
3208 *(ex2694)* 6/4/46.
8588 *(ex1803)* 21/8/48.
27662 *(ex4827)* 24/4/51.
27773 *(ex4770)* 9/1/54.
27653 *(ex4743)* 27/10/56.

SHEDS:
Immingham.
Lincoln 6/11/31.
Immingham 22/12/46.
Colwick 27/4/47.
Tuxford 27/9/53.
Stratford 16/1/55.
Doncaster 20/3/55.
Barnsley 2/6/57.
Mexborough 3/1/60.

RENUMBERED:
4828 29/9/46.
64828 21/8/48.

CONDEMNED:
21/3/60.
Cut up at Stratford.

2968

Darlington.

To traffic 24/11/31.

REPAIRS:
Gor. 7-31/3/34.**G.**
Gor. 23/4-16/5/36.**G.**
Gor. 15/8-13/9/38.**G.**
Gor. 4/10-16/11/40.**G.**
Gor. 4-13/12/40.**L.**
Str. 11/11/42-6/2/43.**G.**
Gor. 28/3-23/6/45.**G.**
Str. 29/7-16/11/47.**G.**
Str. 15/8-15/9/48.**L.**
Gor. 21/10-24/12/49.**G.**
Gor. 13-21/1/50.**C/L.**
Dby. 8/8-8/9/52.**L/I.**
Str. 8-26/3/54.**C/L.**
Str. 18/1-26/2/55.**G.**
Str. 23/9-26/10/57.**G.**

BOILERS:
8586.
8589 *(ex2971)* 31/3/34.
2296 *(ex2711)* 16/5/36.
8023 *(ex2770)* 13/9/38.
2688 *(ex2987)* 16/11/40.
8018 *(ex2988)* 6/2/43.
2672 *(ex2708)* 23/6/45.
2114 *(ex2719)* 24/12/49.
2114 Reno.27718 8/9/52.
27724 *(ex4885)* 26/2/55.
27824 *(ex4761)* 26/10/57.

SHEDS:
March.
Norwich 6/10/43.
Ipswich 26/4/46.

RENUMBERED:
4829 5/1/47.
64829 15/9/48.

CONDEMNED:
18/5/59.
Cut up at Stratford.

2969

Darlington.

To traffic 16/12/31.

REPAIRS:
Gor. 13/4-5/5/34.**G.**
Gor. 6-27/8/36.**G.**
Gor. 26/1-18/2/39.**G.**
Gor. 30/3-31/5/41.**G.**
Str. 15/7-30/9/42.**H/I.**
Gor. 27/4-24/6/44.**G.**
Gor. 29/8-25/5/47.**G.**
Gor. 9/11/49-14/1/50.**G.**
Gor. 17-18/1/50.**N/C.**
Dby. 1/11/51-9/1/52.**G.**
Str. 24/5-30/6/54.**G.**
Gor. 10/10-15/11/56.**G.**
Gor. 19-20/11/56.**N/C.**
Gor. 9/1-2/3/57.**C/H.**
Gor. 5-7/3/57.**N/C.**

BOILERS:
8587.
8593 *(ex2975)* 5/5/34.
8582 *(ex1495)* 27/8/36.
8020 *(ex1295)* 18/2/39.
2770 *(ex2997)* 31/5/41.
2299 *(ex2692)* 24/6/44.
2669 *(ex2982)* 25/5/47.
2287 *(ex4809)* 14/1/50.
27687 *(ex4789)* 9/1/52.
27887 *(ex4715)* 30/6/54.
27789 *(ex4901)* 15/11/56.

SHEDS:
March.
Doncaster 7/8/34.
Stratford 15/10/34.
Ipswich 24/10/41.
March 4/1/42.
New England 4/7/43.
Grantham 31/12/45.
Retford 28/9/46.

RENUMBERED:
4830 16/12/46.
64830 14/1/50.

CONDEMNED:
8/2/60.
Cut up at Gorton.

2970

Darlington.

To traffic 24/12/31.

REPAIRS:
Gor. 26/3-21/4/34.**G.**
Dar. 25/5-7/7/36. *Not repaired. Sent to Gorton.*
Gor. 16/7-8/8/36.**G.**
Gor. 14/12/38-14/1/39.**G.**
Gor. 28/12/40-1/2/41.**G.**
Cow. 24/2-30/3/44.**G.**
Gor. 30/8-27/10/45.**G.**
Gor. 18/7-21/12/46.**G.**
Gor. 9/2-21/3/48.**L.**
Gor. 12/5-6/8/49.**G.**
Gor. 22-23/8/49.**N/C.**
Dby. 2/1-13/2/52.**G.**
Gor. 13/11-24/12/54.**G.**
Gor. 3-5/1/55.**N/C.**
Gor. 15/1-15/2/58.**G.**
Gor. 9/5/61.*Not repaired.*

BOILERS:
8588.
2189 *(ex1282)* 21/4/34.
2094 *(ex2699)* 7/7/36.
2296 *(ex2968)* 14/1/39.
2685 *(ex2981)* 1/2/41.
2601 *(ex1471)* 30/3/44.
2216 *(ex2996)* 21/12/46.
2660 *(ex4902)* 6/8/49.
27691 *(ex4720)* 13/2/52.
27694 *(ex4741)* 24/12/54.
27675 *(ex4719)* 15/2/58.

SHEDS:
March.
Doncaster 20/5/37.
Colwick 4/6/37.
Grantham 22/8/40.
Colwick 6/9/40.
Ardsley 1/4/51.
Hull Dairycoates 10/5/59.

RENUMBERED:
4831 29/8/46.
64831 20/3/48.

CONDEMNED:
20/6/61.
Cut up at Gorton.

2971

Darlington.

To traffic 22/1/32.

REPAIRS:
Gor. 23/2-16/3/34.**G.**
Dar. 27/12/35-25/1/36.**G.**
Gor. 28/2-26/3/38.**G.**
Gor. 4/8-14/9/40.**G.**
Gor. 12/12/42-27/3/43.**G.**
Gor. 13/8-3/11/45.**G.**
Gor. 28/7-28/12/46.**G.**
Gor. 5/4-7/6/48.**G.**
Dby. 1/12/50-7/2/51.**G.**
Dby. 27/2-4/3/51.**N/C.**
Dby. 14/5-18/6/52.**C/L.**
Gor. 2/7-22/8/53.**G.**
Gor. 26/8-3/9/53.**N/C.**
Gor. 8-9/9/53.**N/C.**
Gor. 29/12/55-3/3/56.**G.**
Str. 16/9/59.*Not repaired.*

BOILERS:
8589.
2194 *(ex2776)* 16/3/34.
2132 *(ex1255)* 25/1/36.
8007 *(ex2705)* 26/3/38.
2681 *(ex2942)* 14/9/40.
2097 *(ex1286)* 27/3/43.
4910 *(ex3081)* 3/11/45.
3199 *(ex1922)* 7/6/48.
27654 *(new)* 7/2/51.
27768 *(ex4903)* 22/8/53.
27753 *(ex4824)* 3/3/56.

SHEDS:
March.
Colwick 28/4/36.
Leicester 5/5/38.
Colwick 14/9/40.

RENUMBERED:
4832 2/11/46.
64832 5/6/48.

CONDEMNED:
28/9/59.
Cut up at Stratford.

2972

Darlington.

To traffic 29/1/32.

REPAIRS:
Dar. 3/2-5/3/32.**N/C.**
Gor. 29/3-21/4/34.**G.**
Gor. 20/4-9/5/36.**G.**
Gor. 19/7-6/8/38.**G.**
Gor. 15-23/8/38.**N/C.**
Gor. 29/9-16/11/40.**G.**
Str. 21/12/42-18/8/43.**G.**
Str. 1/7-8/9/45.**G.**
Str. 14/9-31/12/47.**G.**
Str. 27/5-13/8/49.**G.**
Dby. 21/2-3/4/52.**G.**
Dby. 10/4-1/5/52.**N/C.**
Dby. 6/7-8/8/52.**C/L.**
Dby. 12-22/8/52.**N/C.**
Gor. 19/3-28/4/55.**G.**
Gor. 23/5-22/6/55.**N/C.**
Gor. 6/5-14/6/58.**G.**
Gor. 28/3-15/5/61.**H/I.**

BOILERS:
8590.
2146 *(ex2719)* 21/4/34.
2184 *(ex1498)* 9/5/36.
2121 *(ex1457)* 6/8/38.
8007 *(ex2971)* 16/11/40.
8012 *(ex2724)* 18/8/43.
2772 *(ex1497)* 8/9/45.
4974 *(new)* 13/8/49.
27693 *(ex4886)* 3/4/52.
27836 *(new)* 28/4/55.
27515 *(ex4947)* 14/6/58.

SHEDS:
March.
Norwich 16/9/43.
Yarmouth 8/10/46.
Norwich 27/12/46.
Ardsley 21/1/51.
Peterborough 21/6/53.
New England 13/9/53.
Ardsley 27/9/53.
Hull Dairycoates 10/5/59.
Sunderland 13/12/59.

RENUMBERED:
4833 25/8/46.
64833 13/8/49.

CONDEMNED:
26/11/62.
Cut up at Darlington.

2973

Darlington.

To traffic 17/2/32.

REPAIRS:
Gor. 18/5-9/6/34.**G.**
Gor. 16/3-3/4/37.**G.**
Gor. 19/8-2/9/38.**L.**
Gor. 16/8-7/10/39.**G.**
Gor. 29/12/42-24/4/43.**G.**
Str. 2/8-13/10/45.**G.**
Str. 4-28/11/47.**L.**
Str. 13/6-15/8/48.**G.**
Dby. 6/10-27/11/50.**H/I.**
Dby. 29/9-3/11/51.**C/L.**
Str. 7/8-5/9/53.**G.**
Str. 23/9-1/10/53.**N/C.**
Str. 13/1-26/2/55.**C/L.**
Str. 3/6-21/7/56.**G.**

BOILERS:
8591.
8018 *(ex1263)* 9/6/34.
8583 *(ex1268)* 3/4/37.
2300 *(ex2694)* 7/10/39.
8024 *(ex2697)* 24/4/43.
2104 *(ex2995)* 13/10/45.
2779 *(ex2697)* 15/8/48.
27875 *(ex4905)* 5/9/53.
25836 *(new)* 21/7/56.

SHEDS:
Sheffield.
Ardsley 2/5/34.
Bradford 5/5/34.
Ardsley 2/2/41.
Stratford 9/9/43.
Ipswich 12/9/43.
Norwich 19/6/49.
Ipswich 19/10/49.

RENUMBERED:
4834 23/11/46.
64834 14/8/48.

CONDEMNED:
20/11/59.
Cut up at Stratford.

2974

Darlington.

To traffic 19/2/32.

REPAIRS:
Gor. 27/4-17/5/34.**G.**
Gor. 16/2-13/3/37.**G.**
Gor. 25/4-4/5/40.**G.**
Str. 3-20/11/43.**G.**
Gor. 22/10-13/11/46.**G.**
Gor. 2-27/9/47.**G.**
Gor. 7/9-8/10/49.**G.**
Gor. 28/10-28/11/53.**G.**
Dar. 1-15/6/54.**C/L.**
Cow. 2/10-3/11/56.**H/I.**
Cow. 19/12/58-17/1/59.**G.**

BOILERS:
8592.
8590 *(ex2972)* 17/5/34.
2109 *(ex1274)* 13/3/37.
2203 *(ex1269)* 4/5/40.
2660 *(ex2986)* 20/11/43.
2284 *(ex2997)* 13/11/46.
8026 *(ex1233)* 27/9/47.
1916 *(ex4881)* 8/10/49.
25804 *(ex4760)* 28/11/53.
27661 *(ex64914)* 17/1/59.

SHEDS:
Sheffield.
Bradford 18/4/34.
Doncaster 30/7/45.
Neville Hill 2/9/51.
Thornaby 13/12/59.
West Auckland 11/9/60.

RENUMBERED:
4835 13/11/46.
64835 8/10/49.

CONDEMNED:
3/12/62.
Cut up at Darlington.

2975

Darlington.

To traffic 10/3/32.

REPAIRS:
Dar. 16-23/3/32.**N/C.**
Gor. 6/4-5/5/34.**G.**
Gor. 10/11-5/12/36.**G.**
Gor. 4/11-30/12/39.**G.**
Gor. 12/7-22/8/42.**G.**
Gor. 8/3-23/7/43.**L.**
After collision.
Gor. 29/1-7/4/45.**G.**
Str. 2/1-6/4/46.**G.**
Gor. 8/11/48-8/1/49.**G.**
Dby. 21/12/50-19/2/51.**L/I.**
Gor. 22/12/52-28/2/53.**C/H.**
Gor. 3-7/3/53.**N/C.**
Gor. 14/3-1/4/53.**N/C.**
Gor. 10/4-8/5/53.**N/C.**
Gor. 22/5-20/6/53.**C/L.**
Gor. 23-26/6/53.**N/C.**
Gor. 13/11-24/12/54.**G.**
Gor. 30/6-27/8/55.**C/L.**
After collision.
Gor. 29/4-7/6/58.**G.**
Dar. 27/3/62. *Not repaired.*

BOILERS:
8593.
8588 *(ex2970)* 5/5/34.
8003 *(ex1281)* 5/12/36.
8017 *(ex2691)* 30/12/39.
2776 *(ex1824)* 22/8/42.
2214 *(ex2718)* 7/4/45.
4944 *(new)* 8/1/49.
4944 Reno.27759 28/2/53.
27699 *(ex4823)* 24/12/54.
27523 *(ex4711)* 7/6/58.

SHEDS:
Annesley.
Leicester 4/4/32.
Annesley 2/3/41.
Colwick 9/8/43.
Ardsley 18/8/46.

RENUMBERED:
4836 18/8/46.
64836 8/1/49.

CONDEMNED:
25/4/62.
Cut up at Darlington.

2976

Darlington.

To traffic 15/3/32.

REPAIRS:
Gor. 30/10-25/11/33.**G.**
Dar. 3/10-1/11/35.**G.**
Gor. 22/2-19/3/38.**G.**
Gor. 14/3-27/4/40.**G.**
Gor. 14/9-10/10/42.**G.**
Cow. 5/3-15/4/44.**G.**
Gor. 15/5-5/10/46.**G.**
Gor. 25/11/48-12/2/49.**G.**
Dby. 24/4-13/6/52.**G.**
Gor. 24/1-31/3/55.**G.**
Gor. 28/7-6/9/58.**G.**
Gor. 25/10-10/12/60.**C/H.**
Gor. 31/10/61.*Not repaired.*

BOILERS:
8594.
8772 *(new)* 25/11/33.
2136 *(ex2725)* 1/11/35.
2674 *(ex2946)* 19/3/38.
825 *(ex2965)* 27/4/40.
8017 *(ex2975)* 10/10/42.
8020 *(ex1282)* 15/4/44.
4920 *(ex3087)* 5/10/46.
4965 *(new)* 12/2/49.
27701 *(ex4735)* 13/6/52.
27835 *(new)* 31/3/55.
25843 *(new)* 6/9/58.

SHEDS:
Colwick.
Grantham 17/3/42.
Colwick 14/5/42.
Ardsley 20/5/51.
Heaton 13/12/59.

RENUMBERED:
4837 15/12/46.
64837 12/2/49.

CONDEMNED:
17/11/61.
Cut up at Gorton.

2977

Darlington.

To traffic 27/5/32.

REPAIRS:
Cow. 3-10/6/32.**N/C.**
Cow. 27/7-24/8/34.**G.**
Cow. 30/7-28/8/36.**G.**
Cow. 15-17/3/37.**N/C.**
Tender only.
Cow. 25/1-16/3/38.**G.**
Cow. 19/3-11/4/40.**G.**

Cow. 16-17/8/40.**N/C.**
Cow. 3/10-3/11/41.**G.**
Cow. 2-4/6/42.**L.**
Cow. 7-29/5/43.**G.**
Cow. 26-31/10/44.**L.**
Cow. 7/10-30/11/46.**G.**
W.P.U. off 5/47.
Gor. 13/10-3/12/49.**G.**
Gor. 8-9/12/49.**N/C.**
Dby. 28/4-19/6/51.**G.**
Str. 15/11-19/12/53.**G.**
Gor. 6/6-11/8/56.**G.**

BOILERS:
C1796.
C1716 *(ex2738)* 28/8/36.
C1834 *(ex1894)* 3/11/41.
2116 *(ex1468)* 30/11/46.
4903 *(ex2981)* 3/12/49.
27668 *(ex2980)* 19/6/51.
27879 *(ex4723)* 19/12/53.
27744 *(ex4954)* 11/8/56.

SHEDS:
Eastfield.
Aberdeen 13/4/43.
Carlisle 12/12/43.
Ipswich 24/3/47.
Norwich 20/4/47.
Woodford 16/4/50.
Colwick 8/10/50.
Tuxford 27/9/53.
Stratford 16/1/55.
Doncaster 20/3/55.

RENUMBERED:
4838 17/11/46.
64838 3/12/49.

CONDEMNED:
26/1/60.
Cut up at Doncaster.

2978

Darlington.

To traffic 7/6/32.

REPAIRS:
Cow. 13-22/6/32.**N/C.**
Cow. 20/12/33-31/1/34.**G.**
Cow. 6/8-6/9/35.**G.**
Cow. 19/10-12/11/37.**G.**
Cow. 28/2-11/3/39.**G.**
Cow. 23-25/10/39.**L.**
Cow. 20/2-18/3/40.**G.**
Cow. 11/9-17/10/42.**G.**
Cow. 27-31/10/42.**N/C.**
Cow. 17-19/2/43.**L.**
Inv. 15-25/9/43.**L.**
Cow. 28/8-15/9/44.**G.**
Cow. 30/8-19/9/45.**L.**
Cow. 19-30/10/46.**L.**
Gor. 2/3-3/5/48.**G.**
Dby. 19/11/51-22/1/52.**G.**
Gor. 22/11/54-14/1/55.**H/I.**
Gor. 15-17/1/55.**N/C.**
Gor. 12/3-12/4/58.**G.**
Gor. 5-10/5/58.**N/C.**
Gor. 19/9/61. *Not repaired.*

BOILERS:
C1797.
C1799 *(ex2980)* 12/11/37.
2926 *(ex1862)* 17/10/42.
2697 *(ex2699)* 3/5/48.
27690 *(ex4777)* 22/1/52.
27689 *(ex4806)* 12/4/58.

SHEDS:
Eastfield.
Aberdeen 17/4/43.
Stratford 23/9/47.
Ardsley 18/9/49.

RENUMBERED:
4839 17/11/46.
64839 1/5/48.

CONDEMNED:
9/10/61.
Cut up at Gorton.

2979

Darlington.

To traffic 15/6/32.

REPAIRS:
Cow. 22-24/6/32.**N/C.**
Cow. 5-15/7/34.**L.**
Cow. 28/8-15/10/34.**G.**
Cow. 13/10-20/11/36.**G.**
Cow. 25/5-11/7/38.**G.**
Cow. 18-19/5/39.**N/C.**
Cow. 19/3-13/4/40.**G.**
Cow. 29/9-29/10/42.**G.**
Cow. 7-29/8/44.**G.**
Cow. 30/6-19/7/45.**G.**
Cow. 21/11-7/12/45.**L.**
Cow. 24-25/1/47.**L.**
Cow. 14/8-11/9/47.**G.**
Gor. 19/1-4/2/49.**L.**
Dby. 18/2-20/4/51.**G.**
Gor. 12/12/52-21/2/53.**C/L.**
Gor. 24-28/2/53.**N/C.**
Gor. 1/1-20/2/54.**G.**
Gor. 23/2-2/3/54.**N/C.**
Gor. 30/8-16/9/55.**C/L.**
Gor. 12/3-13/4/57.**G.**
Gor. 12/4-4/6/60.**G.**

BOILERS:
C1798.
C1796 *(ex2977)* 20/11/36.
C1798 *(ex2980)* 29/10/42.
2277 *(ex1472)* 19/7/45.
27803 *(new)* 20/4/51.
27531 *(ex4817)* 20/2/54.
27671 *(ex4804)* 13/4/57.
27698 *(ex4739)* 4/6/60.

SHEDS:
Eastfield.
Aberdeen 17/4/43.
Dundee 12/12/43.
Carlisle 15/6/46.
Stratford 24/9/47.
Ardsley 18/9/49.

RENUMBERED:
4840 25/8/46.
64840 4/2/49.

CONDEMNED:
27/11/62.
Cut up at Gorton.

2980

Darlington.

To traffic 16/6/32.

REPAIRS:
Dar. 27/6-1/7/32.**N/C.**
Cow. 8-12/7/32.**N/C.**
Cow. 11/12/34-28/1/35.**G.**
Cow. 20/4-22/5/37.**G.**
Cow. 12/4-15/5/39.**G.**
Cow. 17/2-17/3/41.**G.**
Cow. 1/9-3/10/42.**G.**
Cow. 21-26/2/44.**L.**
Cow. 26/4-18/5/45.**G.**
Cow. 28/6-23/8/46.**L.**
Cow. 23-24/1/47.**N/C.**
Spark arrestor fitted.
Removed April 1947.
Cow. 16/2-1/3/47.**L.**
Str. 28/8-6/12/47.**G.**
Dby. 5/11-28/12/50.**G.**
Str. 26/7-5/9/53.**G.**
Str. 29/1-3/3/56.**G.**
Str. 21-29/3/56.**N/C.**

BOILERS:
C1799.
C1798 *(ex2979)* 22/5/37.
C1740 *(ex2738)* 3/10/42.
27650 *(ex4980)* 28/12/50.
27873 *(ex4969)* 5/9/53.
27777 *(ex4776)* 3/3/56.

SHEDS:
Eastfield.
Aberdeen 17/4/43.
Dundee 12/12/43.
Carlisle 15/6/46.
Ipswich 15/4/47.

RENUMBERED:
4841 8/12/46.
64841 28/12/50.

CONDEMNED:
6/10/59.
Cut up at Stratford.

1453

Darlington.

To traffic 31/8/32.

REPAIRS:
Dar. 20-25/9/33.**N/C.** *Cleaned for Shildon Exhibition.*
Dar. 24/5-22/6/34.**G.**
Dar. 30/9-13/11/36.**G.**
Dar. 16-26/11/36.**N/C.**
Dar. 23/11-5/12/38.**N/C.**
Tender change.
Gor. 27/6-22/7/39.**G.**
Dar. 17/3-18/4/42.**G.**
Cow. 1/2-23/12/44.**G.**
Cow. 5/3-13/4/46.**L.**
Cow. 18/2-7/6/47.**G.**
Cow. 18/11-17/12/49.**L/I.**
Cow. 31/3-10/5/52.**G.**
Cow. 3/7-11/8/52.**N/C.**
Cow. 11/1-13/2/54.**H/I.**
Ghd. 15-23/9/55.**C/L.**
Cow. 23/1-23/2/57.**G.**
Cow. 2/4/62. *Not repaired.*

BOILERS:
3176/5D.
1913 *(ex1455)* 22/6/34.
1916 *(ex1466)* 13/11/36.
2223 *(ex1281)* 22/7/39.
2571 *(ex1459)* 18/4/42.
C1715 *(ex2737)* 23/12/44.
C1739 *(ex2742)* 7/6/47.
27543 *(ex4822)* 10/5/52.
27631 *(new)* 23/2/57.

SHEDS:
Neville Hill.
Haverton Hill 28/3/43.
Blaydon 19/6/43.
Heaton 15/1/61.

RENUMBERED:
4842 10/2/46.
64842 31/1/49.

CONDEMNED:
18/4/62.
Cut up at Darlington.

1469

Darlington.

To traffic 6/10/32.

REPAIRS:
Dar. 16/10-13/11/34.**G.**
Dar. 5/8-3/9/37.**G.**
Dar. 21/9-3/11/39.**G.**
Dar. 9-27/11/39.**N/C.**
Dar. 17-26/1/42.**N/C.**
Dar. 29/6-8/8/42.**G.**
Dar. 28/7-4/8/43.**N/C.**
Cow. 19/1-10/2/45.**G.**
Cow. 15/2-5/4/47.**G.**

Not all the circular covers were lost, despite their peregrinations through the various workshops for more than thirty years. When Inverurie gave 64795 a heavy repair (and fitted it with Automatic Warning System) as late as March 1961, they found a circular cover to fit round the safety valves, as seen here at Portobello on 17th May 1961. The boiler is that fitted to no.1808 when new in 1938, ten years after those covers had ceased to be put on as original equipment. *A.G.Ellis*

Some engines coming out of Cowlairs in late LNER days had new cover made for the base of the safety valves, but those could be identified easily because they were rectangular as seen here on 64978 when ex works on 30th December 1950. Note that the engine got British Railways numbering (with correct Gill Sans 6 and 9) but the tender still kept the L N E R which had been painted on it in November 1947. *A.G.Ellis*

With only 1448 of the twelve for N. E. Area getting a Westinghouse standpipe, No.1449 and the other ten acquired the more usual connection for that brake by a union under the buffer beam - shown clearly in this view of 1455 - which allowed front number to be displayed in the accustomed style. The other pipe is for train heating. *Photomatic*

The 28 engines which Beyer, Peacock built in September 1936 to May 1937 were all delivered with single red lining on their black paint, that style having been shown on the drawing supplied to them, although LNER paint shops had stopped

applying it in 1928. Note the maker's works plate on the side of the smokebox. Here at Gorton shed for its first three weeks, they were running-in no.1856 before it went to its allocated shed at Colwick near Nottingham. *W.H.Whitworth*

The first thirty of those built in 1928/29, nos. 2691 to 2720 were painted when numbers were still being put on the tender, shown here on 2712 at Stratford. *WBY collection*

Beginning with No.2721, new in March 1929, number position on cab side was made standard, to which all the rest of the J39 class then conformed.

Nos. 2731-42 were allocated to Scottish Area, and went there with L N E R on tender in 12" shaded transfers. When repaired at Cowlairs in the mid-1930's, that works saw fit to use up some 7½" transfers for L N E R on them. No.2737 here on 16th June 1935 at its home shed of St Margarets had been so done when ex Cowlairs from May 1934 repair. *A.G.Ellis*

1469 cont.
Ghd. 4-29/6/48.**L.**
Cow. 31/1-26/3/49.**G.**
Inv. 27/9-9/11/51.**H/I.**
Cow. 7/4-14/5/53.**G.**
Cow. 16-31/12/54.**C/L.**
Cow. 27/4-26/5/56.**H/I.**
Cow. 30/7-6/9/58.**G.**
Dar. 8-29/12/60.**C/L.**

BOILERS:
3176/6D.
3176/6D Reno.119 13/11/34.
1909 *(ex1451)* 3/9/37.
2141 *(ex1451)* 3/11/39.
2846 *(ex1537)* 8/8/42.
2625 *(ex1466)* 10/2/45.
2625 Reno.27498 9/11/51.
27540 *(ex4932)* 14/5/53.
27486 *(ex4912)* 6/9/58.

SHEDS:
Neville Hill.
Haverton Hill 28/3/43.
Blaydon 19/6/43.
Tweedmouth 5/6/49.
Sunderland 20/8/61.

RENUMBERED:
4843 27/10/46.
64843 26/3/49.

CONDEMNED:
29/3/62.
Cut up at Darlington.

1471

Darlington.

To traffic 13/10/32.

REPAIRS:
Dar. 14/3-10/4/34.**G.**
Dar. 23/9-23/10/35.**G.**
Dar. 17/6-6/8/37.**G.**
Dar. 29/8-6/9/38.**N/C.**
Tender change.
Dar. 15/3-3/5/39.**G.**
Dar. 4/5-3/6/39.**N/C.**
Dar. 7-15/11/40.**N/C.**
Tender only.
Dar. 26/2-9/4/41.**G.**
Cow. 26/1-4/3/44.**G.**
Cow. 29/9-20/10/45.**L.**
Cow. 27/7-7/9/46.**G.**
Cow. 15-22/2/47.**L.**
Cow. 23/9-30/10/48.**G.**
Cow. 13/3-18/4/52.**L/I.**
Cow. 8/12/53-15/1/54.**G.**
Cow. 23/5-22/6/57.**H/I.**
Cow. 28/10-5/12/59.**G.**

BOILERS:
3176/7D.
8021 *(ex1233)* 23/10/35.
1920 *(ex1458)* 6/8/37.
2601 *(ex1418)* 9/4/41.
C1713 *(ex2739)* 4/3/44.
2842 *(ex1534)* 7/9/46.
1907 *(ex1412)* 30/10/48.
1907 Reno.27452 18/4/52.
27493 *(ex4859)* 15/1/54.
25835 *(new)* 5/12/59.

SHEDS:
Darlington.
Blaydon 26/6/43.
Tweedmouth 14/8/49.

RENUMBERED:
4844 10/11/46.
64844 30/10/48.

CONDEMNED:
3/12/62.
Cut up at Cowlairs.

1480

Darlington.

To traffic 9/11/32.

REPAIRS:
Dar. 9/4-4/5/34.**G.**
Dar. 9-12/5/34.**N/C.**
Dar. 31/1-5/3/36.**G.**
Dar. 10/7/36.*Weigh.*
Dar. 14-16/7/37.**N/C.**
Tender change.
Dar. 22/11/37-7/1/38.**G.**
Dar. 15/12/39-17/1/40.**G.**
Dar. 19/6-30/7/42.**G.**
Cow. 15/5-3/6/44.**L.**
Cow. 7-28/4/45.**G.**
Cow. 29/3-31/5/47.**G.**
Cow. 6-22/5/48.**L.**
Cow. 30/9-29/10/49.**L/I.**
Cow. 4/1-2/2/52.**G.**
Gor. 28/6-21/8/54.**G.**
Cow. 23/8-19/9/57.**H/I.**
Cow. 4-15/4/60.**N/C.**
Cow. 8-26/8/60.**C/L.**

BOILERS:
3176/8D.
3176/8D Reno.121 5/3/36.
1904 *(ex1452)* 7/1/38.
RS119 *(ex1412)* 17/1/40.
1904 *(ex1466)* 30/7/42.
C1715 *(ex1453)* 31/5/47.
27516 *(ex4914)* 2/2/52.
27758 *(ex4806)* 21/8/54.

SHEDS:
Darlington.
Starbeck 5/7/43.
York 13/9/59.
Thornaby 13/12/59.

RENUMBERED:
4845 15/9/46.
64845 22/5/48.

CONDEMNED:
21/7/61.
Cut up at Cowlairs.

1482

Darlington.

To traffic 24/5/33.

REPAIRS:
Dar. 14/11-10/12/34.**G.**
Dar. 17/2-21/3/36.**G.**
Dar. 8/4-20/5/38.**G.**
Dar. 20-24/5/38.**N/C.**
Don. 6/11-8/12/39.**N/C.**
Tender only.
Dar. 3/7-1/8/40.**G.**
Dar. 29/8-28/9/42.**G.**
Dar. 30/11-17/12/43.**L.**
Cow. 30/10-25/11/44.**G.**
Cow. 20/4-25/5/46.**G.**
Cow. 5-12/4/47.**L.**
Cow. 12/12/47-21/2/48.**G.**
Cow. 3/6-1/7/50.**H/I.**
Ghd. 11/10-20/11/50.**C/L.**
Cow. 19/12/50-22/2/51.**C/L.**
Gor. 23/6-5/9/53.**G.**
Gor. 2-31/10/53.**C/L.**
Cow. 29/7-8/8/55.**N/C.**
Cow. 19-29/9/55.**N/C.**
Ghd. 13-19/11/58.**C/L.**
Cow. 27/1-21/2/59.**G.**
Cow. 23/4-11/5/59.**N/C.**
Cow. 25/8-14/10/60.**C/L.**

BOILERS:
3176/9D.
3176/9D Reno.122 10/12/34.
2573 *(ex1472)* 1/8/40.
RS121 *(ex1489)* 28/9/42.
2712 *(ex1490)* 21/2/48.
25800 *(ex4734)* 5/9/53.
27437 *(ex62746)* 21/2/59.

SHEDS:
Heaton.
Darlington 28/3/43.
Blaydon 23/6/43.
Borough Gardens 22/1/50.
Gateshead 14/6/59.
North Blyth 15/1/61.
Tyne Dock 30/7/61.
Sunderland 20/8/61.

RENUMBERED:
4846 5/1/47.
64846 1/7/50.

CONDEMNED:
16/11/62.
Cut up at Darlington.

1483

Darlington.

To traffic 19/5/33.

REPAIRS:
Dar. 18/2-22/3/35.**G.**
Dar. 6/10-26/11/36.**G.**
Dar. 26/11-16/12/36.**N/C.**
Dar. 26/5-1/7/39.**G.**
Dar. 6/12/39-15/2/40.**L.**
Dar. 12-25/8/41.**H.**
Dar. 8/12/41-15/1/42.**G.**
Dar. 6-27/11/43.**L.**
Cow. 13/12/44-20/1/45.**G.**
Cow. 25-27/3/45.**N/C.**
Cow. 4-25/5/46.**L.**
Cow. 6/10-20/12/47.**G.**
Cow. 6/8-4/9/48.**L.**
Cow. 9/8-2/9/50.**H/I.**
Cow. 13-17/11/50.**N/C.**
Cow. 11/3-2/5/53.**G.**
Cow. 12/1-18/2/56.**L/I.**
Cow. 28/11-20/12/58.**G.**
Cow. 27/7-26/8/61.**L/I.**
Cow. 31/8-9/9/61.**C/L.**

BOILERS:
3176/10D.
3176/10D Reno.123 22/3/35.
2340 *(ex1481)* 26/11/36.
2713 *(ex1587)* 15/1/42.
C1738 *(ex2741)* 20/1/45.
2708 *(ex1548)* 20/12/47.
27528 *(ex4936)* 2/5/53.
27454 *(ex64857)* 20/12/58.

SHEDS:
Heaton.
Darlington 28/3/43.
Middlesbrough 25/7/48.
Starbeck 27/9/53.
Selby 14/6/59.
York 13/9/59.
Sunderland 8/11/59.

RENUMBERED:
4847 5/1/47.
64847 4/9/48.

CONDEMNED:
16/11/62.
Cut up at Darlington.

1412

Darlington.

To traffic 15/3/34.

REPAIRS:
Dar. 11-14/4/34.**N/C.**
Water scoop fitted.
Dar. 18/10-27/11/35.**G.**
Dar. 20/8-1/10/37.**G.**
Dar. 12/9-13/10/39.**G.**
Dar. 6/10-22/11/41.**G.**
Cow. 26/5-24/6/44.**G.**
Cow. 11/5-1/6/46.**G.**
Ghd. 9/12/47-8/1/48.**L.**
Cow. 23/9-23/10/48.**G.**
Cow. 13/6-7/7/51.**L/I.**
Cow. 2-31/10/53.**G.**

Cow. 17-26/11/53.**N/C.**
Cow. 11-20/2/54.**N/C.**
Cow. 23/8-22/9/56.**H/I.**
Dar. 1/1-11/2/57.**C/L.**
Cow. 3/11-3/12/60.**G.**
Dar. 31/10/61.**C/L.**
Cow. 4/1-9/2/62.**C/L.**

BOILERS:
3077/20D.
3077/20D Reno.129 27/11/35.
RS119 *(ex1469)* 1/10/37.
1919 *(ex1418)* 13/10/39.
RS123 *(ex1476)* 22/11/41.
1907 *(ex1449)* 1/6/46.
4909 *(ex4975)* 23/10/48.
4909 Reno.27546 7/7/51.
27524 *(ex4854)* 31/10/53.
27428 *(ex62701)* 3/12/60.

SHEDS:
Newport.
Darlington 28/3/43.
Starbeck 8/7/43.
Darlington 14/1/46.
West Auckland 4/1/48.
Middlesbrough 29/8/54.
West Auckland 6/3/55.
Middlesbrough 3/4/55.
West Auckland 26/6/55.

RENUMBERED:
4848 31/5/46.
64848 23/10/48.

CONDEMNED:
3/12/62.
Cut up at Darlington.

1463

Darlington.

To traffic 19/3/34.

REPAIRS:
Dar. 9-11/4/34.**N/C.**
Water scoop fitted.
Dar. 2/10-11/11/35.**G.**
Dar. 1/2-8/3/38.**G.**
Dar. 9/1-7/2/40.**G.**
Dar. 17/2-18/3/41.**L.**
Dar. 27/1-21/2/42.**G.**
Dar. 10/2-2/3/43.**L.**
Cow. 18/10-11/11/44.**G.**
Cow. 18/5-15/6/46.**L.**
Cow. 3/5-19/7/47.**G.**
Cow. 1-17/7/48.**L.**
Cow. 4/11-3/12/49.**L/I.**
Cow. 11/4-6/5/50.**C/H.**
Cow. 8/2-17/3/51.**G.**
Cow. 9/10-21/11/53.**H/I.**
Ghd. 24/2-4/3/55.**C/L.**
Cow. 21/11-15/12/56.**G.**

BOILERS:
2564.
1918 *(ex1418)* 8/3/38.
2099 *(ex1449)* 7/2/40.
2712 *(ex1465)* 21/2/42.
BP135 *(ex1563)* 11/11/44.
2917 *(ex1508)* 19/7/47.
27465 *(ex4794)* 17/3/51.
27629 *(new)* 15/12/56.

SHEDS:
Newport.
Darlington 28/3/43.
Blaydon 26/6/43.
Heaton 30/6/57.
Blaydon 10/11/57.
West Hartlepool 9/10/60.

RENUMBERED:
4849 10/11/46.
64849 15/7/48.

CONDEMNED:
16/11/62.
Cut up at Darlington.

1467

Darlington.

To traffic 22/3/34.

REPAIRS:
Dar. 18-20/4/34.**N/C.**
Water scoop fitted.
Dar. 9/12/35-23/1/36.**G.**
Dar. 11/5-16/6/38.**G.**
Dar. 26/3-29/4/40.**G.**
Dar. 31/5-3/7/43.**L.**
Cow. 25/4-20/5/44.**G.**
Cow. 18/1-19/4/47.**G.**
Cow. 12/10-19/11/49.**L/I.**
Cow. 10-27/10/52.**G.**
Cow. 20-28/11/52.**N/C.**
Cow. 18/8-17/9/55.**H/I.**
Cow. 31/12/58-24/1/59.**G.**

BOILERS:
2568.
2317 *(ex1425)* 16/6/38.
RS129 *(ex1425)* 29/4/40.
3194 *(ex3094)* 20/5/44.
3191 *(ex1505)* 19/4/47.
27564 *(ex64888)* 27/10/52.
27827 *(ex62771)* 24/1/59.

SHEDS:
Newport.
Tweedmouth 19/6/39.
Gateshead 20/1/40.
Darlington 28/3/43.
Neville Hill 29/1/50.
Selby 26/9/54.
Neville Hill 7/8/55.
Thornaby 1/11/59.
Malton 9/7/61.
Hull Dairycoates 25/2/62.

RENUMBERED:
4850 17/11/46.
64850 17/11/49.

CONDEMNED:
3/12/62.
Cut up at Darlington.

1468

Darlington.

To traffic 17/3/34.

REPAIRS:
Dar. 5-9/4/34.**N/C.**
Water scoop fitted.
Dar. 13/1-8/2/36.**G.**
Dar. 9/12/37-9/2/38.**G.**
Dar. 10-16/2/38.**N/C.**
Dar. 16/11-23/12/39.**G.**
Dar. 28/12/39-12/1/40.**N/C.**
Dar. 17/12/41-22/1/42.**G.**
Cow. 24/4-27/5/44.**G.**
Cow. 9/2-17/3/45.**L.**
Cow. 19/10/46-25/1/47.**G.**
Cow. 19/2-25/6/49.**G.**
Cow. 27/7-25/8/51.**H/I.**
Cow. 10/6-10/7/54.**G.**
Cow. 20/10-19/11/60.**G.**
Cow. 6-10/12/60.**C/L.**

BOILERS:
2571.
8021 *(ex1471)* 9/2/38.
2100 *(ex2725)* 23/12/39.
1909 *(ex1429)* 22/1/42.
2116 *(ex1505)* 27/5/44.
RS125 *(ex279)* 25/1/47.
2699 *(ex1880)* 25/6/49.
2699 Reno.27505 25/8/51.
27533 *(ex4949)* 10/7/54.
27651 *(ex65909)* 19/11/60.

SHEDS:
Newport.
Darlington 5/11/38.
Stockton 16/7/40.
Blaydon 21/6/43.
Darlington 23/7/45.
Alston 2/1/49.
Borough Gardens 4/1/53.
Gateshead 14/6/59.
Tyne Dock 26/2/61.
Sunderland 20/8/61.

RENUMBERED:
4851 9/11/46.
64851 25/6/49.

CONDEMNED:
3/12/62.
Cut up at Darlington.

1472

Darlington.

To traffic 27/3/34.

REPAIRS:
Dar. 20-23/4/34.**N/C.**
Water scoop fitted.
Dar. 28/11/35-3/1/36.**G.**
Dar. 14/2-28/3/38.**G.**
Dar. 1-29/6/40.**G.**
Dar. 1/8-5/9/42.**G.**
Cow. 5/5-2/6/45.**G.**
Cow. 3/9-25/10/47.**G.**
Cow. 3/9-8/10/49.**L/I.**
Cow. 5/6-5/7/52.**G.**
Ghd. 14-22/12/54.**N/C.**
Cow. 8/11-8/12/56.**G.**
Inv. 7/5-21/7/60.**H/I.**
Cow. 16-18/3/61.**C/L.**

BOILERS:
2573.
8580 *(ex1466)* 29/6/40.
2277 *(ex1458)* 5/9/42.
2715 *(ex1548)* 2/6/45.
2940 *(ex1585)* 25/10/47.
27514 *(ex4986)* 5/7/52.
27628 *(new)* 8/12/56.

SHEDS:
Middlesbrough.
Haverton Hill 12/10/36.
Blaydon 19/6/43.
Gateshead 4/3/51.
Heaton 5/11/61.

RENUMBERED:
4852 3/11/46.
64852 5/10/49.

CONDEMNED:
3/12/62.
Cut up at Darlington.

1488

Darlington.

To traffic 14/12/34.

REPAIRS:
Dar. 19/1-16/2/37.**G.**
Dar. 17-18/2/37.**N/C.**
Gor. 12/9-7/10/39.**G.**
Dar. 11/6-5/7/40.**N/C.**
Dar. 30/6-12/8/41.**G.**
Dar. 1/1-3/2/43.**G.**
Cow. 14/8-9/9/44.**G.**
Str. 23/3-25/5/46.**G.**
Cow. 6/4-29/5/48.**G.**
Cow. 16/11-8/12/51.**L/I.**
Cow. 8/7-21/8/54.**G.**
Cow. 8-31/8/57.**H/I.**
Cow. 8/3-25/5/60.**G.**

BOILERS:
2623.
2579 *(ex1476)* 16/2/37.
2623 *(ex1458)* 7/10/39.
C1797 *(ex2736)* 12/8/41.
8580 *(ex1472)* 3/2/43.
8009 *(ex1274)* 25/5/46.
E1358 *(ex1804)* 29/5/48.
E1358 Reno.27526 8/12/51.

It has not been established whether Cowlairs had reduced its stock of the 7½" transfers to its satisfaction, or whether it had been instructed to come into line and use 12", but it was certainly doing so when it turned out 2733 in August 1935. Here in May 1937 it is at its home shed of Eastfield in Glasgow. *WBY coll.*

27452 *(ex4844)* 21/8/54.
27431 *(ex4784)* 25/5/60.

SHEDS:
Ferryhill.
Blaydon 24/8/38.
Gateshead 18/9/49.
Heaton 18/10/53.
Sunderland 13/12/59.
Tyne Dock 30/7/61.
Sunderland 20/8/61.

RENUMBERED:
4853 27/10/46.
64853 29/5/48.

CONDEMNED:
3/12/62.
Cut up at Darlington.

1490

Darlington.

To traffic 20/12/34.

REPAIRS:
Dar. 15/2-17/3/37.**G.**
Dar. 19/3-1/4/37.**N/C.**
Dar. 24/4-12/6/39.**G.**
Dar. 14/5-12/7/41.**G.**
Dar. 18/7-14/8/41.**L.**
Dar. 10/7-20/8/42.**N/C.**
Tender only.
Dar. 30/6-9/8/43.**G.**
Cow. 21/4-19/5/45.**G.**
Cow. 5-19/10/46.**L.**
Cow. 14/1-20/3/48.**G.**
Cow. 18/4-6/5/50.**L/I.**
Cow. 1-4/5/51.**C/L.**
Gor. 23/6-8/8/53.**G.**
Cow. 27/1-14/2/59.**G.**
Cow. 23/4-6/5/59.**N/C.**

BOILERS:
2625.
1913 *(ex1448)* 12/6/39.
C1797 *(ex1488)* 9/8/43.
2712 *(ex1463)* 19/5/45.
E1353 *(ex2984)* 20/3/48.
27767 *(ex4813)* 8/8/53.
27429 *(ex62772)* 14/2/59.

SHEDS:
Ferryhill.
Darlington 7/11/38.
Stockton 16/7/40.
Blaydon 21/6/43.
Tweedmouth 17/7/49.
Borough Gardens 4/1/53.
Gateshead 14/6/59.
Sunderland 11/9/60.

RENUMBERED:
4854 1/12/46.
64854 20/3/48.

CONDEMNED:
3/12/62.
Cut up at Darlington.

1475

Darlington.

To traffic 19/10/34.

REPAIRS:
Dar. 26/8-8/10/36.**G.**
Dar. 24/2-6/4/39.**G.**
Dar. 11-20/4/39.**N/C.**
Dar. 21/4-22/5/41.**G.**
Dar. 9/10-11/11/42.**H/I.**
Cow. 1/1-5/2/44.**G.**
Cow. 12/5-2/6/45.**G.**
Ghd. 1-26/11/46.**L.**
Cow. 29/10/47-10/1/48.**G.**
Cow. 4-21/5/48.**L.**
Cow. 13/8-10/9/49.**L/I.**
Cow. 29/1-1/3/52.**G.**
Cow. 17/12/54-5/2/55.**H/I.**
Cow. 8-22/11/56.**C/L.**
Cow. 7/6-6/7/57.**G.**
Cow. 16-17/8/57.**N/C.**
Cow. 4/4-7/5/60.**L/I.**

BOILERS:
2591.
2564 *(ex1463)* 6/4/39.
RS122 *(ex1482)* 22/5/41.
2714 *(ex1436)* 5/2/44.
4931 *(new)* 10/1/48.
27558 *(ex4706)* 1/3/52.
27538 *(ex64816)* 6/7/57.

SHEDS:
Newport.
Darlington 28/3/43.
Starbeck 10/7/43.
York 13/9/59.
Thornaby 13/12/59.
Heaton 24/12/61.

RENUMBERED:
4855 20/10/46.
64855 4/5/48.

CONDEMNED:
20/8/62.
Cut up at Cowlairs.

1476

Darlington.

To traffic 24/10/34.

REPAIRS:
Dar. 3/12/36-15/1/37.**G.**
Dar. 22/4-25/5/39.**G.**
Dar. 15/9-25/10/41.**G.**
Dar. 10/6-13/7/43.**G.**
Cow. 24/3-14/4/45.**G.**
Cow. 19-26/10/46.**L.**
Cow. 4/12/47-14/2/48.**G.**
Cow. 25/3-22/4/50.**H/I.**
Cow. 21/2-19/4/52.**G.**
Cow. 1/9-8/10/55.**H/I.**
Cow. 9/4-17/5/58.**G.**
Dar. 8/12/59-19/1/60.**C/L.**
Cow. 9-18/12/60.**N/C.**
Cow. 15/10/62.*Not repaired.*

BOILERS:
2579.
RS123 *(ex1483)* 15/1/37.
2591 *(ex1478)* 25/10/41.
7946 *(ex1470)* 13/7/43.
BP141 *(ex1835)* 14/4/45.
C1738 *(ex1483)* 14/2/48.
27551 *(ex4709)* 19/4/52.
27557 *(ex4986)* 17/5/58.

SHEDS:
Newport.
Darlington 28/3/43.
Blaydon 3/8/43.
Heaton 23/10/49.

RENUMBERED:
4856 26/10/46.
64856 22/4/50.

CONDEMNED:
15/10/62.
Cut up at Cowlairs.

1477

Darlington.

To traffic 29/10/34.

REPAIRS:
Dar. 6/7-17/8/36.**G.**
Dar. 18/9-12/10/36.**N/C.**
Dar. 16/6-3/8/38.**G.**
Dar. 27/5-18/6/40.**G.**
Dar. 29/1-27/2/43.**G.**
Cow. 31/3-28/4/45.**G.**
Cow. 9/11-7/12/46.**L.**
Cow. 6/11/47-17/1/48.**G.**
Cow. 4/8-1/9/50.**G.**
Cow. 24/3-8/6/53.**G.**
Cow. 2-21/11/53.**C/L.**
Cow. 3/9-2/10/54.**C/L.**
Cow. 3-26/11/55.**L/I.**

Cow. 9/9-11/10/58.**G.**
Cow. 21/11-8/12/58.**C/L.**

BOILERS:
2595.
2317 *(ex1467)* 18/6/40.
2573 *(ex1482)* 27/2/43.
4932 *(new)* 17/1/48.
27454 *(ex4704)* 8/6/53.
27477 *(ex64938)* 11/10/58.

SHEDS:
Newport.
Selby 31/7/39.
York 23/10/39.
Selby 27/2/40.
Starbeck 20/7/40.
York 13/9/59.
Thornaby 22/11/59.
Neville Hill 17/6/62.

RENUMBERED:
4857 3/11/46.
64857 1/9/50.

CONDEMNED:
3/12/62.
Cut up at Darlington.

1478

Darlington.

To traffic 14/11/34.

REPAIRS:
Dar. 21/8-30/9/36.**G.**
Dar. 2/3-22/4/39.**G.**
Dar. 29/4-27/5/40.**L.**
Dar. 20/5-21/6/41.**G.**
Dar. 27/3-23/5/42.**L.**
Cow. 14/4-13/5/44.**G.**
Cow. 18/1-8/3/47.**G.**
Cow. 27/5-25/6/49.**L/I.**
Cow. 26/10-17/11/51.**G.**
Cow. 19/12/53-30/1/54.**L/I.**
Cow. 20/9-27/10/56.**G.**
Cow. 22/7-17/9/60.**G.**
Cow. 23/11-2/12/61.**C/L.**

BOILERS:
2617.
2591 *(ex1475)* 22/4/39.
2564 *(ex1475)* 21/6/41.
2636 *(ex2785)* 13/5/44.
C1713 *(ex1471)* 8/3/47.
27592 *(new)* 17/11/51.
27580 *(ex65915)* 27/10/56.
27711 *(ex64799)* 17/9/60.

SHEDS:
Newport.
Darlington 28/3/43.
Blaydon 29/8/48.
Hull Dairycoates 4/9/49.
Blaydon 2/10/49.
Sunderland 15/1/61.

RENUMBERED:
4858 31/5/46.
64858 25/6/49.

CONDEMNED:
29/3/62.
Cut up at Darlington.

1479

Darlington.

To traffic 7/12/34.

REPAIRS:
Dar. 23/9-26/11/35.**H.**
After collision.
Dar. 24/2-24/3/37.**G.**
Dar. 13/9-18/10/37.**L.**
Dar. 18/9-25/10/39.**G.**
Dar. 31/10-13/11/39.**N/C.**
Dar. 18/5-18/6/42.**G.**
Dar. 17/12/42-8/1/43.**L.**
Dar. 14-27/8/43.**L.**
Cow. 1-27/7/44.**G.**
Dar. 23/6-7/7/45.**L.**
Cow. 28/7-4/8/45.**L.**
Cow. 12/10-14/12/46.**G.**
Cow. 14/1-5/3/49.**G.**
Cow. 6/9-5/10/51.**H/I.**
Don. 1-8/5/52.**N/C.**
Cow. 6-27/2/53.**C/L.**
Cow. 28/5-17/6/53.**C/L.**
Cow. 16/10-21/11/53.**G.**
Cow. 21/6-3/8/57.**H/I.**
Cow. 7/9-23/10/59.**G.**

BOILERS:
2622.
2306 *(ex1474)* 25/10/39.
1919 *(ex1412)* 18/6/42.
2597 *(ex1896)* 14/12/46.
2597 Reno.27493 5/10/51.
27478 *(ex4933)* 21/11/53.
25830 *(new)* 23/10/59.

SHEDS:
Newport.
Middlesbrough 23/1/36.
Darlington 28/3/43.
Starbeck 10/7/43.
York 13/9/59.
Thornaby 13/12/59.
West Auckland 24/12/61.
Mirfield 15/4/62.
Ardsley 18/11/62.

RENUMBERED:
4859 27/10/46.
64859 4/3/49.

CONDEMNED:
3/12/62.
Cut up at Darlington.

1436

Darlington.

To traffic 31/10/35.

REPAIRS:
Don. 16/8-17/9/38.**G.**
Dar. 13/12/40-15/1/41.**G.**
Cow. 20/10-6/11/43.**G.**
Cow. 17/11/43.**L.**
Cow. 11/1/44.**L.**
Cow. 2/6-14/7/45.**L.**
Cow. 6/7-31/8/46.**G.**
Dar. 13/9-11/10/46.**L.**
Ghd. 6/12/47-7/1/48.**L.**
Cow. 26/7-21/8/48.**G.**
Cow. 10/1-3/2/51.**H/I.**
Cow. 19/1-23/2/52.**C/L.**
Cow. 28/5-11/7/53.**G.**
Cow. 3/7-23/8/56.**L/I.**
Cow. 4/4-4/5/57.**C/L.**
Cow. 11/11-6/12/58.**G.**

BOILERS:
2708.
2714 *(ex1487)* 15/1/41.
3173 *(ex3088)* 6/11/43.
3192 *(ex3092)* 31/8/46.
C1797 *(ex1460)* 21/8/48.
C1797 Reno. 27482 3/2/51.
27474 *(ex4756)* 11/7/53.
27567 *(ex64819)* 6/12/58.

SHEDS:
Neville Hill.
Starbeck 28/3/43.
Neville Hill 13/6/54.
Selby 7/8/55.
Gateshead 30/8/59.

RENUMBERED:
4860 30/8/46.
64860 21/8/48.

CONDEMNED:
3/12/62.
Cut up at Darlington.

1460

Darlington.

To traffic 4/11/35.

REPAIRS:
Dar. 21/9-10/11/38.**G.**
Dar. 19/6-12/7/40.**G.**
Dar. 8-24/9/41.**N/C.**
Dar. 16/2-19/3/43.**G.**
Dar. 20-27/3/43.**N/C.**
Dar. 1-23/4/43.**L.**
Cow. 1/9-6/10/45.**G.**
Cow. 2-16/11/46.**L.**
Ghd. 23/4-10/5/47.**L.**
Cow. 30/3-1/5/48.**G.**
Cow. 22/9-21/10/50.**H/I.**
Cow. 14/11/52-30/1/53.**G.**
Cow. 4/5-4/6/55.**H/I.**
Cow. 4/7-22/8/58.**G.**

BOILERS:
2710.
2946 *(new)* 10/11/38.
BP136 *(ex1543)* 12/7/40.
2925 *(ex1577)* 19/3/43.
C1797 *(ex1496)* 6/10/45.
C1712 *(ex1862)* 1/5/48.
27456 *(ex4950)* 30/1/53.
27804 *(ex64713)* 22/8/58.

SHEDS:
Neville Hill.
Starbeck 21/7/37.
Scarborough 25/9/49.
Starbeck 23/7/50.
York 13/9/59.
Thornaby 13/12/59.
Neville Hill 26/11/61.

RENUMBERED:
4861 12/10/46.
64861 1/5/48.

CONDEMNED:
3/12/62.
Cut up at Darlington.

1464

Darlington.

To traffic 8/11/35.

REPAIRS:
Dar. 29/4-11/6/38.**G.**
Dar. 14/6-10/7/40.**G.**
Dar. 12-30/7/40.**N/C.**
Dar. 19/1-17/2/43.**G.**
Cow. 25/8-6/10/45.**G.**
Cow. 5-19/10/46.**L.**
Cow. 15/3-27/4/48.**G.**
Cow. 27/2-31/3/51.**H/I.**
Cow. 26/1-26/2/52.**L/I.**
Cow. 23/8-18/9/54.**G.**
Cow. 5-8/10/54.**N/C.**
Cow. 14-23/10/54.**N/C.**
Cow. 23/1-23/2/57.**L/I.**

BOILERS:
2711.
2129 *(ex1455)* 10/7/40.
2723 *(ex1548)* 17/2/43.
2622 *(ex1560)* 27/4/48.
2622 Reno.27496 31/3/51.
27460 *(ex4814)* 18/9/54.

SHEDS:
Neville Hill.
Starbeck 25/10/37.
Darlington 14/1/46.
West Hartlepool 12/12/48.
Middlesbrough 25/2/51.
West Hartlepool 14/9/52.
West Auckland 6/3/55.

RENUMBERED:
4862 5/1/47.
64862 27/4/48.

CONDEMNED:
22/10/61.
Cut up at Cowlairs.

1465

Darlington.

To traffic 13/11/35.

REPAIRS:
Dar. 28/3-16/5/39.**G.**
Dar. 28/10-29/11/41.**G.**
Cow. 19/11-8/12/43.**G.**
Cow. 25/5-3/8/46.**G.**
Cow. 23/2-7/5/49.**G.**
Cow. 31/1-23/2/52.**H/I.**
Cow. 17/12/54-15/1/55.**G.**
Cow. 27-29/1/55.**C/L.**
Cow. 19/9-22/10/58.**H/I.**

BOILERS:
2712.
8022 *(ex1450)* 29/11/41.
2716 *(ex1539)* 8/12/43.
2716 Reno.27512 23/2/52.
27553 *(ex64975)* 15/1/55.

SHEDS:
Sunderland.
Consett 15/6/36.
Darlington 28/3/43.
Tweedmouth 4/1/48.
Blaydon 28/2/48.
Heaton 7/11/48.
Neville Hill 12/2/50.

RENUMBERED:
4863 27/10/46.
64863 7/5/49.

CONDEMNED:
31/1/62.
Cut up at Cowlairs.

1473

Darlington.

To traffic 15/11/35.

REPAIRS:
Dar. 2/5-3/6/39.**G.**
Dar. 29/7-6/9/41.**G.**
Dar. 6-31/7/43.**L.**
Cow. 8/3-15/4/44.**G.**
Cow. 5/10-30/11/46.**G.**
Dar. 30/6-6/8/48.**L.**
Dar. 9-27/8/48.**N/C.**
Cow. 20/6-20/8/49.**G.**
Ghd. 11-14/10/50.**C/L.**
Cow. 16/10-1/12/51.**L/I.**
Cow. 2/8-17/9/52.**C/H.**
Ghd. 16-31/10/53.**C/L.**
Ghd. 22-31/12/53.**C/L.**
Str. 14/4-5/6/54.**G.**
Cow. 13/12/56-12/1/57.**L/I.**
Cow. 23/5-14/7/61.**G.**

BOILERS:
2713.
8005 *(ex1454)* 3/6/39.
1907 *(ex1456)* 6/9/41.
3174 *(ex3086)* 15/4/44.
C1834 *(ex2977)* 30/11/46.
3194 *(ex4915)* 20/8/49.
3194 Reno.27554 1/12/51.
27679 *(ex4882)* 5/6/54.
27525 *(ex64817)* 14/7/61.

SHEDS:
Sunderland.
Consett 28/11/38.
Tyne Dock 14/11/41.
Darlington 28/3/43.
Hull Dairycoates 4/1/48.
Borough Gardens 3/12/50.
Blaydon 4/1/53.
Hull Dairycoates 13/6/54.
Heaton 16/6/57.

RENUMBERED:
4864 27/10/46.
64864 6/8/48.

CONDEMNED:
3/12/62.
Cut up at Darlington.

1474

Darlington.

To traffic 20/11/35.

REPAIRS:
Dar. 29/6-16/8/37.**G.**
Dar. 15/5-26/6/39.**G.**
Dar. 6/2/41.**N/C.** *Tender only.*
Dar. 27/9-31/10/41.**G.**
Dar. 3-11/11/41.**N/C.**
Cow. 7/7-12/8/44.**G.**
Cow. 9-23/11/46.**L.**
Cow. 24/5-27/9/47.**G.**
Cow. 19/4-13/5/50.**L/I.**
Cow. 27/1-18/4/53.**G.**
Cow. 26/8-9/10/54.**C/H.**
Ghd. 11-15/11/54.**N/C.**
Cow. 19/4-11/6/60.**G.**

BOILERS:
2714.
2306 *(ex1456)* 16/8/37.
2625 *(ex1490)* 26/6/39.
2623 *(ex1488)* 31/10/41.
4905 *(ex1863)* 12/8/44.
27463 *(ex4964)* 18/4/53.
27660 *(ex64965)* 11/6/60.

SHEDS:
Darlington.
Blaydon 15/2/48.
Heaton 7/11/48.
Gateshead 4/3/51.

RENUMBERED:
4865 23/11/46.
64865 13/5/50.

CONDEMNED:
3/12/62.
Cut up at Darlington.

1485

Darlington.

To traffic 26/11/35.

REPAIRS:
Dar. 7/2-18/3/38.**G.**
Dar. 8/1-6/2/40.**G.**
Dar. 12/12/40.*Weigh.*
Dar. 19/8-19/9/42.**G.**
Cow. 19/9-7/10/44.**G.**
Cow. 12/1-2/2/46.**L.**
Cow. 15/3-17/5/47.**G.**
Cow. 10/2-11/3/50.**H/I.**
Cow. 26/4-6/5/50.**C/L.**
Cow. 16/11-29/12/50.**H/I.**
Cow. 14/11/52-7/2/53.**G.**
Cow. 18/8-17/9/55.**H/I.**
Cow. 9/9-11/10/58.**G.**

BOILERS:
2715.
BP141 *(ex1577)* 6/2/40.
BP138 *(ex1545)* 19/9/42.
2568 *(ex1546)* 17/5/47.
27742 *(ex64784)* 7/2/53.
27522 *(ex64922)* 11/10/58.

SHEDS:
Darlington.
Starbeck 14/7/43.
York 13/9/59.
Sunderland 8/11/59.
Heaton 13/12/59.

RENUMBERED:
4866 16/6/46.
64866 11/3/50.

CONDEMNED:
24/9/62.
Cut up at Cowlairs.

1486

Darlington.

To traffic 5/12/35.

REPAIRS:
Dar. 2/4-14/5/38.**G.**
Dar. 3/9-8/10/40.**G.**
Dar. 28/11/42-5/1/43.**L.**
Cow. 8/1-12/2/44.**G.**
Cow. 8/9-6/10/45.**G.**
Cow. 6-27/7/46.**L.**
Cow. 2-9/11/46.**L.**
Cow. 9/9-16/10/48.**G.**
Cow. 6/9-20/10/51.**G.**
Cow. 23/9-22/10/55.**G.**
Cow. 11/1-9/2/57.**C/H.**
Cow. 11/2-6/3/59.**L/I.**

BOILERS:
2716.
2922 *(ex1560)* 8/10/40.
8022 *(ex1465)* 12/2/44.
2095 *(ex1971)* 16/10/48.
27589 *(new)* 20/10/51.
27532 *(ex64703)* 22/10/55.
27511 *(ex64949)* 9/2/57.

SHEDS:
Newport.
Middlesbrough 23/1/36.
Darlington 28/3/43.
Hull Dairycoates 28/12/47.
Neville Hill 20/5/51.
Malton 10/6/51.

RENUMBERED:
4867 24/11/46.
64867 15/10/48.

CONDEMNED:
18/2/62.
Cut up at Cowlairs.

1504

Darlington.

To traffic 3/12/35.

REPAIRS:
Dar. 14/7-27/8/36.**L.**
After collision.
Dar. 2/12/37-28/1/38.**G.**
Dar. 20/3-19/4/40.**G.**
Dar. 11/8-18/9/42.**G.**
Dar. 24/6-16/7/43.**L.**
Cow. 6/9-7/10/44.**G.**
Dar. 8/1/46.*Weigh.*
Cow. 8/3-10/5/47.**G.**
Cow. 16/4-13/5/50.**H/I.**
Cow. 16/2-21/3/52.**G.**
Cow. 19/9-19/10/55.**H/I.**
Cow. 1-17/12/55.**N/C.**
Cow. 28/6-7/7/56.**C/L.**
Cow. 17/10-8/11/58.**G.**

BOILERS:
2717.
RS121 *(ex1480)* 28/1/38.
2622 *(ex1479)* 19/4/40.
RS119 *(ex1480)* 18/9/42.
BP138 *(ex1485)* 10/5/47.
27484 *(ex4875)* 21/3/52.
27519 *(ex65929)* 8/11/58.

SHEDS:
Heaton.
Darlington 28/3/43.
Alnmouth 26/10/47.

Starting in July 1942 only N E instead of L N E R was used, the saving in labour for its application being more important during the war than the reduced cost of the transfers. 2699 was so altered when ex Cowlairs on 30th May 1943, and here at Stratford on 13th October 1945 it had just completed its next repair. *H.C.Casserley*

A start on using L N E R again was able to be made in January 1946, but very few J39s had it restored whilst still in their original numbering. In that same month the general renumbering also began, in which this class took 4700 to 4988. Parkeston shed changed 2778 to 4804 on Sunday 15th June 1946, but it kept just N E on tender until it went to works on 2nd March 1947. When sending it back to traffic on 4th June Stratford had been able to find normal 12" shaded transfers both for the number and for L N E R. *E.Haigh collection*

To keep up with the momentum of changing engine numbers, normally done at sheds on Sundays, outside painters had to be employed, and they often did the job in only 6" high stencils and white paint. No.4965 was so changed at Grantham shed on 23rd September 1946 under instructions from Doncaster, hence the curled tails on figures 9 and 6. "MALLARD" - no less - also got that same undignified change to 22 during that week at Grantham shed. *A.G.Ellis*

New England shedded no.1996 went into Gorton works for general repair on 5th November 1946 and would be in many different parts and places when, on Saturday 23rd November it was notionally renumbered 4969 to clear 1996 to be taken by a K4. When the general repair was completed on 8th February 1947, Gorton curiously used only 9" figures for the new number, although normal 12" for LNER on tender. *WBY collection*

1504 cont.
Darlington 18/4/48.
Alnmouth 16/5/48.

RENUMBERED:
4868 12/10/46.
64868 13/5/50.

CONDEMNED:
18/4/62.
Cut up at Darlington.

1505

Darlington.

To traffic 6/12/35.

REPAIRS:
Dar. 25/1-25/2/37.**G.**
Dar. 25/5-29/6/39.**G.**
Dar. 16/6-29/7/41.**G.**
Cow. 5/4-13/5/44.**G.**
Cow. 25/1-3/5/47.**G.**
Ghd. 2-12/11/48.**L.**
Cow. 23/2-23/4/49.**G.**
Ghd. 31/8-7/10/49.**C/L.**
Cow. 24/8-15/9/51.**H/I.**
Ghd. 26-29/11/51.**C/L.**
Cow. 13/3-2/4/52.**C/L.**
Ghd. 16-18/4/52.**C/L.**
Ghd. 16-29/9/53.**C/L.**
Cow. 1/9-8/10/55.**G.**
Cow. 22/7-3/9/60.**G.**

BOILERS:
2719.
2116 *(ex2725)* 29/7/41.
3191 *(ex3091)* 13/5/44.
2607 *(ex222)* 3/5/47.
2607 Reno.27495 15/9/51.
27512 *(ex64863)* 8/10/55.
25813 *(ex64732)* 3/9/60.

SHEDS:
Heaton.
Darlington 28/3/43.
Blaydon 14/11/48.
Gateshead 9/7/50.
North Blyth 8/10/61.
Alnmouth 8/4/62.

RENUMBERED:
4869 6/9/46.
64869 12/11/48.

CONDEMNED:
3/12/62.
Cut up at Cowlairs.

1506

Darlington.

To traffic 13/12/35.

REPAIRS:
Dar. 28/2-14/4/38.**G.**
Dar. 9/9-21/10/40.**G.**
Dar. 1-28/1/43.**G.**
Cow. 9/6-11/7/45.**G.**
Cow. 4/12/47-7/2/48.**G.**
Cow. 21/9-22/10/49.**H/I.**
Cow. 20/6-14/7/51.**G.**
Cow. 19/4-14/5/55.**G.**
Cow. 30/8-22/9/56.**C/L.**
Cow. 20/3-3/5/58.**H/I.**

BOILERS:
2720.
2717 *(ex1491)* 21/10/40.
1918 *(ex1455)* 28/1/43.
7946 *(ex1476)* 11/7/45.
2935 *(ex1491)* 7/2/48.
27587 *(new)* 14/7/51.
27483 *(ex64943)* 14/5/55.

SHEDS:
West Hartlepool.
Darlington 28/3/43.
Hull Dairycoates 15/2/48.
Borough Gardens 24/12/50.
Blaydon 4/1/53.
Neville Hill 26/6/55.
Thornaby 13/12/59.

RENUMBERED:
4870 16/6/46.
64870 22/10/49.

CONDEMNED:
18/1/62.
Cut up at Cowlairs.

1584

Darlington.

To traffic 20/12/35.

REPAIRS:
Dar. 24/2-13/4/38.**G.**
Dar. 13/2-9/3/40.**G.**
Dar. 13/3-7/6/41.**H.**
Dar. 13/5-12/6/42.**G.**
Cow. 8-30/9/44.**G.**
Cow. 29/6-27/7/46.**G.**
Cow. 8-16/8/47.**L.**
Cow. 17/12/48-26/2/49.**G.**
Cow. 15/5-13/6/51.**L/I.**
Cow. 31/10-5/11/51.**C/L.**
Cow. 21/11-15/12/51.**L/I.**
Cow. 22-27/9/52.**C/L.**
Ghd. 6-14/8/53.**C/L.**
Cow. 2-28/11/53.**G.**
Cow. 9/10-6/11/58.**G.**

BOILERS:
2723.
2715 *(ex1485)* 9/3/40.
2099 *(ex1463)* 12/6/42.
2623 *(ex1474)* 30/9/44.
C1796 *(ex2993)* 26/2/49.
C1796 Reno.27481 13/6/51.
27508 *(ex4846)* 28/11/53.
27476 *(ex4778)* 6/11/58.

SHEDS:
Blaydon.
Gateshead 18/9/49.
Heaton 7/7/57.

RENUMBERED:
4871 1/12/46.
64871 26/2/49.

CONDEMNED:
15/10/62.
Cut up at Cowlairs.

2941

Darlington.

To traffic 7/6/35.

REPAIRS:
Don. 21/8-15/10/38.**G.**
Gor. 14/12/39-17/2/40.**L.**
Don. 25/11/41-3/1/42.**G.**
Str. 22/12/42-9/1/43.**L.**
Str. 6/2-1/4/44.**G.**
Str. 23/6-14/11/46.**G.**
Str. 27/11-21/12/46.**L.**
Str. 20/8-26/9/48.**L.**
Gor. 1/3-7/5/49.**G.**
Gor. 21-23/5/49.**N/C.**
Gor. 31/8-10/9/49.**C/L.**
Gor. 5-12/10/49.**C/L.**
Gor. 16-19/10/49.**N/C.**
Dby. 26/7-10/9/51.**H/I.**
Gor. 25/2-27/3/54.**G.**
Gor. 30/3-8/4/54.**N/C.**
Gor. 15/1-23/2/57.**G.**
Gor. 12/11-20/12/58.**C/H.**
Gor. 13/12/60-11/2/61.**G.**

BOILERS:
2663.
2695 *(ex2944)* 1/4/44.
2767 *(ex2706)* 7/5/49.
27705 *(ex4746)* 27/3/54.
27877 *(ex4759)* 23/2/57.
27565 *(ex4886)* 11/2/61.

SHEDS:
Doncaster.
Ardsley 9/8/35.
Doncaster 19/8/35.
Retford 26/8/35.
March 13/2/36.
Ipswich 25/2/36.
Norwich 16/4/50.
Ardsley 30/4/50.
Bradford 16/6/57.
Low Moor 12/1/58.

RENUMBERED:
4872 5/12/46.
64872 25/9/48.

CONDEMNED:
26/11/62.
Cut up at Darlington.

2942

Darlington.

To traffic 8/6/35.

REPAIRS:
Gor. 18/11-24/12/37.**G.**
Gor. 1-6/1/38.**N/C.**
Gor. 29/6-10/8/40.**G.**
Str. 27/2-7/8/43.**G.**
Str. 16/12/45-19/1/46.**G.**
Gor. 19/9-13/11/48.**G.**
Dby. 20/12/51-8/2/52.**H/I.**
Str. 22/7-15/8/53.**C/L.**
Str. 22/1-6/2/54.**C/L.**
Str. 28/2-14/4/55.**G.**
Str. 22/7-6/8/55.**N/C.**
Str. 23/7-30/8/57.**G.**

BOILERS:
2665.
2681 *(ex2951)* 24/12/37.
2665 *(ex1273)* 10/8/40.
1921 *(ex2722)* 7/8/43.
3175 *(ex2717)* 19/1/46.
2294 *(ex2948)* 13/11/48.
2294 Reno. 27883 6/2/54.
27806 *(ex4765)* 14/4/55.
27497 *(ex4780)* 30/8/57.

SHEDS:
Doncaster.
Ardsley 9/8/35.
Doncaster 22/8/35.
Stratford 28/8/35.
Parkeston 24/6/44.
Stratford 23/6/45.
Parkeston 16/10/49.
New England 28/10/56.
Stratford 14/4/57.

RENUMBERED:
4873 29/11/46.
64873 13/11/48.

CONDEMNED:
18/5/59.
Cut up at Stratford. Boiler retained and sent to Cowlairs.

2943

Darlington.

To traffic 13/6/35.

REPAIRS:
Gor. 13/1-11/2/38.**G.**
Gor. 13/10-7/12/40.**G.**
Cow. 25/6-26/8/43.**G.**
Str. 10/2-3/4/46.**G.**
Gor. 24/6-27/8/49.**G.**
Gor. 27/4-22/7/50.**C/H.**
Dby. 11/6-5/8/52.**H/I.**
Dby. 15/8-2/9/52.**N/C.**
Str. 22/10-7/11/53.**N/C.**
Str. 10/11-24/12/54.**G.**

Str. 14/12/55-28/2/56.**C/L.**
Str. 4/11-7/12/57.**G.**

BOILERS:
2666.
2660 *(ex1273)* 11/2/38.
2684 *(ex2949)* 7/12/40.
C7963 *(ex1450)* 3/4/46.
4975 *(new)* 27/8/49.
4975 Reno.27711 5/8/52.
27708 *(ex4800)* 24/12/54.
25828 *(new)* 7/12/57.

SHEDS:
Doncaster.
Stratford 30/8/35.
Parkeston 24/6/51.
New England 28/10/56.
Stratford 14/4/57.
Lincoln 21/12/58.
Doncaster 1/3/59.

RENUMBERED:
4874 22/12/46.
64874 27/8/49.

CONDEMNED:
17/4/61.
Cut up at Doncaster.

2944

Darlington.

To traffic 19/6/35.

REPAIRS:
Gor. 7-21/5/38.**G.**
Gor. 19/3-2/4/41.**G.**
Str. 3-22/12/43.**G.**
Str. 16/1-1/2/46.**G.**
Cow. 16/5-20/6/47.**G.**
Cow. 23/10-21/11/50.**G.**
Cow. 1-24/4/53.**H/I.**
Cow. 7-16/3/55.**C/L.**
Cow. 27/4-26/5/56.**G.**
Cow. 8-30/8/58.**L/I.**
Inv. 21/3-12/5/61.**G.**

BOILERS:
2667.
2678 *(ex2950)* 21/5/38.
2695 *(ex2945)* 2/4/41.
2282 *(ex2702)* 22/12/43.
8591 *(ex2771)* 1/2/46.
C2026 *(new)* 21/11/50.
C2026 Reno.27576 24/4/53.
27500 *(ex65920)* 26/5/56.
27574 *(ex4897)* 12/5/61.

SHEDS:
Doncaster.
Stratford 13/9/35.
Carlisle 20/3/47.
Gorton 8/11/58.
Woodford 30/7/62.

RENUMBERED:
4875 20/12/46.
64875 19/9/48.

CONDEMNED:
15/10/62.
Cut up at Darlington.

2945

Darlington.

To traffic 21/6/35.

REPAIRS:
Gor. 20/2-8/4/38.**G.**
Gor. 22/4-5/5/38.**N/C.**
Gor. 7/1-8/2/41.**G.**
Cow. 20/4-30/8/43.**G.**
Str. 17/6-22/8/45.**G.**
Str. 19/5-31/7/46.**H.**
Gor. 16/10-31/12/49.**G.**
Gor. 6-7/1/50.**N/C.**
Dby. 15/2-20/3/52.**G.**
Str. 21/9-10/10/53.**N/C.**
Str. 13/4-27/5/55.**G.**
Gor. 20/2-9/3/57.**C/L.**
Gor. 12-13/3/57.**N/C.**
Str. 24/9/59.*Not repaired.*

BOILERS:
2671.
2695 *(ex2987)* 8/4/38.
2145 *(ex2704)* 8/2/41.
E1355 *(ex2772)* 31/7/46.
2116 *(ex2977)* 31/12/49.
27431 *(new)* 20/3/52.
27715 *(ex4782)* 27/5/55.

SHEDS:
Doncaster.
Ardsley 9/8/35.
Doncaster 19/8/35.
Stratford 29/8/35.
Ardsley 24/6/51.
Stratford 22/9/52.
Doncaster 27/11/55.

RENUMBERED:
4876 25/7/46.
64876 31/12/49.

CONDEMNED:
28/9/59.
Cut up at Stratford.

2946

Darlington.

To traffic 28/6/35.

REPAIRS:
Gor. 11-24/2/38.**G.**
Gor. 1-10/6/40.**G.**
Str. 22/6-4/7/42.**G.**
Gor. 28/3-21/4/45.**G.**
Cow. 5/3-16/4/48.**G.**
Cow. 28/1-24/2/50.**G.**
Cow. 7/9-2/10/51.**L/I.**
Cow. 3-23/8/53.**G.**
Cow. 23/11-10/12/55.**H/I.**
Cow. 14-17/12/55.**N/C.**
Cow. 9/10-9/11/57.**G.**
Cow. 20-21/11/57.**N/C.**
Cow. 23/10-28/11/59.**H/I.**

BOILERS:
2674.
2666 *(ex2943)* 24/2/38.
2273 *(ex1266)* 10/6/40.
8581 *(ex2728)* 4/7/42.
2302 *(ex2965)* 21/4/45.
BP141 *(ex4856)* 16/4/48.
BP141 Reno.27527 2/10/51.
27487 *(ex4924)* 23/8/53.
27635 *(new)* 9/11/57.

SHEDS:
Doncaster.
Lincoln 24/7/35.
March 8/11/35.
Stratford 13/6/43.
Carlisle 18/9/47.

RENUMBERED:
4877 12/12/46.
64877 16/4/48.

CONDEMNED:
22/10/62.
Cut up at Cowlairs.

2947

Darlington.

To traffic 3/7/35.

REPAIRS:
Gor. 15/9-16/10/37.**G.**
Gor. 12/9-2/11/40.**G.**
Gor. 18/10/43-8/1/44.**G.**
Str. 9/12/46-26/2/47.**G.**
Gor. 16/6-20/8/49.**G.**
Gor. 6-13/9/49.**N/C.**
Dby. 11/4-25/5/52.**H/I.**
Gor. 6/8-18/9/54.**G.**
Gor. 23-24/9/54.**N/C.**
Gor. 9/3-13/4/57.**G.**

BOILERS:
2675.
2318 *(ex1298)* 16/10/37.
2696 *(ex2948)* 2/11/40.
2121 *(ex2981)* 8/1/44.
2109 *(ex2990)* 26/2/47.
4973 *(new)* 20/8/49.
4973 Reno.27698 25/5/52.
27684 *(ex4748)* 18/9/54.
25839 *(new)* 13/4/57.

SHEDS:
Doncaster.
Sheffield 9/8/35.

RENUMBERED:
4878 21/12/46.
64878 20/8/49.

CONDEMNED:
18/2/61.
Cut up at Doncaster.

2948

Darlington.

To traffic 5/7/35.

REPAIRS:
Gor. 15/11-18/12/37.**G.**
Gor. 29/7-28/9/40.**G.**
Cow. 28/3-4/7/43.**G.**
Str. 24/3-20/7/46.**G.**
Gor. 12/6-10/8/47.**L.**
Gor. 25/7-15/9/48.**G.**
Dby. 21/4-14/6/51.**G.**
Dby. 22/8-9/10/52.**H/I.**
Dby. 12-14/10/52.**N/C.**
Gor. 23/12/54-15/1/55.**C/L.**
Gor. 18-20/1/55.**N/C.**
Gor. 22/9-19/11/55.**G.**
Gor. 23-25/11/55.**N/C.**
Gor. 3/3-15/4/59.**H/I.**
A.W.S. part fitted.

BOILERS:
2672.
2696 *(ex2988)* 18/12/37.
2686 *(ex2951)* 28/9/40.
2294 *(ex2698)* 4/7/43.
8586 *(ex2728)* 15/9/48.
27667 *(ex4956)* 14/6/51.
27798 *(new)* 19/11/55.

SHEDS:
Doncaster.
Sheffield 9/8/35.
Gorton 23/5/44.
Barnsley 24/10/46.
Gorton 27/4/47.
Liverpool 12/6/49.
Gorton 14/8/49.
Sheffield 8/4/51.
Ardsley 3/2/52.

RENUMBERED:
4879 3/11/46.
64879 15/9/48.

CONDEMNED:
12/11/62.
Cut up at Darlington.

2949

Darlington.

To traffic 10/7/35.

REPAIRS:
Gor. 28/10-11/11/37.**G.**
Gor. 2-12/11/40.**G.**

Str. 17/2-5/3/43.**G.**
Gor. 30/7-9/8/45.**G.**
Cow. 6/2-26/3/48.**G.**
Cow. 27/1-22/2/50.**H/I.**
Cow. 14/11-7/12/50.**G.**
Cow. 15-27/6/53.**G.**
Cow. 19/3-19/9/56.**G.**
Cow. 20/2-13/3/59.**H/I.**

BOILERS:
2669.
2684 *(ex2953)* 11/11/37.
2672 *(ex2983)* 12/11/40.
823 *(ex2965)* 5/3/43.
2665 *(ex2777)* 9/8/45.
C2028 *(new)* 7/12/50.
C2028 Reno.27578 27/6/53.
27759 *(ex64836)* 19/9/56.

SHEDS:
Doncaster.
Gorton 29/8/35.
March 8/11/35.
Parkeston 7/2/36.
Stratford 29/9/39.
Ipswich 29/10/41.
Carlisle 13/4/47.
Gorton 20/12/60.

RENUMBERED:
4880 13/10/46.
64880 26/3/48.

CONDEMNED:
15/10/62.
Cut up at Cowlairs.

2950

Darlington.

To traffic 11/7/35.

REPAIRS:
Gor. 26/2-22/4/38.**G.**
Gor. 14/2-29/3/41.**G.**
Str. 20/12/42-30/1/43.**L.**
Gor. 9/1-15/4/44.**G.**
Gor. 26/1-8/2/47.**G.**
Gor. 28/7-3/9/49.**G.**
Dby. 1/1-13/2/52.**L/I.**
Str. 4/1-12/2/55.**G.**
Str. 23/9/59.*Not repaired.*

BOILERS:
2678.
2671 *(ex2945)* 22/4/38.
2312 *(ex1457)* 29/3/41.
C1710 *(ex2731)* 15/4/44.
1916 *(ex1484)* 8/2/47.
C7963 *(ex2943)* 3/9/49.
27808 *(ex4775)* 12/2/55.

SHEDS:
Doncaster.
Ardsley 7/8/35.
Doncaster 19/8/35.
Gorton 4/9/35.
March 31/10/35.
Ipswich 12/2/36.
March 2/9/42.
New England 5/7/43.
Lincoln 1/7/45.
Tuxford 15/11/53.
Lincoln 14/2/54.

RENUMBERED:
4881 22/11/46.
64881 3/9/49.

CONDEMNED:
28/9/59.
Cut up at Stratford.

2951

Darlington.

To traffic 6/8/35.

REPAIRS:
Gor. 7/11-11/12/37.**G.**
Gor. 11/7-17/8/40.**G.**
Str. 13/7-30/10/42.**G.**
Str. 18-22/7/43.**L.**
Gor. 22/3-2/6/45.**G.**
Str. 11/3-30/4/47.**L.**
Str. 8/7-8/11/47.**H.**
Str. 26/9-27/11/48.**G.**
Dby. 1/9-29/10/51.**G.**
Str. 14/2-26/3/54.**G.**
Str. 17/1-2/2/55.**C/L.**
Str. 14/10-21/11/56.**G.**

BOILERS:
2681.
2686 *(ex2982)* 11/12/37.
2188 *(ex1255)* 17/8/40.
8015 *(ex2719)* 30/10/42.
2701 *(ex2713)* 2/6/45.
3209 *(ex2694)* 27/11/48.
27679 *(ex4801)* 29/10/51.
27669 *(ex4796)* 26/3/54.
27876 *(ex4726)* 21/11/56.

SHEDS:
Doncaster.
Colwick 10/9/35.
March 4/10/35.
Stratford 15/6/43.
Norwich 8/12/46.
Ipswich 7/6/53.
Norwich 20/9/53.
Ipswich 18/2/55.
Norwich 13/10/57.
Lincoln 30/11/58.
Colwick 4/1/59.
Retford 1/3/59.

RENUMBERED:
4882 15/12/46.
64882 27/11/48.

CONDEMNED:
11/4/61.
Cut up at Doncaster.

2952

Darlington.

To traffic 7/8/35.

REPAIRS:
Gor. 3/4-21/5/37.**G.**
Gor. 4/3-21/5/38.**G.**
Gor. 13/10-14/12/40.**G.**
Don. 10/8-9/10/43.**G.**
Gor. 30/9-1/12/45.**G.**
Gor. 14/12/47-16/2/48.**G.**
Gor. 15/6-30/7/49.**C/L.**
Dby. 23/8-27/10/50.**G.**
Str. 23/3-6/5/53.**G.**
Gor. 9/7-22/9/56.**G.**

BOILERS:
2683.
2318 *(ex2947)* 14/12/40.
2114 *(ex1255)* 9/10/43.
8772 *(ex2776)* 1/12/45.
2766 *(ex1493)* 16/2/48.
2299 *(ex4960)* 27/10/50.
27776 *(ex4779)* 6/5/53.
27665 *(ex4808)* 22/9/56.

SHEDS:
Doncaster.
March 12/3/38.
Grantham 29/4/42.
New England 21/7/44.
Lincoln 1/7/45.
Peterborough 12/10/52.
Plaistow 7/4/57.
Doncaster 26/5/57.

RENUMBERED:
4883 8/12/46.
E4883 16/2/48.
64883 30/7/49.

CONDEMNED:
11/3/60.
Cut up at Stratford.

2953

Darlington.

To traffic 13/8/35.

REPAIRS:
Gor. 20/9-15/10/37.**G.**
Gor. 23/9-4/11/39.**G.**
Gor. 1-15/8/42.**G.**
Str. 20/7-30/8/45.**G.**
Str. 5-9/8/47.**L.**
Cow. 15/9-15/10/48.**G.**
Cow. 2-25/5/51.**L/I.**
Cow. 10/10-9/11/53.**G.**
Cow. 14/12/55-21/1/56.**L/I.**
Cow. 30/4-25/5/57.**N/C.**
Cow. 11-27/11/58.**G.**

BOILERS:
2684.
8018 *(ex2973)* 15/10/37.
2772 *(ex2996)* 4/11/39.
8586 *(ex1289)* 15/8/42.
8584 *(ex2771)* 30/8/45.
1918 *(ex4701)* 15/10/48.
1918 Reno.27455 25/5/51.
27539 *(ex65914)* 9/11/53.
27742 *(ex64866)* 27/11/58.

SHEDS:
Doncaster.
Stratford 14/9/43.
Norwich 25/9/44.
Carlisle 23/9/47.

RENUMBERED:
4884 16/12/46.
64884 2/10/48.

CONDEMNED:
21/3/62.
Cut up at Cowlairs.

2981

Darlington.

To traffic 21/8/35.

REPAIRS:
Gor. 11/4-12/6/37.**G.**
Gor. 7/11/40-4/1/41.**G.**
Gor. 26/6-16/10/43.**G.**
Gor. 10-18/11/43.**L.**
Str. 3/3-1/6/46.**G.**
Gor. 11/5-12/9/47.**L.**
Gor. 15/10-20/11/48.**L.**
Gor. 8/8-17/9/49.**G.**
Gor. 29-30/9/49.**N/C.**
Dby. 18/8-6/10/52.**G.**
Str. 1/1-12/2/55.**G.**
Gor. 20/8-28/9/57.**G.**
Gor. 7-8/10/57.**N/C.**

BOILERS:
2685.
2121 *(ex2972)* 4/1/41.
2132 *(ex2695)* 16/10/43.
4903 *(ex2698)* 1/6/46.
3210 *(ex4740)* 17/9/49.
27724 *(ex4757)* 6/10/52.
27730 *(ex4761)* 12/2/55.
27823 *(ex4976)* 28/9/57.

WORKS CODES:- Cow - Cowlairs. Dar - Darlington. Dby - Derby. Don - Doncaster. Ghd - Gateshead. Gor - Gorton. Inv - Inverurie. Str - Stratford.
REPAIR CODES:- **C/H** - Casual Heavy. **C/L** - Casual Light. **G** - General. **H**- Heavy. **H/I** - Heavy Intermediate. **L** - Light. **L/I** - Light Intermediate. **N/C** - Non-Classified.

Stocks of the shaded transfers were becoming exhausted during 1947, and with the known demise of the LNER at the end of that year, it made sense not to buy more. 4761 ex Stratford on 14th August 1947 was an early example of the change to 12" yellow painted and unshaded letters and figures. *Photomatic*

SHEDS:
Doncaster.
Bradford 22/2/38.
Ardsley 24/7/40.
Doncaster 30/7/45.

RENUMBERED:
4885 20/12/46.
64885 20/11/48.

CONDEMNED:
17/2/61.
Cut up at Doncaster.

2982

Darlington.

To traffic 30/8/35.

REPAIRS:
Gor. 2-27/11/37.**G.**
Don. 30/9-20/10/38.**L.**
Don. 22-29/7/39.**L.**
Gor. 20/7-17/8/40.**G.**
Gor. 12-20/5/43.**G.**
Gor. 29/9-4/10/45.**L.**
Gor. 24/4-7/5/47.**G.**
Gor. 21/2/48.**C/L.**
Gor. 20/8/49.**C/L.**
Dby. 22/2-12/4/51.**G.**
Cow. 9/2-6/3/54.**H/I.**
Cow. 30/8-13/10/56.**G.**
Gor. 19/4-3/6/60.**G.**

BOILERS:
2686.
2669 *(ex2949)* 27/11/37.
2193 *(ex2717)* 17/8/40.
2669 *(ex2987)* 20/5/43.
2203 *(ex2783)* 7/5/47.
27800 *(new)* 12/4/51.
27565 *(ex4822)* 13/10/56.
27836 *(ex4833 & spare)* 3/6/60.

SHEDS:
Doncaster.
Mexborough 7/12/35.
Doncaster 30/1/37.
Ardsley 4/8/39.
New England 23/2/40.
Grantham 18/1/43.
Retford 13/10/46.
Copley Hill 10/4/49.
Lincoln 4/6/50.
Neville Hill 2/9/51.
Bradford 15/9/57.
Low Moor 12/1/58.
Ardsley 18/11/62.

RENUMBERED:
4886 10/12/46.
64886 7/4/51.

CONDEMNED:
27/11/62.
Cut up at Darlington.

2983

Darlington.

To traffic 4/9/35.

REPAIRS:
Gor. 18/11-25/12/37.**G.**
Gor. 22/8-5/10/40.**G.**
Gor. 5/11/42-30/1/43.**G.**
Gor. 7-13/2/43.**G.**
Str. 26/1-27/4/46.**G.**
Gor. 24/8-7/10/47.**L.**
Don. 25/5-23/7/48.**G.**
Gor. 18/1-19/3/49.**C/L.**
Dby. 22/4-4/7/51.**H/I.**
Str. 11/1-26/2/54.**G.**
Str. 22/6-26/7/54.**C/L.**
Gor. 10/2-16/3/57.**G.**

BOILERS:
2688.
2672 *(ex2948)* 25/12/37.
8019 *(ex2695)* 5/10/40.
2617 *(ex3082)* 27/4/46.
27662 *(ex4828)* 26/2/54.
27803 *(ex4717)* 16/3/57.

SHEDS:
Doncaster.
Mexborough 7/12/35.
Doncaster 21/7/36.
New England 11/4/42.
Grantham 17/3/43.
New England 29/8/43.
Grantham 6/1/46.
New England 17/1/46.
Retford 7/10/46.
Copley Hill 10/4/49.
Lincoln 4/6/50.
Boston 9/11/58.
Colwick 1/3/59.

RENUMBERED:
4887 8/12/46.
64887 23/7/48.

CONDEMNED:
20/1/60.
Cut up at Stratford.

2984

Darlington.

To traffic 10/9/35.

REPAIRS:
Gor. 2-27/3/37.**G.**
Gor. 17/6-15/7/39.**G.**
Str. 19/7-19/9/42.**G.**
Gor. 14/4-9/6/45.**G.**
Cow. 26/1-1/4/48.**G.**
Cow. 15/2-9/3/51.**L/I.**
Cow. 5-28/9/52.**G.**
Cow. 18/2-15/3/55.**H/I.**
Cow. 27/2-23/3/57.**G.**
Cow. 5-29/1/59.**H/I.**

BOILERS:
2690.
2779 *(ex2995)* 15/7/39.
2273 *(ex2946)* 19/9/42.
E1353 *(ex1898)* 9/6/45.
3803 *(new)* 1/4/48.
3803 Reno. 27564 9/3/51.
27560 *(ex64922)* 28/9/52.
27532 *(ex64867)* 23/3/57.

SHEDS:
Doncaster.
Stratford 12/10/35.
Parkeston 3/7/43.
Carlisle 17/3/47.

RENUMBERED:
4888 19/12/46.
64888 1/4/48.

CONDEMNED:
22/10/62.
Cut up at Cowlairs.

2985

Darlington.

To traffic 13/9/35.

REPAIRS:
Gor. 3/10-6/11/37.**G.**
Gor. 7/5-8/6/40.**G.**
Str. 28/3-14/8/43.**G.**
Str. 17/4-22/7/46.**G.**
Str. 13/11-24/12/47.**L.**
Str. 6/1-24/2/48.**L.**
Str. 20/2-9/4/49.**G.**
Dby. 22/11/51-7/1/52.**H/I.**
Str. 27/3-30/4/54.**G.**
Str. 23/9-7/11/56.**G.**
Str. 6/1-21/3/58.**C/H.**

BOILERS:
2691.
2675 *(ex2947)* 6/11/37.
2641 *(ex1290)* 8/6/40.
8003 *(ex2700)* 14/8/43.
2595 *(ex1869)* 22/7/46.
4969 *(new)* 9/4/49.
27885 *(ex4953)* 30/4/54.
27650 *(ex4731)* 7/11/56.

64944 was ex Cowlairs from a general repair on 3rd April 1948 still with L N E R on tender because that works did not begin using BRITISH RAILWAYS until the end of April. It had number on buffer beam, and for that, the usual 4½" shaded transfers had been used whereas 64845, amongst others, had come out with 6" size on the bufferbeam (Cowlairs were no stickler for uniformity). 64944's L N E R is believed to have been retained until it went to works at the end of November 1952. *WBY collection*

SHEDS:
Doncaster.
Stratford 14/10/35.
Ipswich 6/9/44.
Lowestoft 6/10/46.
Norwich 26/3/47.
Lincoln 21/12/58.
Colwick 8/11/59.

RENUMBERED:
4889 1/12/46.
64889 9/4/49.

CONDEMNED:
20/8/60.
Cut up at Doncaster.

2986

Darlington.

To traffic 13/9/35.

REPAIRS:
Gor. 9/10-20/11/37.**G.**
Gor. 7/11/40-4/1/41.**G.**
Gor. 4/6-25/9/43.**G.**
Gor. 16-27/10/43.**N/C.**
Gor. 5/9-24/10/47.**G.**
Gor. 9/1-18/2/50.**G.**
Gor. 22/2-2/3/50.**N/C.**
Dby. 28/10-30/12/52.**G.**
Str. 5/3-27/4/56.**G.**

BOILERS:
2689.
2691 *(ex2985)* 20/11/37.
2660 *(ex2943)* 4/1/41.
2675 *(ex2693)* 25/9/43.
BP145 *(ex2989)* 24/10/47.
2104 *(ex4983)* 18/2/50.
27738 *(ex4902)* 30/12/52.
27786 *(ex4797)* 27/4/56.

SHEDS:
Doncaster.
March 16/10/35.
Sheffield 13/5/38.
Stratford 17/10/54.
Cambridge 25/9/55.
March 12/10/58.
Lincoln 7/12/58.

RENUMBERED:
4890 24/11/46.
64890 18/2/50.

CONDEMNED:
21/3/60.
Cut up at Stratford.

2987

Darlington.

To traffic 18/9/35.

REPAIRS:
Gor. 28/2-19/3/38.**G.**
Gor. 15/8-5/10/40.**G.**
Gor. 6/12/42-13/2/43.**G.**
Gor. 4-20/4/44.**L.**
Gor. 8/7-15/9/45.**G.**
Gor. 30/4-25/6/48.**G.**
Dby. 26/7-7/9/51.**G.**
Str. 29/10-11/12/54.**G.**

BOILERS:
2695.
2688 *(ex2983)* 19/3/38.
2669 *(ex2982)* 5/10/40.
2182 *(ex2964)* 13/2/43.
8025 *(ex1496)* 15/9/45.
4939 *(new)* 25/6/48.
27674 *(ex4747)* 7/9/51.
27658 *(ex4751)* 11/12/54.

SHEDS:
Doncaster.
March 21/10/35.
New England 14/5/38.
Boston 17/5/38.
Colwick 3/8/39.
Grantham 14/7/40.
Colwick 23/10/40.
Doncaster 23/8/46.
Colwick 27/4/52.
Peterborough 12/4/53.
Plaistow 7/4/57.
Ipswich 26/5/57.
March 25/10/59.

RENUMBERED:
4891 29/12/46.
64891 25/6/48.

CONDEMNED:
8/2/60.
Cut up at Stratford.

2988

Darlington.

To traffic 26/9/35.

REPAIRS:
Gor. 2/11-4/12/37.**G.**
Gor. 13/4-4/5/40.**G.**
Str. 30/11-19/12/42.**G.**
Str. 21-28/8/43.**L.**
Gor. 28/4-15/5/45.**G.**
Str. 7-21/12/46.**L.**
Str. 3-17/5/47.**L.**
Gor. 29/1-28/2/48.**G.**
Cow. 17-24/4/48.**L.**
Cow. 14/3-10/4/51.**L/I.**
Cow. 6/7-10/8/53.**G.**
Cow. 17/12/54-8/1/55.**H/I.**
Cow. 11-15/1/55.**N/C.**
Cow. 27/5-6/7/57.**G.**

BOILERS:
2696.
2689 *(ex2986)* 4/12/37.
8018 *(ex2953)* 4/5/40.
2779 *(ex2984)* 19/12/42.
2776 *(ex2975)* 15/5/45.
2720 *(ex1927)* 28/2/48.
2720 Reno.27515 10/4/51.
27509 *(ex64707)* 10/8/53.
27560 *(ex4888)* 6/7/57.

SHEDS:
Doncaster.
March 12/10/35.
Norwich 16/7/43.
Ipswich 7/11/46.
Carlisle 10/6/47.

RENUMBERED:
4892 19/12/46.
E4892 28/2/48.
64892 24/4/48.

CONDEMNED:
12/5/61.
Cut up at Cowlairs.

2989

Darlington.

To traffic 1/10/35.

REPAIRS:
Gor. 31/7-30/9/38.**G.**
Don. 9/5-1/8/41.**G.**
Cow. 29/1-18/3/44.**G.**
Gor. 11/12/45-23/3/46.**L.**
Gor. 14/3-10/10/47.**G.**
Dar. 17/2-16/4/48.**L.**
Dby. 2/11-22/12/50.**H/I.**
Str. 29/4-6/6/53.**G.**
Gor. 26/8-13/10/56.**G.**
Gor. 15-27/10/56.**N/C.**
Str. 21/4/60.*Not repaired.*

BOILERS:
2697.
2699 *(ex2992)* 30/9/38.
BP145 *(ex1535)* 18/3/44.
4926 *(new)* 10/10/47.
27780 *(ex4883)* 6/6/53.
27762 *(ex4969)* 13/10/56.

SHEDS:
Doncaster.
March 11/10/35.
Parkeston 28/12/35.
Stratford 3/12/39.
Ipswich 5/11/41.
Doncaster 17/10/43.
Retford 4/3/51.

RENUMBERED:
4893 20/12/46.
64893 16/4/48.

CONDEMNED:
11/7/60.
Cut up at Stratford.

2990

Darlington.

To traffic 4/10/35.

REPAIRS:
Gor. 15/2-22/4/39.**G.**
Gor. 2/2-16/5/42.**G.**
Gor. 22/10-25/11/44.**G.**
Str. 28/11/46-4/4/47.**G.**
Str. 29/5-3/7/47.**L.**
Gor. 3/2-1/4/50.**G.**
Gor. 5-13/4/50.**N/C.**
Str. 17/5-20/6/53.**G.**
Str. 3/9-8/10/55.**G.**

BOILERS:
2698.
E1352 *(ex1870)* 16/5/42.
2109 *(ex2705)* 25/11/44.
2121 *(ex2947)* 4/4/47.
8593 *(ex2708)* 1/4/50.
27783 *(ex4956)* 20/6/53.
27434 *(ex4784)* 8/10/55.

SHEDS:
Doncaster.
Ipswich 30/10/35.

RENUMBERED:
4894 10/1/47.
64894 1/4/50.

CONDEMNED:
19/10/59.
Cut up at Stratford.

2991

Darlington.

To traffic 9/10/35.

REPAIRS:
Gor. 4-23/7/38.**G.**
Don. 14/6-19/7/41.**G.**
Str. 14/11/42.**H.**
Str. 2/1/43.**L.**
Str. 5-27/5/44.**G.**
Str. 27/1-1/2/45.**L.**
Str. 17/3-14/4/45.**L.**
Str. 16-23/2/46.**L.**
Cow. 9/5-13/6/47.**G.**
Dar. 20/12/47-13/3/48.**H.**
Cow. 21/3-7/4/50.**G.**
Cow. 2/5-2/6/52.**G.**
Cow. 11/6-12/7/54.**H/I.**
Cow. 2-14/8/54.**N/C.**
Cow. 20/4-25/6/57.**G.**
Cow. 11/9-3/10/59.**L/I.**

BOILERS:
2701.
2704 *(ex2993)* 23/7/38.
2663 *(ex2941)* 27/5/44.
3802 *(new)* 13/3/48.
27517 *(ex64897)* 2/6/52.
27514 *(ex64852)* 25/6/57.

SHEDS:
Doncaster.
Parkeston 28/10/35.
Stratford 8/9/40.
Ipswich 28/1/46.
Lowestoft 17/4/46.
Ipswich 29/7/46.
Carlisle 28/3/47.

RENUMBERED:
4895 22/12/46.
64895 19/9/48.

CONDEMNED:
22/10/62.
Cut up at Cowlairs.

2992

Darlington.

To traffic 11/10/35.

REPAIRS:
Gor. 18/7-20/8/38.**G.**
Gor. 23/2-5/4/41.**G.**
Cow. 28/2-19/4/44.**G.**
Gor. 16/7-25/8/45.**L.**
Gor. 5-13/9/45.**L.**
Gor. 2/5-7/9/46.**G.**
Gor. 27/3-9/5/49.**G.**
Gor. 1-9/6/49.**N/C.**
Dby. 4/2-13/3/52.**H/I.**
Dby. 19-27/3/52.**N/C.**
Dby. 10/4-7/5/52.**N/C.**
Str. 9/4-2/5/53.**N/C.**
Str. 17/9-6/10/54.**C/L.**
Gor. 1/7-25/8/55.**G.**

BOILERS:
2699.
2701 *(ex2991)* 20/8/38.
2691 *(ex2986)* 5/4/41.
3169 *(ex3082)* 19/4/44.
3171 *(ex4715)* 9/5/49.
3171 Reno.27700 13/3/52.
27790 *(new)* 25/8/55.

SHEDS:
Doncaster.
Parkeston 4/11/35.
Stratford 25/9/39.
Parkeston 3/12/39.
Stratford 8/9/40.
Ardsley 7/9/43.
Peterborough 28/12/52.
Plaistow 7/4/57.
Parkeston 26/5/57.
Stratford 9/3/58.
Lincoln 7/12/58.

RENUMBERED:
4896 21/12/46.
64896 7/5/49.

CONDEMNED:
27/8/60.
Cut up at Doncaster.

2993

Darlington.

To traffic 17/10/35.

REPAIRS:
Gor. 25/5-18/6/38.**G.**
Gor. 8/3-3/5/41.**G.**
Str. 21/5-17/6/44.**G.**
Cow. 19/6-5/10/46.**G.**
Cow. 14/1-26/3/49.**G.**
Cow. 21/2-19/4/52.**G.**
Cow. 6/1-11/2/56.**G.**
Inv. 15/8-30/9/60.**G.**
Dar. 21/12/61-16/1/62.**C/L.**

BOILERS:
2704.
2667 *(ex2944)* 18/6/38.
2678 *(ex2944)* 3/5/41.
1931 *(ex2773)* 17/6/44.
C1796 *(ex2732)* 5/10/46.
BP130 *(ex4814)* 26/3/49.
27542 *(ex4946)* 19/4/52.
27574 *(ex65927)* 11/2/56.
27566 *(ex64921)* 30/9/60.

SHEDS:
Doncaster.
Parkeston 28/1/36.
Stratford 8/9/40.
Darlington 7/1/45.
Hull Dairycoates 4/1/48.
Borough Gardens 24/12/50.
Blaydon 4/1/53.
Alnmouth 28/3/54.

RENUMBERED:
4897 1/12/46.
64897 26/3/49.

CONDEMNED:
3/12/62.
Cut up at Cowlairs.

2994

Darlington.

To traffic 22/10/35.

REPAIRS:
Don. 9/11/38-19/1/39.**G.**
Don. 24-31/1/39.**N/C.**
Don. 2-13/2/39.**N/C.**
Don. 30/6-12/9/41.**G.**
Gor. 2/1-11/3/44.**G.**
Gor. 20/10-18/11/44.**L.**
Gor. 20/5-31/8/46.**G.**
Gor. 5/10-5/12/47.**L.**
Gor. 7/4-14/5/49.**G.**
Dby. 5/8-29/9/52.**L/I.**
Gor. 1/1-25/2/56.**G.**
Gor. 28/2-6/3/56.**N/C.**
Gor. 9/10-23/11/56.**C/H.**
Gor. 3/1-23/2/57.**C/H.**

BOILERS:
2706.
3203 *(new)* 12/9/41.
2696 *(ex2947)* 11/3/44.
4970 *(new)* 14/5/49.
4970 Reno.27722 29/9/52.
27736 *(ex4754)* 25/2/56.

SHEDS:
Doncaster.
Ipswich 13/3/36.
Doncaster 15/9/43.
Retford 5/10/47.

RENUMBERED:
4898 5/1/47.
64898 14/5/49.

CONDEMNED:
19/2/60.
Cut up at Stratford.

2995

Darlington.

To traffic 6/8/36.

REPAIRS:
Gor. 27/5-1/7/39.**G.**
Str. 27/4-6/6/42.**G.**
Str. 8-20/6/42.**L.**
Str. 10/9-20/10/45.**G.**
Cow. 9/3-1/4/48.**G.**
Cow. 30/3-22/4/50.**H/I.**
Cow. 12/10-5/11/51.**H/I.**
Cow. 4-24/5/53.**G.**
Cow. 22/6-10/7/54.**C/L.**
Cow. 14/9-7/10/54.**C/L.**
Cow. 3/4-12/5/56.**H/I.**
Cow. 28-30/5/56.**N/C.**
Cow. 8-20/4/57.**C/L.**
Cow. 21/3-3/4/58.**N/C.**
Cow. 15/1-5/2/59.**G.**

BOILERS:
2779.
2104 *(ex2726)* 1/7/39.
8024 *(ex2973)* 20/10/45.
RS121 *(ex4846)* 1/4/48.
RS121 Reno.27479 5/11/51.
27545 *(ex64865)* 24/5/53.
27416 *(ex62735)* 5/2/59.

SHEDS:
Doncaster.
Stratford 21/1/37.
Carlisle 15/4/47.

RENUMBERED:
4899 19/12/46.
64899 1/4/48.

CONDEMNED:
22/10/62.
Cut up at Cowlairs.

2996

Darlington.

To traffic 5/8/36.

REPAIRS:
Gor. 21/7-13/9/39.**G.**
Don. 24/8-8/11/41.**G.**
Str. 3/1-12/2/44.**G.**
Gor. 16/7-19/8/44.**L.**
Gor. 28/7-14/12/46.**G.**
Str. 7-20/1/48.**L.**
Gor. 24/4-24/6/48.**G.**
Gor. 13/12/49-11/2/50.**G.**
Gor. 16-17/2/50.**N/C.**
Dby. 7/2-3/4/51.**H/I.**
Dby. 6-13/4/51.**N/C.**
Str. 4/6-8/8/53.**G.**
Str. 16/9-26/10/56.**G.**
Str. 15/10-6/12/57.**C/L.**

BOILERS:
2772.
2690 *(ex2984)* 13/9/39.
2706 *(ex2994)* 8/11/41.
2216 *(ex2777)* 12/2/44.
2094 *(ex2774)* 14/12/46.
3201 *(ex3097)* 24/6/48.
4985 *(new)* 11/2/50.
27871 *(ex4909)* 8/8/53.
27822 *(ex4953)* 26/10/56.

SHEDS:
Doncaster.
Ipswich 4/9/36.
Yarmouth 15/1/39.
Norwich 14/5/39.
Ipswich 2/7/39.
Norwich 24/6/51.
Melton Constable 7/11/54.
Norwich 6/3/55.

RENUMBERED:
4900 7/12/46.
64900 19/6/48.

CONDEMNED:
27/7/59.
Cut up at Stratford. Boiler retained and sent to Cowlairs.

2997

Darlington.

To traffic 12/8/36.

REPAIRS:
Don. 5/11-21/12/38.**G.**
Gor. 24/2-23/4/41.**G.**
Gor. 1/4-2/5/42.**L.**
Gor. 2/4-27/5/44.**G.**
Gor. 23/5-12/10/46.**G.**
Gor. 10/10/47-23/1/48.**G.**
Gor. 9-18/1/50.**G.**
Gor. 14-30/6/51.**C/L.**
Str. 7/6-8/8/53.**G.**
Gor. 30/8-20/10/56.**G.**
Str. 29-31/7/59.**N/C.**

BOILERS:
2770.
2287 *(ex1298)* 23/4/41.
2284 *(ex1298)* 27/5/44.
4918 *(ex1287)* 12/10/46.
2681 *(ex2966)* 23/1/48.
E1351 *(ex4743)* 18/1/50.
27789 *(ex4785)* 8/8/53.
27872 *(ex4737)* 20/10/56.

SHEDS:
Doncaster.
Gorton 25/9/36.
Trafford Park 30/4/41.
Northwich 1/4/51.
Peterborough 12/10/52.
Plaistow 7/4/57.
Peterborough 26/5/57.
March 31/1/60.

RENUMBERED:
4901 12/10/46.
E4901 23/1/48.
64901 29/1/49.

CONDEMNED:
13/10/61.
Cut up at Doncaster.

2998

Darlington.

To traffic 14/8/36.

REPAIRS:
Don. 6/11-10/12/38.**G.**
Don. 5/6-27/8/41.**G.**
Don. 18/4-17/6/44.**G.**
Gor. 30/7-6/10/45.**L.**
Gor. 10/3-18/4/46.**L.**
Gor. 26/9/46-8/3/47.**G.**
Gor. 20/4-18/6/49.**G.**
Dby. 30/5-8/7/52.**G.**
Gor. 27/7-17/9/55.**G.**
Gor. 27/9-13/10/55.**N/C.**

BOILERS:
2771.
2287 *(ex2997)* 17/6/44.
2660 *(ex2974)* 8/3/47.
3169 *(ex2992)* 18/6/49.
27703 *(ex4839)* 8/7/52.
27792 *(new)* 17/9/55.

SHEDS:
Doncaster.
Gorton 11/9/36.
Ardsley 30/6/39.
Doncaster 30/7/45.
Peterborough 5/10/52.
Barnsley 25/11/56.
Mexborough 3/1/60.

RENUMBERED:
4902 16/12/46.
64902 18/6/49.

CONDEMNED:
11/3/60.
Cut up at Stratford.

2999

Darlington.

To traffic 19/8/36.

REPAIRS:
Gor. 1/12/38-14/1/39.**G.**
Gor. 1/1-7/2/42.**G.**
Gor. 23/11/42-30/1/43.**L.**
Gor. 19/6-5/8/44.**G.**
Gor. 18-22/8/44.**N/C.**
Gor. 10/12/45-12/1/46.**L.**
Gor. 8/6-30/9/47.**G.**
Gor. 22-31/10/47.**N/C.**
Dby. 1/6-1/9/50.**G.**
Dby. 11-13/9/50.**N/C.**
Gor. 24/4-23/5/53.**G.**
Gor. 8-17/6/53.**N/C.**
Gor. 1-18/7/53.**N/C.**
Gor. 30/7-17/8/53.**N/C.**
Gor. 1-19/9/53.**N/C.**

WORKS CODES:- Cow - Cowlairs. Dar - Darlington. Dby - Derby. Don - Doncaster. Ghd - Gateshead. Gor - Gorton. Inv - Inverurie. Str - Stratford.
REPAIR CODES:- **C/H** - Casual Heavy. **C/L** - Casual Light. **G** - General. **H**- Heavy. **H/I** - Heavy Intermediate. **L** - Light. **L/I** - Light Intermediate. **N/C** - Non-Classified.

Gor. 9-30/10/53.**N/C.**
Gor. 16/4-9/6/56.**G.**
Gor. 28/7-30/9/59.**H/I.**
Gor. 21/3-8/4/61.**C/L.**
Gor. 27/3/62.*Not repaired.*

BOILERS:
2776.
2697 *(ex2989)* 14/1/39.
8006 *(ex1282)* 7/2/42.
2312 *(ex2950)* 5/8/44.
4906 *(ex1974)* 30/9/47.
2132 *(ex1287)* 1/9/50.
27761 *(ex4824)* 23/5/53.
25803 *(ex4747)* 9/6/56.

SHEDS:
Doncaster.
Sheffield 18/9/36.
Barnsley 20/10/46.
Gorton 27/4/47.
Sheffield 17/10/47.
Ardsley 23/12/51.
Bradford 16/3/52.
Low Moor 12/1/58.

RENUMBERED:
4903 24/11/46.
64903 1/9/50.

CONDEMNED:
13/4/62.
Cut up at Gorton.

3000

Darlington.

To traffic 21/8/36.

REPAIRS:
Gor. 16/12/38-14/1/39.**G.**
Don. 4/10-8/11/41.**G.**
Gor. 20/6-8/7/44.**G.**
Gor. 30/4-9/5/46.**G.**
Gor. 1-9/10/47.**G.**
Gor. 23/5-12/6/48.**H.**
Gor. 5-29/4/50.**G.**
Gor. 13/11-15/12/53.**G.**
Cow. 24/4-25/5/57.**H/I.**
Cow. 11/12/58-8/1/59.**G.**
Cow. 8/3-2/4/60.**C/L.**
Cow. 19/9-21/10/60.**C/H.**

BOILERS:
2769.
2110 *(ex2967)* 14/1/39.
RS120 *(ex2770)* 8/7/44.
4917 *(ex1980)* 9/10/47.
3215 *(ex2774)* 29/4/50.
25805 *(ex4762)* 15/12/53.
27484 *(ex64868)* 8/1/59.
27512 *(ex4869)* 21/10/60.

SHEDS:
Doncaster.
Sheffield 14/9/36.
Lincoln 1/7/45.
Darlington 2/9/51.
Hull Dairycoates 6/7/52.
Heaton 7/12/52.
Hull Dairycoates 13/6/54.
Selby 10/10/54.
York 13/9/59.
Hull Dairycoates 22/11/59.
Scarborough 11/9/60.
Hull Dairycoates 9/10/60.

RENUMBERED:
4904 18/5/46.
64904 12/6/48.

CONDEMNED:
22/10/61.
Cut up at Cowlairs.

1803

Beyer Peacock 6802.

To traffic 2/9/36.

REPAIRS:
Gor. 30/10-4/11/37.**L.**
Don. 28/8-19/10/38.**G.**
Gor. 16/8-21/10/39.**H.**
Str. 26/4-23/7/42.**G.**
Str. 20/1-5/2/43.**L.**
Str. 8/11-16/12/44.**L.**
Gor. 6/5-20/7/45.**G.**
Gor. 19/4-18/6/48.**G.**
Dby. 3/1-21/2/51.**H/I.**
Dby. 28/2-10/3/51.**N/C.**
Str. 19/6-22/8/53.**G.**
Str. 21/8-5/10/56.**G.**
Str. 23/9/59.*Not repaired.*

BOILERS:
E1350.
BP140 *(ex1463)* 21/10/39.
8774 *(ex1269)* 23/7/42.
8588 *(ex1286)* 20/7/45.
4938 *(new)* 18/6/48.
27874 *(ex4900)* 22/8/53.
27657 *(ex4788)* 5/10/56.

SHEDS:
Gorton.
March 2/10/36.
Ipswich 14/7/41.

RENUMBERED:
4905 5/9/46.
64905 18/6/48.

CONDEMNED:
28/9/59.
Cut up at Stratford.

1813

Beyer Peacock 6803.

To traffic 4/9/36.

REPAIRS:
Gor. 10-18/11/37.**L.**
Gor. 19/11/38-21/1/39.**G.**
Gor. 27/10-28/12/40.**G.**
Gor. 20/10-18/12/43.**G.**
Gor. 23/3-8/8/47.**G.**
Gor. 17/1-12/3/49.**C/L.**
Dby. 19/6-21/9/50.**H/I.**
Dby. 19/3-9/5/52.**G.**
Str. 5/10-14/11/53.**C/L.**
Str. 3/4-21/5/55.**G.**
Gor. 8/3-8/4/58.**G.**
Gor. 11-16/4/58.**N/C.**

BOILERS:
E1351.
E1356 *(ex1857)* 28/12/40.
3210 *(new)* 18/12/43.
4919 *(ex1943)* 8/8/47.
27696 *(ex4882)* 9/5/52.
27721 *(ex4973)* 21/5/55.
27831 *(ex4825)* 8/4/58.

SHEDS:
Gorton.
March 30/9/36.
Grantham 2/5/42.
Retford 28/9/46.

RENUMBERED:
4906 1/9/46.
64906 12/3/49.

CONDEMNED:
12/4/61.
Cut up at Doncaster.

1824

Beyer Peacock 6804.

To traffic 23/9/36.

REPAIRS:
Gor. 28/10-2/11/37.**L.**
Gor. 26/11/38-4/2/39.**G.**
Gor. 18/2-1/3/39.**N/C.**
Gor. 16/1-28/2/42.**G.**
Gor. 1/10-18/11/44.**G.**
Str. 15/8-29/10/46.**G.**
Dby. 26/1-8/3/51.**G.**
Gor. 30/7-5/9/53.**G.**
Gor. 8-22/9/53.**N/C.**
Gor. 4-19/10/53.**N/C.**
Gor. 22/3-5/5/56.**G.**
Gor. 11-12/5/56.**N/C.**
Gor. 27/1-3/3/59.**H/I.**
Gor. 9-18/3/59.**N/C.**

BOILERS:
E1352.
2776 *(ex2999)* 4/2/39.
2316 *(ex2785)* 28/2/42.
8589 *(ex1274)* 18/11/44.
27659 *(new)* 8/3/51.
27654 *(ex4832)* 5/9/53.
27757 *(ex4955)* 5/5/56.

SHEDS:
Gorton.
Stratford 20/10/36.
Ardsley 18/9/49.
Bradford 16/3/52.
Low Moor 12/1/58.

RENUMBERED:
4907 19/8/46.
64907 8/3/51.

CONDEMNED:
26/11/62.
Cut up at Crewe.

1828

Beyer Peacock 6805.

To traffic 23/9/36.

REPAIRS:
Gor. 23/8-3/9/37.**L.**
Don. 18/9-22/10/38.**G.**
Gor. 11/7-17/8/40.**G.**
Gor. 12/12/42-13/2/43.**G.**
Gor. 5-17/3/43.**N/C.**
Gor. 16/4-21/7/45.**G.**
Gor. 9-18/8/45.**N/C.**
Gor. 14/4-10/8/46.**G.**
Gor. 10/6-7/8/48.**G.**
Dby. 3/8-15/9/51.**H/I.**
Str. 26/5-26/6/54.**G.**
Gor. 10/2-23/3/57.**G.**

BOILERS:
E1353.
4908 *(ex1922)* 17/8/40.
3168 *(ex3081)* 13/2/43.
E1350 *(ex1290)* 21/7/45.
4940 *(new)* 7/8/48.
27888 *(ex4889)* 26/6/54.
25838 *(new)* 23/3/57.

SHEDS:
Gorton.
Colwick 23/10/36.
Doncaster 23/8/46.
Retford 5/10/47.

RENUMBERED:
4908 20/3/46.
64908 7/8/48.

CONDEMNED:
22/3/61.
Cut up at Doncaster.

1854

Beyer Peacock 6806.

To traffic 25/9/36.

REPAIRS:
Gor. 15-16/9/37.**L.**
Don. 21/9-5/11/38.**G.**
Gor. 29/1-22/3/41.**G.**

Ex Cowlairs on 25th January 1947 the tender of 64851 had been fortunate to get 12" shaded transfers for its L N E R, and they were retained when the B.R. numbering and smokebox number plate were applied at the June 1949 repair. Indeed they also survived the heavy repair of August 1951, so would be seen to June 1954! *W.A.Brown*

When they did really consider it necessary, Cowlairs could do a decent painting job as here on 64861 which was ex works on 1st May 1948 from general repair. They were then still using 12" on cab, but 8 ½ " lettering on tender. *A.G.Ellis*

Gorton's first nationalisation style did include the E prefix to 12" figures but tender lettering was in only 6" as shown by E4892 ex works on 28th February 1948. Stratford also used the same sizes on the four J39s to which it gave E prefix. *L&GRP*

The last one on to which Gorton put the prefix was E4752 ex works on 14th March 1948. The same figure sizes were used but the tender lettering had been increased to 9". *H.C.Casserley*

64745 must be regarded as a 'freak' from the painting it got in June 1949. Correct Gill Sans 6 was used on cab, and on the smokebox number plate, but those on the cab were only 8½" and did not match the standard 10" used on the tender. Although 64745 got a heavy repair at Derby in October-December 1950, it did *not* include any painting correction because this photograph is dated September 1951. *Photomatic*

The tender lettering was discarded in August 1949 in favour of a transfer-applied emblem of a lion over a wheel. Supplies must have been late arriving at Gorton because 64811 ex works on 12th November had not been so changed, the matching 10" letters and figures still appearing, but including the correct 6. *L.W.Perkins*

When Derby repaired 159 members of the class from 1st May 1950 until the end of December 1952, Gorton clearly guided them as to painting. 64891 is shown ex Derby on 7th September 1951 with correct 6 on cab but in 8½" against the 10" then standard. The smokebox number plate had been put on at Gorton's June 1949 general repair, and so has a 6 with a curled tail. With one known exception Derby did however otherwise use the large size emblem. *WBY collection*

64984 was the exception on which Derby applied only the 15½" size emblem, when ex works on 10th August 1951. The smokebox number plate with curled 6 and 9 had been fitted by Gorton at the December 1948 general repair. *WBY collection*

1854 cont.
Cow. 14/3-11/7/43.**G.**
Gor. 12/6-25/8/45.**H.**
Gor. 18/2-1/4/47.**G.**
Gor. 10/8-22/10/48.**G.**
Dby. 28/2-3/4/51.**L/I.**
Str. 26/5-25/7/53.**G.**
Gor. 9/10/56-26/1/57.**G.**
Gor. 31/1-16/2/57.**N/C.**

BOILERS:
E1354.
2945 *(ex1997)* 22/3/41.
3168 *(ex1828)* 25/8/45.
4937 *(new)* 22/10/48.
27787 *(ex4793)* 25/7/53.
25806 *(ex4796)* 26/1/57.

SHEDS:
Gorton.
Colwick 14/11/36.
Ardsley 31/3/46.
Sheffield 28/7/46.
Doncaster 22/9/46.

RENUMBERED:
4909 18/8/46.
64909 22/10/48.

CONDEMNED:
5/4/61.
Cut up at Doncaster.

1856

Beyer Peacock 6807.

To traffic 30/9/36.

REPAIRS:
Gor. 1-22/9/38.**G.**
Gor. 31/8-14/9/40.**G.**
Gor. 17-25/2/43.**G.**
Gor. 18-26/10/44.**G.**
Gor. 30/6-23/7/47.**G.**
Dby. 30/11/50-8/2/51.**G.**
Cow. 21/5-24/6/54.**H/I.**
Cow. 26/7-22/9/56.**G.**
Cow. 28/4-23/5/59.**G.**
Dar. 30/12/59-29/1/60.**C/L.**

BOILERS:
E1355.
4915 *(ex1971)* 14/9/40.
4908 *(ex1828)* 25/2/43.
3197 *(ex3098)* 26/10/44.
2301 *(ex1942)* 23/7/47.
27652 *(new)* 8/2/51.
27550 *(ex64786)* 22/9/56.
25804 *(ex64835)* 23/5/59.

SHEDS:
Gorton.
Colwick 24/10/36.
Doncaster 23/8/46.
Hull Dairycoates 2/9/51.
Middlesbrough 18/11/51.
West Hartlepool 14/9/52.
Northallerton 19/9/54.
West Auckland 6/3/55.
Sunderland 25/9/55.
Hull Dairycoates 10/6/56.
Neville Hill 11/9/60.
Heaton 15/1/61.
Alnmouth 19/8/62.

RENUMBERED:
4910 18/8/46.
64910 8/2/51.

CONDEMNED:
23/11/62.
Cut up at Cowlairs.

1857

Beyer Peacock 6808.

To traffic 2/10/36.

REPAIRS:
Gor. 15/12/36.*Weigh.*
Don. 20/12/36-2/1/37.**N/C.**
For weighing.
Gor. 16-20/10/37.**L.**
Gor. 4/12/37-29/1/38.**G.**
Don. 8/11/38-5/1/39.**G.**
Gor. 16/10-14/12/40.**G.**
Cow. 25/6-16/9/43.**H.**
Gor. 29/8-8/12/45.**G.**
Gor. 8/6-30/7/48.**G.**
Gor. 22/8-18/9/48.**L.**
Dby. 12/1-10/3/51.**H/I.**
Gor. 10/8-19/9/53.**G.**
Gor. 22-29/9/53.**N/C.**
Gor. 2/4-4/5/57.**G.**
Gor. 28/6-13/7/57.**N/C.**
Gor. 9/8-21/9/57.**C/L.**

BOILERS:
E1356.
4916 *(ex1974)* 14/12/40.
2720 *(ex1532)* 16/9/43.
2290 *(ex2700)* 8/12/45.
2769 *(ex2709)* 30/7/48.
25801 *(ex 4714 & spare)* 19/9/53.
25840 *(new)* 4/5/57.

SHEDS:
Gorton.
Colwick 12/11/36.
Ardsley 31/3/46.
Copley Hill 9/5/54.
Ardsley 9/3/58.
Copley Hill 14/9/58.
Ardsley 6/11/60.

RENUMBERED:
4911 12/8/46.
64911 30/7/48.

CONDEMNED:
12/11/62.
Cut up at Darlington.

1869

Beyer Peacock 6809.

To traffic 6/10/36.

REPAIRS:
Gor. 7-26/7/39.**G.**
Cow. 1/6-5/8/43.**G.**
Str. 22-24/10/45.**C/L.**
Str. 12/8-5/9/46.**H.**
Cow. 5/7-13/8/48.**G.**
Cow. 21/6-11/8/50.**G.**
Cow. 7-26/10/52.**H/I.**
Cow. 19/10-24/11/53.**C/H.**
Cow. 14/2-11/3/55.**G.**
Cow. 12/12/56-19/1/57.**H/I.**
Cow. 9/5-7/6/58.**G.**
Cow. 29-30/11/59.**N/C.**

BOILERS:
E1357.
BP139 *(ex1547)* 26/7/39.
2595 *(ex2736)* 5/8/43.
2691 *(ex3094)* 5/9/46.
C2023 *(new)* 11/8/50.
27486 *(ex64920)* 11/3/55.
27473 *(ex4821)* 7/6/58.

SHEDS:
Gorton.
Stratford 14/11/36.
Ipswich 22/10/41.
Lowestoft 6/10/46.
Carlisle 24/3/47.

RENUMBERED:
4912 17/3/46.
64912 13/8/48.

CONDEMNED:
5/12/59.
Cut up at Cowlairs.

1870

Beyer Peacock 6810.

To traffic 10/10/36.

REPAIRS:
Gor. 10-19/10/37.**L.**
Gor. 16/4-27/5/39.**G.**
Str. 14/11/41-16/1/42.**G.**
Gor. 24/9-11/11/44.**G.**
Str. 18/5-1/9/47.**G.**
Gor. 22/11/49-28/1/50.**G.**
Gor. 7-9/2/50.**N/C.**
Str. 22/2-18/4/53.**G.**
Str. 11/8-17/9/55.**G.**
Str. 14/6-23/8/57.**C/L.**

BOILERS:
E1358.
E1352 *(ex1824)* 27/5/39.
2671 *(ex2950)* 16/1/42.
2310 *(ex2729)* 11/11/44.
8585 *(ex4758)* 28/1/50.
27746 *(ex4876)* 18/4/53.
27740 *(ex4722)* 17/9/55.

SHEDS:
Gorton.
Stratford 12/11/36.
Norwich 11/12/46.
Melton Constable 22/4/56.
Norwich 7/10/56.
Melton Constable 6/1/57.
Norwich 3/2/57.

RENUMBERED:
4913 16/3/46.
64913 28/1/50.

CONDEMNED:
21/10/59.
Cut up at Stratford.

1532

Beyer Peacock 6811.

To traffic 14/10/36.

REPAIRS:
Gor. 13-15/9/37.**L.**
Dar. 2/8-5/9/38.**G.**
Dar. 27/11/39-16/1/40.**L.**
Dar. 2/12/40-18/1/41.**G.**
Dar. 7/5/41.**N/C.**
Dar. 14/5-19/6/43.**G.**
Cow. 17/8-9/9/44.**G.**
Cow. 27/7-24/8/46.**G.**
Cow. 18/6-17/7/48.**G.**
Cow. 16/1-10/2/51.**G.**
Cow. 11-24/2/51.**N/C.**
Cow. 28/8-25/9/53.**H/I.**
Cow. 31/1-31/3/56.**G.**
Cow. 29/10-15/11/58.**G.**

BOILERS:
BP130.
2720 *(ex1506)* 18/1/41.
2129 *(ex1464)* 19/6/43.
2723 *(ex1464)* 17/7/48.
27562 *(ex4941)* 10/2/51.
27661 *(ex4725)* 31/3/56.
27535 *(ex65907)* 15/11/58.

SHEDS:
Gorton.
Newport 8/11/36.
Middlesbrough 6/2/37.
Darlington 28/3/43.
Starbeck 14/7/43.
Darlington 13/4/47.
Hull Dairycoates 28/12/47.

RENUMBERED:
4914 16/6/46.
64914 17/7/48.

CONDEMNED:
21/7/61.
Cut up at Cowlairs.

1533

Beyer Peacock 6812.

To traffic 17/10/36.

REPAIRS:
Gor. 22-23/9/37.**L.**
Don. 31/8-29/9/38.**G.**
Dar. 15/4-29/5/41.**G.**
Cow. 8/1-19/2/44.**G.**
Cow. 11/1-12/4/47.**G.**
Dar. 24/6-16/7/48.**L.**
Cow. 8/6-9/7/49.**G.**
Cow. 1-6/8/49.**N/C.**
Cow. 8-31/1/53.**H/I.**
Cow. 4/8-5/9/53.**C/L.**
Cow. 14/1-11/2/55.**G.**
Ghd. 29/11-7/12/55.**C/L.**
Dar. 9/4-7/5/57.**C/L.**
Cow. 29/10-15/11/58.**L/I.**

BOILERS:
BP131.
BP133 *(ex1454)* 29/5/41.
BP130 *(ex1451)* 19/2/44.
3194 *(ex1467)* 12/4/47.
2685 *(ex1558)* 9/7/49.
2685 Reno.27503 31/1/53.
27526 *(ex4853)* 11/2/55.

SHEDS:
Gorton.
Neville Hill 12/11/36.
Newport 19/11/36.
Middlesbrough 6/2/37.
Darlington 28/3/43.
Blaydon 26/6/43.
Heaton 7/11/48.

RENUMBERED:
4915 3/4/46.
64915 16/7/48.

CONDEMNED:
29/3/62.
Cut up at Darlington.

1534

Beyer Peacock 6813.

To traffic 21/10/36.

REPAIRS:
Gor. 13-14/10/37.**L.**
Don. 26/8-28/9/38.**G.**
Dar. 11/10-6/11/40.**G.**
Dar. 17/3-1/5/42.**L.**
Dar. 11/2-13/3/43.**G.**
Cow. 29/9-27/10/45.**G.**
Ghd. 11/2-1/3/47.**L.**
Cow. 9/7-6/9/47.**G.**
Cow. 1/11-9/12/50.**G.**
Cow. 11-22/12/50.**N/C.**
Cow. 24/12/53-16/1/54.**L/I.**
Cow. 7/9-13/10/56.**G.**

BOILERS:
BP132.
2711 *(ex1464)* 6/11/40.
2842 *(ex1560)* 13/3/43.
2141 *(ex1481)* 27/10/45.
C2027 *(new)* 9/12/50.
C2027 Reno.27577 16/1/54.
27576 *(ex4875)* 13/10/56.

SHEDS:
Gorton.
Newport 11/11/36.
Hull Dairycoates 4/7/38.
Newport 12/10/38.
Selby 12/6/39.
York 21/10/39.
Selby 29/2/40.
Darlington 28/3/43.
Starbeck 8/7/43.
Darlington 13/4/47.
West Hartlepool 12/12/48.
Heaton 19/9/54.
Alnmouth 26/6/55.

RENUMBERED:
4916 11/8/46.
64916 27/11/48.

CONDEMNED:
25/8/61.
Cut up at Inverurie.

1536

Beyer Peacock 6814.

To traffic 23/10/36.

REPAIRS:
Gor. 10-12/11/37.**L.**
Dar. 29/10-9/12/38.**G.**
Dar. 23/7-27/8/40.**G.**
Dar. 23/1-20/2/43.**G.**
Ghd. 7-28/12/44.**L.**
Cow. 27/7-31/8/46.**G.**
Cow. 19/10-27/12/47.**G.**
Cow. 18/4-13/5/50.**L/I.**
Cow. 15/5-2/6/51.**C/H.**
Cow. 14/1-18/2/54.**G.**
Cow. 22-26/2/54.**N/C.**
Cow. 4-8/3/54.**N/C.**
Cow. 17/1-8/2/58.**H/I.**
Inv. 8/3-19/4/61.**G.**

BOILERS:
BP133.
2950 *(new)* 9/12/38.
BP144 *(ex1580)* 20/2/43.
3196 *(ex3096)* 31/8/46.
2573 *(ex1477)* 27/12/47.
27506 *(ex4912)* 2/6/51.
27583 *(ex4733)* 18/2/54.
27573 *(ex65908)* 19/4/61.

SHEDS:
Gorton.
Neville Hill 18/11/36.
Newport 19/11/36.
Darlington 28/3/43.
Blaydon 27/7/43.
Tweedmouth 23/10/49.
Alnmouth 9/9/62.

RENUMBERED:
4917 17/3/46.
64917 11/5/50.

CONDEMNED:
3/12/62.
Cut up at Darlington.

1539

Beyer Peacock 6815.

To traffic 28/10/36.

REPAIRS:
Gor. 25-27/10/37.**L.**
Dar. 20/1-25/2/39.**G.**
Dar. 14/11-12/12/40.**G.**
Cow. 28/8-18/9/43.**G.**
Gor. 31/3-7/6/46.**G.**
Gor. 12/9-5/11/49.**G.**
Gor. 10-12/11/49.**N/C.**
Bow 5-14/3/52.**C/L.**
Gor. 20/6-15/8/53.**G.**
Cow. 18-22/8/53.**N/C.**
Gor. 28/7-25/8/56.**G.**
Gor. 25/10-22/12/60.**G.**

BOILERS:
BP134.
2716 *(ex1486)* 12/12/40.
8592 *(ex2701)* 18/9/43.
4913 *(ex3084)* 7/6/46.
4978 *(new)* 5/11/49.
27766 *(ex4744)* 15/8/53.
27659 *(ex4760)* 25/8/56.
27796 *(ex4824)* 22/12/60.

SHEDS:
Gorton.
Newport 24/11/36.
Darlington 28/3/43.
Gorton 22/6/44.
Cricklewood 14/12/49.
Ardsley 16/3/52.

RENUMBERED:
4918 7/6/46.
64918 5/11/49.

CONDEMNED:
30/11/62.
Cut up at Darlington.

1540

Beyer Peacock 6816.

To traffic 31/10/36.

REPAIRS:
Gor. 15-16/9/37.**L.**
Dar. 22/3-9/5/39.**G.**
Dar. 5/6-10/7/40.**L.**
Dar. 3/11-3/12/41.**G.**
Cow. 1-22/7/44.**G.**
Cow. 24/5-6/9/47.**G.**
Cow. 14/1-11/2/50.**H/I.**
Cow. 29/10-21/11/52.**G.**
Dar. 8-24/9/54.**C/L.**
Ghd. 14/3-1/4/55.**C/L.**
Cow. 24/5-23/6/56.**H/I.**
Cow. 5/6-8/8/59.**G.**
Dar. 11/2-26/3/60.**C/L.**

BOILERS:
BP135.
2939 *(ex1551)* 3/12/41.
2686 *(ex3088)* 22/7/44.
27559 *(ex4923)* 21/11/52.
27564 *(ex64850)* 8/8/59.

SHEDS:
Gorton.
Starbeck 14/11/36.
West Hartlepool 19/11/36.
Darlington 28/3/43.
Starbeck 29/8/48.
Scarborough 25/9/49.
Neville Hill 1/10/50.
Borough Gardens 1/7/51.
Sunderland 1/2/53.
Low Moor 25/1/59.

RENUMBERED:
4919 5/5/46.
64919 11/2/50.

CONDEMNED:
3/12/62.
Cut up at Darlington.

1543

Beyer Peacock 6817.

To traffic 4/11/36.

REPAIRS:
Gor. 22-23/11/37.**L.**
Gor. 28/2-19/3/38.**G.**
Cracked cyl. casting.
Dar. 28/3-24/4/40.**G.**
Dar. 1/5-12/6/42.**G.**
Cow. 15/5-10/6/44.**G.**
Dar. 2/8-13/9/45.**L.**
Cow. 18/1-8/2/47.**G.**
Cow. 16/3-14/5/49.**G.**
Cow. 28/3-26/4/52.**H/I.**
Cow. 7-16/7/53.**C/L.**
Cow. 23/9-1/11/54.**G.**
Cow. 30/9-2/11/57.**L/I.**
Cow. 30/5-25/6/60.**N/C.**

BOILERS:
BP136.
2938 *(ex1548)* 24/4/40.
2154 *(ex234)* 12/6/42.
C1799 *(ex2734)* 10/6/44.
RS125 *(ex4851)* 14/5/49.
RS125 Reno.27486 26/4/52.

27494 *(ex64790)* 1/11/54.

SHEDS:
Gorton.
Newport 30/11/36.
Darlington 28/3/43.
Blaydon 16/7/43.
Heaton 7/11/48.
Neville Hill 12/2/50.

RENUMBERED:
4920 5/5/46.
64920 14/5/49.

CONDEMNED:
16/11/61.
Cut up at Cowlairs.

1544

Beyer Peacock 6818.

To traffic 9/11/36.

REPAIRS:
Gor. 7-9/12/37.**L.**
Dar. 22/3-9/5/39.**G.**
Dar. 24/1-28/2/41.**G.**
Cow. 8-30/12/43.**G.**
Cow. 24/11-29/12/45.**G.**
Dar. 8-30/1/46.**L.**
Cow. 16/3-23/4/48.**G.**
Cow. 6/11-6/12/50.**H/I.**
Cow. 15-22/2/52.**C/L.**
Cow. 24/4-4/7/53.**G.**
Cow. 21/6-13/7/55.**L/I.**
Inv. 2/5-7/7/60.**G.**

BOILERS:
BP137.
BP134 *(ex1539)* 28/2/41.
4911 *(ex1984)* 30/12/43.
8024 *(ex2995)* 23/4/48.
27566 *(ex64857)* 4/7/53.
27489 *(ex4704)* 7/7/60.

SHEDS:
Gorton.
Neville Hill 12/11/36.
Newport 19/11/36.
Darlington 28/3/43.
Blaydon 26/6/43.
Darlington 23/7/45.
Neville Hill 29/1/50.
Borough Gardens 1/7/51.
Gateshead 14/6/59.
Tyne Dock 26/2/61.
Sunderland 20/8/61.
Heaton 12/11/61.

RENUMBERED:
4921 16/6/46.
64921 23/4/48.

CONDEMNED:
3/12/62.
Cut up at Darlington.

1545

Beyer Peacock 6819.

To traffic 13/11/36.

REPAIRS:
Gor. 27-29/1/38.**L.**
Gor. 8-11/3/38.**L.**
Cracked cyl. casting.
Dar. 3/5-17/6/39.**G.**
Dar. 29/5-2/7/42.**G.**
Cow. 1-25/11/44.**G.**
Cow. 10/6-27/9/47.**G.**
Cow. 31/1-25/2/50.**G.**
Cow. 27/7-22/8/52.**G.**
Dar. 11-19/5/54.**C/L.**
Cow. 12/5-29/6/55.**H/I.**
Cow. 10/7-23/8/58.**G.**

BOILERS:
BP138.
2936 *(ex1508)* 2/7/42.
4924 *(new)* 27/9/47.
27522 *(ex4868)* 22/8/52.
27499 *(ex65912)* 23/8/58.

SHEDS:
Gorton.
West Hartlepool 11/12/36.
Darlington 28/3/43.
Starbeck 5/7/43.
Neville Hill 1/10/50.
Selby 26/9/54.
Neville Hill 26/6/55.

RENUMBERED:
4922 11/8/46.
64922 25/2/50.

CONDEMNED:
23/11/62.
Cut up at Darlington.

1547

Beyer Peacock 6820.

To traffic 26/11/36.

REPAIRS:
Gor. 24-26/3/38.**L.**
Gor. 27/6-15/7/39.**G.**
Dar. 3/3-9/4/42.**G.**
Cow. 3/5-3/6/44.**G.**
Cow. 24/5-23/8/47.**G.**
Cow. 24/10-3/12/49.**L/I.**
Cow. 3-26/10/52.**G.**
Cow. 28/8-12/9/53.**C/L.**
Cow. 15/12/55-28/1/56.**H/I.**
Ghd. 26/6-6/7/56.**C/L.**
Cow. 11/10-16/11/57.**G.**

BOILERS:
BP139.
E1358 *(ex1870)* 15/7/39.
E1357 *(ex1563)* 9/4/42.
2564 *(ex1478)* 3/6/44.
4923 *(new)* 23/8/47.
27459 *(ex4928)* 26/10/52.
27636 *(new)* 16/11/57.

SHEDS:
Gorton.
West Hartlepool 19/12/36.
Darlington 28/3/43.
Blaydon 27/7/43.
Heaton 7/11/48.

RENUMBERED:
4923 28/6/46.
64923 1/12/49.

CONDEMNED:
15/10/62.
Cut up at Cowlairs.

1563

Beyer Peacock 6821.

To traffic 31/3/37.

REPAIRS:
Gor. 7-11/3/38.**L.**
Gor. 20/7-23/9/39.**G.**
Dar. 1/12/41-5/1/42.**G.**
Cow. 23/9-21/10/44.**G.**
Cow. 4/12/47-7/2/48.**G.**
Cow. 24/7-16/8/51.**L/I.**
Cow. 8/5-1/6/53.**G.**
Ghd. 15/3-9/4/56.**C/L.**
Cow. 17/4-26/5/56.**L/I.**
Cow. 19/12/58-16/1/59.**G.**

BOILERS:
BP140.
E1357 *(ex1869)* 23/9/39.
BP135 *(ex1540)* 5/1/42.
2223 *(ex1458)* 21/10/44.
7946 *(ex1506)* 7/2/48.
7946 Reno.27487 16/8/51.
27507 *(ex4847)* 1/6/53.
27505 *(ex64943)* 16/1/59.

SHEDS:
Gorton.
Ferryhill 25/4/37.
Blaydon 24/8/38.
Alnmouth 8/9/43.
Blaydon 29/9/46.
Alnmouth 13/4/47.

RENUMBERED:
4924 12/5/46.
64924 15/8/51.

CONDEMNED:
23/11/62.
Cut up at Cowlairs.

1577

Beyer Peacock 6822.

To traffic 7/4/37.

REPAIRS:
Gor. 4-6/4/38.**L.**
Dar. 27/11-30/12/39.**G.**
Dar. 28/4-22/5/41.**L.**
Dar. 8/1-11/2/43.**G.**
Cow. 25/8-15/9/45.**G.**
Cow. 9-30/11/46.**L.**
Cow. 21/5-19/6/48.**G.**
Cow. 7/7-18/8/50.**H/I.**
Cow. 24/8-13/9/52.**G.**
Cow. 15-22/9/52.**N/C.**
Ghd. 15-17/2/55.**C/L.**
Cow. 10/2-10/3/56.**L/I.**
Cow. 11-18/1/57.**C/L.**
Cow. 13/2-13/3/59.**G.**

BOILERS:
BP141.
2925 *(ex1542)* 30/12/39.
2946 *(ex1551)* 11/2/43.
2938 *(ex1586)* 15/9/45.
2223 *(ex1563)* 19/6/48.
27541 *(ex4852)* 13/9/52.
27425 *(ex62736)* 13/3/59.

SHEDS:
Gorton.
Tyne Dock 3/5/37.
Darlington 28/3/43.
Blaydon 29/8/48.
Tweedmouth 14/8/49.

RENUMBERED:
4925 18/8/46.
64925 19/6/48.

CONDEMNED:
3/12/62.
Cut up at Darlington.

1580

Beyer Peacock 6823.

To traffic 12/4/37.

REPAIRS:
Gor. 4-7/5/38.**L.**
Dar. 9/10-4/11/39.**G.**
Dar. 19/12/42-18/1/43.**G.**
Cow. 4/8-8/9/45.**G.**
Cow. 25/8-18/10/47.**G.**
Cow. 16/12/49-14/1/50.**H/I.**
Cow. 23/1-15/2/53.**G.**
Cow. 25/9-7/11/53.**C/L.**
Cow. 18/4-11/5/57.**H/I.**
Cow. 8-30/8/58.**C/L.**
Cow. 19/11-19/12/59.**G.**

BOILERS:
BP142.
BP144 *(ex1586)* 4/11/39.
2913 *(ex1535)* 18/1/43.
1902 *(ex1509)* 8/9/45.
27530 *(ex4812)* 15/2/53.
25833 *(new)* 19/12/59.

SHEDS:
Gorton.
Tyne Dock 6/5/37.
Darlington 28/3/43.
Blaydon 27/7/43.
Hull Dairycoates 9/5/48.
Borough Gardens 4/2/51.
Heaton 16/6/57.

RENUMBERED:
4926 30/3/46.
64926 14/1/50.

CONDEMNED:
15/10/62.
Cut up at Cowlairs.

1585

Beyer Peacock 6824.

To traffic 16/4/37.

REPAIRS:
Gor. 25-27/5/38.**L.**
Gor. 27/6-22/7/39.**G.**
Dar. 27/12/41-27/1/42.**G.**
Dar. 30/1-12/2/42.**N/C.**
Dar. 19/10-4/11/42.**L.**
After collision.
Cow. 15/11-4/12/43.**G.**
Cow. 13/10-3/11/45.**G.**
Cow. 9/9-7/11/47.**G.**
Cow. 15/10-26/11/49.**L/I.**
Cow. 24/11-21/12/52.**G.**
Cow. 14/2-13/4/57.**G.**
Cow. 29/9-8/11/60.**G.**

BOILERS:
BP143.
BP131 *(ex1533)* 27/1/42.
2940 *(ex1454)* 4/12/43.
4928 *(new)* 7/11/47.
27518 *(ex4821)* 21/12/52.
27586 *(ex4812)* 13/4/57.
27568 *(ex64813)* 8/11/60.

SHEDS:
Gorton.
Sunderland 6/5/37.
Tweedmouth 8/7/39.
Blaydon 17/1/40.
Darlington 28/3/43.
Blaydon 16/7/43.
Hull Dairycoates 9/5/48.
Borough Gardens 4/2/51.
West Auckland 10/6/56.
Mirfield 15/4/62.
Ardsley 18/11/62.

RENUMBERED:
4927 1/9/46.
64927 26/11/49.
CONDEMNED:
3/12/62.
Cut up at Darlington.

1586

Beyer Peacock 6825.

To traffic 22/4/37.

REPAIRS:
Gor. 28-30/12/37.**L.**
Dar. 20/9-21/10/39.**G.**
Dar. 17/6-15/8/41.**L.**
Dar. 11/7-17/8/42.**G.**
Cow. 24/5-10/6/44.**L.**
Cow. 5/5-2/6/45.**G.**
Cow. 10/7-20/9/47.**G.**
Cow. 15/9-22/10/49.**L/I.**
Cow. 7/9-4/10/51.**L/I.**
Cow. 20/8-12/9/52.**G.**
Cow. 13-24/10/52.**N/C.**
Cow. 20/8-19/9/54.**H/I.**
Ghd. 22-24/2/55.**C/L.**
Cow. 19/12/56-9/2/57.**G.**
Dar. 24/4-23/5/58.**C/L.**

BOILERS:
BP144.
BP145 *(ex1587)* 21/10/39.
2938 *(ex1543)* 17/8/42.
8021 *(ex1491)* 2/6/45.
8021 Reno.27459 4/10/51.
27513 *(ex4711)* 12/9/52.
27536 *(ex4705)* 9/2/57.

SHEDS:
Gorton.
Stockton 19/5/37.
Middlesbrough 10/1/38.
Darlington 28/3/43.
Hull Dairycoates 1/3/48.
Malton 26/10/52.

RENUMBERED:
4928 6/6/46.
64928 20/10/49.

CONDEMNED:
21/7/61.
Cut up at Cowlairs.

1587

Beyer Peacock 6826.

To traffic 29/4/37.

REPAIRS:
Gor. 13-14/1/38.**L.**
Dar. 3/6-8/7/39.**G.**
Dar. 11/8-23/9/41.**G.**
Cow. 15/5-24/6/44.**G.**
Cow. 1-29/9/45.**L.**
Cow. 5/1-16/2/46.**H.**
Cow. 24/5-16/8/47.**G.**
Cow. 1-27/8/51.**G.**
Cow. 23/12/54-3/2/55.**H/I.**
Cow. 17/1-22/2/58.**G.**

BOILERS:
BP145.
2713 *(ex1473)* 8/7/39.
2719 *(ex1505)* 23/9/41.
2591 *(ex1476)* 24/6/44.
2253 *(ex1456)* 16/2/46.
2306 *(ex1489)* 16/8/47.
27588 *(new)* 27/8/51.
27637 *(new)* 22/2/58.

SHEDS:
Gorton.
Haverton Hill 25/5/37.
Blaydon 28/3/43.
Tweedmouth 8/9/43.
Darlington 23/7/45.
Borough Gardens 16/5/48.
Gateshead 4/1/53.
Alnmouth 16/6/57.

RENUMBERED:
4929 8/9/46.
64929 25/8/51.

CONDEMNED:
23/11/62.
Cut up at Cowlairs.

1875

Beyer Peacock 6827.

To traffic 5/5/37.

REPAIRS:
Gor. 23-25/10/37.**L.**
Cow. 31/12/38.**G.**
Cow. 4/10-15/11/41.**G.**
Cow. 15/12/44.**G.**
Cow. 11-25/8/45.**L.**
Cow. 16/10-19/12/47.**G.**
Cow. 19/9/48.**L.**
Cow. 30/5-18/6/51.**H/I.**
Cow. 24/3-24/4/54.**G.**
Cow. 12/10-3/11/56.**L/I.**
Cow. 24/2-29/3/58.**G.**
Gor. 21-25/5/59.*Weigh.*
Cow. 7/9-1/10/59.**C/L.**

BOILERS:
C1832.
C1716 *(ex2977)* 15/11/41.
2846 *(ex4816)* 19/12/47.
2846 Reno.27535 18/6/51.
27506 *(ex64917)* 24/4/54.
27561 *(ex65917)* 29/3/58.

SHEDS:
Gorton.
Carlisle 28/5/37.
Gorton 8/11/58.

RENUMBERED:
4930 7/7/46.
64930 19/9/48.

CONDEMNED:
3/7/61.
Cut up at Cowlairs.

1880

Beyer Peacock 6828.

To traffic 19/5/37.

REPAIRS:
Gor. 6-8/11/37.**L.**
Cow. 24/6/39.**G.**
Cow. 27/9/39.**L.**
Cow. 31/10/40.**G.**
Cow. 20/12/41.**L.**
Cow. 22/4/44.**G.**
Cow. 24-29/4/44.**N/C.**
Cow. 24/3-28/4/45.**L.**
Cow. 21/9-19/10/46.**G.**
Cow. 14/2-23/4/49.**G.**
Cow. 23/11-19/12/51.**H/I.**
Str. 26/8-9/10/54.**G.**
Cow. 4/1-4/2/56.**C/L.**
Cow. 31/1-8/3/58.**H/I.**

BOILERS:
C1833.
C1719 *(ex2732)* 31/10/40.
2699 *(ex2989)* 22/4/44.
2623 *(ex1584)* 23/4/49.
2623 Reno.27497 19/12/51.
27805 *(ex4987)* 9/10/54.

SHEDS:
Gorton.
Carlisle 19/6/37.
Eastfield 27/5/41.
Darlington 28/8/43.
Hull Dairycoates 4/1/48.
Borough Gardens 24/12/50.
Heaton 16/6/57.

RENUMBERED:
4931 8/9/46.
64931 22/4/49.

CONDEMNED:
22/10/61.
Cut up at Cowlairs.

1894

Beyer Peacock 6829.

To traffic 28/5/37.

REPAIRS:
Gor. 16-18/9/37.**L.**
Cow. 21/5/38.**L.**
Cow. 30/3/39.**G.**
Cow. 24/5/41.**G.**
Cow. 2/9/44.**G.**
Cow. 15/9-15/11/47.**G.**
Cow. 3/11-1/12/50.**G.**
Cow. 11/3-5/4/53.**G.**
Cow. 24/12/54-26/1/55.**H/I.**
Cow. 1-3/2/55.**N/C.**
Cow. 9-17/2/55.**N/C.**
Cow. 16/4-25/5/57.**H/I.**
Str. 15-17/9/57.**C/L.**
Cow. 16/2-20/3/59.**G.**

64960 here at Deadman's Lane, Derby on 30th July 1950 certainly was a 'freak'. It was one of the first J39s to go to Derby for repair, and whilst it had left the erecting shop on 19th July, painting had still to be done. Gorton must have supplied the smokebox number plate (with its wrong 6 and 9) and it was officially changed to 64960 on Monday 30th July, the day it returned to works for painting. But a case of B.R. number on smokebox door, *no* number on cab side, and LNER on tender is unlikely to be paralleled elsewhere. *R.J.Buckley*

BOILERS:
C1834.
C1833 *(ex1880)* 24/5/41.
2939 *(ex4938)* 15/11/47.
27504 *(ex64919)* 5/4/53.
27358 *(ex62761)* 20/3/59.

SHEDS:
Gorton.
Carlisle 21/6/37.

RENUMBERED:
4932 7/7/46.
64932 19/9/48.

CONDEMNED:
3/7/61.
Cut up at Cowlairs.

1508

Darlington.

To traffic 16/12/37.

REPAIRS:
Dar. 21/2-16/3/40.**G.**
Dar. 27/3-29/4/42.**G.**
Cow. 17/6-8/7/44.**G.**
Cow. 24/5-16/8/47.**H.**
Dar. 20/9/47.*Weigh.*
Cow. 1/7-12/8/50.**L/I.**
Gor. 31/3-27/8/53.**G.**
Cow. 16/8-15/9/56.**H/I.**
Cow. 9/9-15/10/60.**G.**

BOILERS:
2913.
2936 *(ex1546)* 16/3/40.
2917 *(ex1538)* 29/4/42.
RS119 *(ex1504)* 16/8/47.
27769 *(ex4918)* 27/8/53.
27546 *(ex64940)* 15/10/60.

SHEDS:
Hull Dairycoates.
Stockton 28/3/43.
Blaydon 21/6/43.
Tweedmouth 8/9/43.
Darlington 23/7/45.
Neville Hill 10/9/50.

RENUMBERED:
4933 11/4/46.
64933 12/8/50.

CONDEMNED:
12/12/62.
Cut up at Darlington.

1509

Darlington.

To traffic 25/1/38.

REPAIRS:
Dar. 27/7-5/8/38.**N/C.**
Welded boiler exam.
Dar. 14/6-11/7/40.**G.**
Dar. 6/7-18/8/42.**G.**
Cow. 26/1-3/3/45.**G.**
Cow. 2/11-7/12/46.**L.**
Cow. 16/12/47-21/2/48.**G.**
Ghd. 20-30/6/49.**C/L.**
Cow. 14/6-10/7/51.**H/I.**
Cow. 7/7-5/9/53.**G.**
Cow. 11/10-17/11/56.**L/I.**
Cow. 22/7-27/8/60.**G.**
Cow. 14/9/60.**N/C.**

BOILERS:
2843.
1902 *(ex1546)* 18/8/42.
2100 *(ex1546)* 3/3/45.
2714 *(ex1475)* 21/2/48.
2714 Reno. 27510 10/7/51.
27482 *(ex4860)* 5/9/53.
27727 *(ex64798)* 27/8/60.

SHEDS:
Hull Dairycoates.
Stockton 28/3/43.
Blaydon 19/6/43.
Heaton 7/11/48.
Neville Hill 12/2/50.

RENUMBERED:
4934 1/9/46.
64934 7/7/51.

CONDEMNED:
17/12/62.
Cut up at Darlington.

1535

Darlington.

To traffic 11/2/38.

REPAIRS:
Dar. 19/8-1/9/38.**N/C.**
Welded boiler exam.
Dar. 14/3-12/4/40.**G.**
Dar. 15-20/4/40.**N/C.**
Dar. 20/5-11/6/41.**N/C.**
Dar. 19/9-15/10/42.**G.**
Dar. 6/4-3/5/43.**H.**
Cow. 1/1-12/2/44.**G.**
Cow. 12-26/5/45.**L.**
Cow. 8/6-6/7/46.**G.**
Cow. 11/5-19/6/48.**G.**
Inv. 27/9-2/11/51.**H/I.**
Cow. 31/10-28/11/52.**C/H.**
Cow. 14/8-14/9/53.**G.**
Cow. 24/5-23/6/56.**H/I.**
Dar. 10-17/3/58.**C/L.**
Cow. 31/8-22/10/60.**G.**
Dar. 15/2-2/3/62.**C/L.**

BOILERS:
2842.
2913 *(ex1508)* 12/4/40.
BP145 *(ex1586)* 15/10/42.

BP131 *(ex1585)* 12/2/44.
C1714 *(ex2787)* 19/6/48.
C1714 Reno. 27469 2/11/51.
27527 *(ex4877)* 14/9/53.
27667 *(ex65933)* 22/10/60.

SHEDS:
York.
Selby 29/2/40.
Starbeck 20/7/40.
Scarborough 25/9/49.
Neville Hill 7/1/51.

RENUMBERED:
4935 2/6/46.
64935 16/6/48.

CONDEMNED:
17/12/62
Cut up at Darlington.

1537

Darlington.

To traffic 16/2/38.

REPAIRS:
Dar. 7-19/9/38.**N/C.**
Welded boiler exam.
Dar. 9/2-7/3/40.**G.**
Dar. 5/3-13/4/42.**G.**
Cow. 24/10-18/11/44.**G.**
Cow. 5/4-26/6/47.**G.**
Cow. 17-31/12/48.**L.**
Cow. 7/9-14/10/50.**H/I.**
Cow. 14/11/52-21/2/53.**C/H.**
Cow. 14/9-16/10/54.**H/I.**
Cow. 2/7-13/8/59.**G.**

BOILERS:
2846.
2340 *(ex1483)* 13/4/42.
BP142 *(ex1455)* 26/6/47.
27537 *(ex4870)* 21/2/53.
25900 was 25800 *(ex4846)* 13/8/59.

SHEDS:
Newport.
Darlington 28/3/43.
Borough Gardens 15/2/48.
Gateshead 14/6/59.

RENUMBERED:
4936 17/3/46.
64936 30/12/48.

CONDEMNED:
3/12/62.
Cut up at Darlington.

1538

Darlington.

To traffic 18/2/38.

REPAIRS:
Dar. 14/6-4/8/39.**G.**
Dar. 26/1-4/3/42.**G.**
Dar. 5/5-7/6/43.**L.**
Cow. 1/9-16/10/43.**G.**
Gor. 17/12/45-2/3/46.**G.**
Gor. 22/2-2/4/48.**G.**
Dby. 10/2-3/4/51.**H/I.**
Str. 18/7-22/8/53.**G.**
Gor. 7/9-27/10/56.**G.**
Gor. 31/10-1/11/56.**N/C.**
Str. 25/2-5/3/59.**N/C.**

BOILERS:
2917.
BP143 *(ex1585)* 4/3/42.
4907 *(ex1997)* 2/3/46.
2698 *(ex1497)* 2/4/48.
27788 *(ex4894)* 22/8/53.
27778 *(ex4721)* 27/10/56.

SHEDS:
Newport.
Darlington 28/3/43.
Lincoln 15/9/44.
Immingham 22/12/46.
Lincoln 27/4/47.

RENUMBERED:
4937 11/5/46.
64937 2/4/48.

CONDEMNED:
15/2/60.
Cut up at Stratford.

1541

Darlington.

To traffic 24/2/38.

REPAIRS:
Dar. 10-21/3/38.**N/C.**
Dar. 31/10-5/12/39.**G.**
Dar. 31/3-4/5/42.**G.**
Cow. 12/9-7/10/44.**G.**
Cow. 12-19/5/45.**L.**
Cow. 25/8-8/9/45.**L.**
Cow. 2-16/3/46.**L.**
Cow. 12/9-18/10/47.**G.**
Cow. 27/2-25/3/50.**H/I.**
Cow. 14/5-23/6/52.**G.**
Cow. 11/11-10/12/55.**L/I.**
Cow. 2/10-3/11/56.**C/L.**
Cow. 15/4-24/5/58.**G.**
Cow. 3-5/6/58.**N/C.**
Cow. 9/9-1/10/60.**C/L.**

BOILERS:
2935.
BP142 *(ex1580)* 5/12/39.
E1358 *(ex1547)* 4/5/42.
2939 *(ex1540)* 7/10/44.
8014 *(ex1487)* 18/10/47.
27477 *(ex4842)* 23/6/52.
27495 *(ex65920)* 24/5/58.

SHEDS:
Newport.
Darlington 28/3/43.
West Auckland 19/1/47.
Darlington 30/1/47.
Starbeck 14/11/48.
Malton 18/4/54.
Selby 14/6/59.
Gateshead 30/8/59.

RENUMBERED:
4938 16/3/46.
64938 23/3/50.

CONDEMNED:
16/11/62.
Cut up at Darlington.

1542

Darlington.

To traffic 2/3/38.

REPAIRS:
Dar. 7/11-9/12/39.**G.**
Dar. 6/2-12/4/40.**L.**
Dar. 7/4-12/5/41.**N/C.**
R.h.Cyl. cracked.
Dar. 28/10-27/11/42.**G.**
Cow. 15/7-19/8/44.**G.**
Cow. 6/7-24/8/46.**G.**
Cow. 18/1-8/2/47.**L.**
Cow. 14/1-9/4/49.**G.**
Cow. 21/10-9/11/52.**L/I.**
Cow. 24/4-22/5/53.**C/H.**
Dar. 24/6-5/8/54.**C/L.**
Cow. 7/9-18/10/54.**G.**
Cow. 7/3-13/4/57.**G.**

BOILERS:
2925.
2935 *(ex1541)* 9/12/39.
4904 *(ex1835)* 27/11/42.
4904 Reno. 27544 9/11/52.
27547 *(ex4948)* 18/10/54.
27468 *(ex64963)* 13/4/57.

SHEDS:
Newport.
Darlington 28/3/43.
Starbeck 14/7/43.
Darlington 14/1/46.
Hull Dairycoates 4/1/48.
Borough Gardens 3/12/50.
Sunderland 1/2/53.
Hull Dairycoates 10/6/56.
Heaton 16/6/57.

RENUMBERED:
4939 16/6/46.
64939 9/4/49.

CONDEMNED:
18/4/62.
Cut up at Darlington.

1546

Darlington.

To traffic 4/3/38.

REPAIRS:
Dar. 9/1-10/2/40.**G.**
Dar. 13/3-15/4/42.**G.**
Dar. 11/1-8/2/43.**L.**
Dar. 14/12/43-14/1/44.**L.**
Cow. 2-25/11/44.**G.**
Cow. 29/3-18/6/47.**G.**
Cow. 6/1-4/2/50.**G.**
Cow. 16/2-24/3/52.**G.**
Cow. 21/6-17/7/54.**L/I.**
Cow. 26/2-5/4/58.**G.**
Cow. 13/6-27/8/60.**G.**
Cow. 31/8-1/9/60.**N/C.**

BOILERS:
2936.
1902 *(ex1452)* 10/2/40.
2100 *(ex1468)* 15/4/42.
2568 *(ex2735)* 25/11/44.
4921 *(new)* 18/6/47.
27555 *(ex4816)* 24/3/52.
27546 *(ex64795)* 5/4/58.
27774 *(ex spare & 4961)* 27/8/60.

SHEDS:
Newport.
Darlington 28/3/43.
Blaydon 29/8/48.
Darlington 19/11/50.
Middlesbrough 7/1/51.
West Auckland 31/8/52.
Sunderland 25/9/55.
Hull Dairycoates 10/6/56.

RENUMBERED:
4940 16/6/46.
64940 3/2/50.

CONDEMNED:
17/12/62.
Cut up at Darlington.

1548

Darlington.

To traffic 9/3/38.

REPAIRS:
Dar. 27/2-27/3/40.**G.**
Dar. 6/10-3/11/42.**G.**
Cow. 22/2-17/3/45.**G.**
Cow. 24/9-6/12/47.**G.**
Cow. 9/11-10/12/49.**G.**
Cow. 20/5-14/6/53.**H/I.**
Cow. 12/1-12/2/55.**G.**
Cow. 14-18/3/55.**N/C.**
Cow. 25/9-25/10/58.**L/I.**
Cow. 28/10-5/12/59.**G.**

BOILERS:
2938.

2723 *(ex1584)* 27/3/40.
2715 *(ex1584)* 3/11/42.
2708 *(ex2725)* 17/3/45.
4930 *(new)* 6/12/47.
4912 *(ex4703)* 10/12/49.
4912 Reno. 27548 14/6/53.
27496 *(ex4862)* 12/2/55.
27497 *(ex64873)* 5/12/59.

SHEDS:
Newport.
Darlington 28/3/43.
Blaydon 14/7/43.
Hull Dairycoates 9/5/48.
Borough Gardens 20/5/51.
Tweedmouth 4/1/53.

RENUMBERED:
4941 10/3/46.
64941 10/12/49.

CONDEMNED:
3/12/62.
Cut up at Darlington.

1551

Darlington.

To traffic 16/3/38.

REPAIRS:
Dar. 24/6-27/7/40.**G.**
Dar. 19/12/41-21/1/42.**L.**
Dar. 17/12/42-15/1/43.**G.**
Cow. 21/9-21/10/44.**G.**
Dar. 7-24/3/45.**L.**
Cow. 19/6-11/10/47.**G.**
Cow. 3/5-3/6/50.**G.**
Cow. 7-26/4/53.**L/I.**
Cow. 16/2-14/4/56.**G.**
Cow. 10/7-22/8/59.**H/I.**
Cow. 12/4-4/5/60.**N/C.**
Cow. 3-4/10/61.**N/C.**

BOILERS:
2939.
2946 *(ex1460)* 27/7/40.
2935 *(ex1542)* 15/1/43.
2099 *(ex1584)* 21/10/44.
2936 *(ex1545)* 11/10/47.
C2020 *(new)* 3/6/50.
C2020 Reno. 27570 26/4/53.
27700 *(ex4896)* 14/4/56.

SHEDS:
Middlesbrough.
Stockton 1/1/40.
Blaydon 19/6/43.
Darlington 23/7/45.
Starbeck 29/8/48.
York 13/9/59.
Sunderland 20/3/60.
Heaton 14/1/62.

RENUMBERED:
4942 18/8/46.
64942 3/6/50.

CONDEMNED:
3/12/62.
Cut up at Darlington.

1558

Darlington.

To traffic 1/4/38.

REPAIRS:
Dar. 20/6-19/9/39.**H.**
Dar. 17/3-17/4/41.**G.**
Dar. 24/6-2/7/41.**N/C.**
Dar. 17-30/7/41.**N/C.**
Dar. 15-26/8/41.**N/C.**
Dar. 4-10/7/42.**N/C.**
Cow. 21/3-29/4/44.**G.**
Cow. 6-27/7/46.**G.**
Cow. 7/9-12/10/46.**N/C.**
Cow. 3-19/7/47.**L.**
Cow. 7/2-11/6/49.**G.**
Cow. 7-30/6/52.**H/I.**
Cow. 26/11-29/12/54.**G.**
Cow. 12/9-11/10/58.**G.**
Don. 20-21/9/60.*Weigh.*
Dar. 31/1-2/3/61.**C/L.**

BOILERS:
2940.
BP137 *(ex1544)* 17/4/41.
2685 *(ex2970)* 29/4/44.
C1799 *(ex1543)* 11/6/49.
C1799 Reno. 27483 30/6/52.
27505 *(ex64851)* 29/12/54.
27595 *(ex64978)* 11/10/58.

SHEDS:
Middlesbrough.
Darlington 28/3/43.
Middlesbrough 10/1/47.
Darlington 1/3/47.
Neville Hill 29/1/50.
Hull Dairycoates 22/11/59.

RENUMBERED:
4943 26/7/46.
64943 9/6/49.

CONDEMNED:
17/12/62.
Cut up at Darlington.

1560

Darlington.

To traffic 7/4/38.

REPAIRS:
Dar. 11-17/11/38.**N/C.**
Change of tender.
Dar. 9/5-4/6/40.**G.**
Dar. 20/1-2/2/42.**N/C.**
Dar. 24/11-22/12/42.**G.**
Dar. 19/6-2/7/43.**L.**
Cow. 3-24/3/45.**G.**
Cow. 18/1-8/2/47.**L.**
Cow. 15/3-3/4/48.**G.**
Cow. 22/9-22/10/49.**L/I.**
Cow. 26/10-5/11/49.**N/C.**
Cow. 30/6-9/8/51.**L/I.**
Cow. 29/11/52-18/1/53.**G.**
Cow. 15/12/54-27/1/55.**H/I.**
Cow. 8/3-7/4/56.**H/I.**
Cow. 29/9-31/10/59.**G.**

BOILERS:
2922.
2842 *(ex1535)* 4/6/40.
2843 *(ex1509)* 22/12/42.
2622 *(ex1470)* 24/3/45.
2571 *(ex1835)* 3/4/48.
2571 Reno. 27490 9/8/51.
25832 *(new)* 31/10/59.

SHEDS:
York.
Selby 29/2/40.
Starbeck 20/7/40.
York 13/9/59.
Neville Hill 13/12/59.

RENUMBERED:
4944 11/8/46.
64944 3/4/48.

CONDEMNED:
12/12/62.
Cut up at Darlington.

1804

Darlington.

To traffic 25/3/38.

REPAIRS:
Cow. 3-20/1/40.**G.**
Cow. 1-4/5/40.**L.**
Cow. 11-30/8/41.**L.**
Cow. 3-28/2/42.**G.**
Cow. 10-11/11/42.**L.**
Cow. 30/9-21/10/44.**G.**
Cow. 29/6-24/8/46.**L.**
Cow. 25/11/47-24/1/48.**G.**
Cow. 1/8-3/9/49.**G.**
Dar. 23/9-28/11/49.**C/L.**
Cow. 28/8-22/9/53.**G.**
Cow. 6-16/10/53.**N/C.**
Cow. 16/10-15/11/56.**H/I.**
Cow. 11/1-16/2/57.**C/H.**
Cow. 22/9-17/10/59.**G.**
Cow. 15/9/62.*Not repaired.*

BOILERS:
4901.
E1358 *(ex1541)* 21/10/44.
2100 *(ex1509)* 24/1/48.
C2018 *(new)* 3/9/49.
27461 *(ex4921)* 22/9/53.
25831 *(new)* 17/10/59.

SHEDS:
St Margarets.
Eastfield 28/9/42.
Parkhead 18/1/43.
Eastfield 17/4/43.
Darlington 18/7/43.
Middlesbrough 12/1/47.
Darlington 29/1/47.
Heaton 14/11/48.

RENUMBERED:
4945 24/8/46.
64945 3/9/49.

CONDEMNED:
15/10/62.
Cut up at Cowlairs.

1808

Darlington.

To traffic 31/3/38.

REPAIRS:
Cow. 17/6/39.**H.**
Cow. 29/8/40.**G.**
Cow. 21/2-21/3/42.**G.**
Cow. 9/12/44.**G.**
Cow. 15/12/45-19/1/46.**L.**
Cow. 30/1-2/5/47.**G.**
Cow. 29/12/48-2/2/49.**H/I.**
Cow. 29/9-30/10/51.**G.**
Cow. 10/2-16/3/54.**L/I.**
Cow. 22-27/3/54.**N/C.**
Cow. 7-10/4/54.**N/C.**
Cow. 22/8-29/9/56.**G.**
Cow. 10/4-1/5/59.**H/I.**
Cow. 13-25/6/59.**C/L.**

BOILERS:
4902.
C1832 *(ex1875)* 21/3/42.
2946 *(ex4778)* 2/5/47.
27590 *(new)* 30/10/51.
27578 *(ex4880)* 29/9/56.

SHEDS:
Carlisle.
St Margarets 22/3/48.
Dalry Road 11/8/58.
St Margarets 27/8/61.
Dunfermline 17/2/62.

RENUMBERED:
4946 7/7/46.
64946 29/1/49.

CONDEMNED:
29/12/62.
Cut up at Inverurie.

1835

Darlington.

To traffic 8/4/38.

REPAIRS:
Cow. 23-25/4/38.**N/C.**
Cow. 3-5/8/38.**N/C.**

Cow. 6-10/10/38.**N/C.**
Cow. 9-11/11/38.**N/C.**
Cow. 14/2-25/3/39.**N/C.**
Cow. 18/4-23/5/40.**G.**
Dar. 6/10-7/11/42.**G.**
Dar. 28/3-11/4/44.**N/C.**
Cow. 18/12/44-20/1/45.**G.**
Dar. 4-25/5/46.**L.**
Cow. 19-24/8/46.**L.**
Cow. 25/11/47-10/4/48.**G.**
Cow. 6/2-3/3/51.**H/I.**
Cow. 10/9-10/10/53.**G.**
Cow. 13/12/56-2/3/57.**G.**
Dar. 14/5-12/6/57.**C/L.**
Cow. 29/8-11/10/58.**C/L.**
Cow. 9/12/59-6/2/60.**G.**

BOILERS:
4903.
4904 *(ex1896)* 23/5/40.
BP141 *(ex1485)* 7/11/42.
2571 *(ex1453)* 20/1/45.
E1357 *(ex3088)* 10/4/48.
E1357 Reno. 27525 3/3/51.
27515 *(ex4892)* 10/10/53.
27552 *(ex4950)* 2/3/57.
27587 *(ex4982)* 6/2/60.

SHEDS:
Carlisle.
Selby 1/1/41.
Darlington 28/3/43.
Blaydon 22/8/43.
Heaton 7/11/48.
Hull Dairycoates 11/2/52.
Malton 25/4/54.
Bradford 15/9/57.
Low Moor 12/1/58.
Hull Dairycoates 8/6/58.
Neville Hill 11/9/60.

RENUMBERED:
4947 25/5/46.
64947 9/4/48.

CONDEMNED:
23/5/62.
Cut up at Cowlairs.

1862

Darlington.

To traffic 12/4/38.

REPAIRS:
Cow. 11/11/39.**H.**
Cow. 18/11/39.**N/C.**
Cow. 12/9/42.**G.**
Cow. 18/12/43.**G.**
Cow. 3-17/2/45.**L.**
Cow. 2/6-7/7/45.**L.**
Cow. 6/1-1/2/46.**G.**
Cow. 15/3-17/4/48.**G.**
Cow. 7-31/8/51.**L/I.**
Cow. 10/5-4/6/54.**G.**
Cow. 11-16/6/54.**N/C.**
Cow. 29/5-6/7/57.**L/I.**

BOILERS:
2926.
C1712 *(ex2786)* 12/9/42.
4911 *(ex4921)* 17/4/48.
4911 Reno. 27547 31/8/51.
27549 *(ex64795)* 4/6/54.

SHED:
Carlisle.

RENUMBERED:
4948 31/3/46.
64948 17/4/48.

CONDEMNED:
11/4/60.
Cut up at Inverurie.

1896

Darlington.

To traffic 21/4/38.

REPAIRS:
Cow. 10/4-9/5/40.**G.**
Dar. 25/8-18/9/41.**L.**
Dar. 8/1-10/2/43.**G.**
Ghd. 12/12/44-4/1/45.**L.**
Cow. 8/6-6/7/46.**G.**
Cow. 28/10-26/11/48.**G.**
Cow. 20/4-12/5/51.**H/I.**
Cow. 4-22/11/52.**C/L.**
Cow. 17/3-16/4/54.**G.**
Cow. 12/10-1/12/56.**C/H.**

BOILERS:
4904.
C1720 *(ex2740)* 9/5/40.
2597 *(ex366)* 10/2/43.
C1717 *(ex2787)* 6/7/46.
2842 *(ex4844)* 26/11/48.
2842 Reno. 27533 12/5/51.
27511 *(ex4819)* 16/4/54.
27592 *(ex64858)* 1/12/56.

SHEDS:
Carlisle.
Consett 20/10/40.
Darlington 28/3/43.
Tweedmouth 4/1/48.
Blaydon 24/2/48.
Neville Hill 20/8/50.
Hull Dairycoates 13/6/54.
Heaton 16/6/57.
Alnmouth 11/5/58.

RENUMBERED:
4949 6/7/46.
64949 26/11/48.

CONDEMNED:
22/8/62.
Cut up at Cowlairs.

1863

Darlington.

To traffic 13/4/38.

REPAIRS:
Cow. 27/1/40.**G.**
Cow. 7/42.**G.**
Cow. 15/7/44.**G.**
Cow. 10/3-2/5/47.**G.**
Cow. 30/8-24/9/49.**H/I.**
Cow. 27/3-15/4/50.**C/H.**
Cow. 5/11-28/12/52.**G.**
Cow. 14/1-6/2/53.**N/C.**
Cow. 6/3-24/4/54.**N/C.**
Cow. 2-26/6/54.**C/L.**
Inv. 23-25/5/56.**C/L.**
Cow. 6/11-7/12/56.**G.**
Cow. 15/9-29/10/60.**G.**
Cow. 13/9-20/10/61.**C/L.**

BOILERS:
4905.
1909 *(ex1468)* 15/7/44.
1922 *(ex4812)* 2/5/47.
27552 *(ex64850)* 28/12/52.
27800 *(ex4886)* 7/12/56.
27842 *(ex4734)* 29/10/60.

SHEDS:
Carlisle.
Eastfield 6/41.
Dundee 11/8/43.

RENUMBERED:
4950 24/3/46.
64950 24/9/49.

CONDEMNED:
29/12/62.
Cut up at Inverurie.

1898

Darlington.

To traffic 25/4/38.

REPAIRS:
Gor. 9/1-16/3/40.**G.**
Gor. 3/9-17/10/42.**G.**
Don. 7/5-7/8/43.**L.**
Gor. 29/8-11/11/44.**G.**
Gor. 18/5-23/6/45.**L.**
Gor. 4/5-14/9/46.**G.**
Gor. 21/1-25/3/47.**H.**
Gor. 7/5-23/7/49.**G.**
Dby. 9/6-7/9/50.**H/I.**
Dby. 20/6-6/8/52.**G.**
Gor. 7-15/11/55.**G.**
Str. 25/8-12/9/57.**C/L.**

BOILERS:
4906.
E1350 *(ex1803)* 16/3/40.
E1353 *(ex1971)* 17/10/42.
4914 *(ex1965)* 11/11/44.
8006 *(ex2726)* 14/9/46.
2138 *(ex1295)* 25/3/47.
2696 *(ex2994)* 23/7/49.
27704 *(ex4976)* 6/8/52.
27712 *(ex4757)* 15/11/55.

SHEDS:
Colwick.
Doncaster 14/9/46.
Peterborough 12/10/52.
Plaistow 7/4/57.
Tilbury 31/10/59.

RENUMBERED:
4951 14/9/46.
64951 23/7/49.

CONDEMNED:
14/3/60.
Cut up at Stratford.

1903

Darlington.

To traffic 29/4/38.

REPAIRS:
Gor. 25/4-25/5/40.**G.**
Gor. 20/12/42-13/3/43.**G.**
Gor. 3/4-2/6/45.**G.**
Gor. 25/10/47-20/1/48.**G.**
Dby. 13/6-6/8/51.**H/I.**
Str. 5/11-12/12/53.**G.**
Gor. 19/4-26/5/56.**H/I.**

BOILERS:
4907.
4920 *(ex1996)* 25/5/40.
E1354 *(ex1927)* 13/3/43.
2932 *(ex1928)* 2/6/45.
RS118 *(ex1289)* 20/1/48.
27656 *(ex4802)* 12/12/53.

SHEDS:
Colwick.
Ardsley 31/3/46.
Sheffield 28/7/46.
Doncaster 22/9/46.
Plaistow 2/6/57.
Tilbury 31/10/59.

RENUMBERED:
4952 20/1/46.
E4952 20/1/48.
64952 6/8/51.

CONDEMNED:
14/3/60.
Cut up at Stratford.

1922

Darlington.

To traffic 4/5/38.

In their final years some J39 class went to Inverurie for repairs, and 64812 here at Tyne Dock on 9th July 1961 has just returned from there. Electrification warning flashes had been added on boiler and on cab because this engine sometimes worked 'under the wires' between Manors East, and Heaton junction near Newcastle. *WBY collection*

Cowlairs proved that they could do an orthodox livery job, as seen here on 64897 ex works on 19th April 1952, in what was standard style for J39 class until the change from emblem to crest in June 1957. Figures 6 and 9, both by foundry and by paint shop are impeccably true Gill Sans, whilst both number on cab, and emblem on tender are the correct size. *John Robertson*

1450 passing Alne on 16th July 1927 is doing exactly what J39 class was designed for viz. the haulage of heavy main line goods trains. Note also that it is able to be routed up the fast line on this high-speed four-track section. *H.G.W. Household*

West Hartlepool shedded 1481 had its Westinghouse brake removed in December 1932 and here is passing through Greatham station with a typical 1930's goods train. *Real Photos*

REPAIRS:
Gor. 4/7-10/8/40.**G.**
Cow. 28/3-27/8/43.**G.**
Str. 21/5-1/7/44.**L.**
Gor. 12/4-30/6/45.**G.**
Str. 20/9-17/10/45.**L.**
Str. 1-22/11/46.**L.**
Gor. 1/2-21/4/48.**G.**
Dby. 2/4-5/6/51.**H/I.**
Str. 8/2-12/3/54.**G.**
Str. 31/8-10/10/56.**G.**
Str. 16-29/4/57.**C/L.**
Str. 8-16/10/57.**C/L.** *A.T.C. & continuous blow-down fitted.*

BOILERS:
4908.
4912 *(ex1940)* 10/8/40.
C1711 *(ex2733)* 27/8/43.
3199 *(ex3097)* 30/6/45.
4935 *(new)* 21/4/48.
27822 *(new)* 12/3/54.
27849 *(new)* 10/10/56.

SHEDS:
Norwich.
Ipswich 22/10/41.
Stratford 2/7/47.
Parkeston 18/1/48.
Plaistow 26/5/57.
Tilbury 30/10/59.

RENUMBERED:
4953 17/3/46.
64953 21/4/48.

CONDEMNED:
14/3/60.
Cut up at Stratford.

1926

Darlington.

To traffic 6/5/38.

REPAIRS:
Gor. 5/6-6/7/40.**G.**
Gor. 15/10-13/11/43.**G.**
Gor. 20/11-16/12/44.**G.**
Gor. 16/9-15/3/47.**G.**
Gor. 10/2-26/4/48.**L.**
Gor. 27/10-9/11/49.**G.**
Str. 19/1-28/2/53.**G.**
Gor. 16/3-5/5/56.**G.**
Str. 26/9-2/10/57.**C/L.** *A.T.C. & continuous blow-down fitted.*

BOILERS:
4909.
4907 *(ex1903)* 6/7/40.
3177 *(ex3090)* 13/11/43.
C1710 *(ex2950)* 15/3/47.
4979 *(new)* 9/11/49.
27744 *(ex4810)* 28/2/53.
27739 *(ex4749)* 5/5/56.

SHEDS:
Doncaster.
New England 11/4/42.
Gorton 18/6/43.
Liverpool 6/4/47.
Trafford Park 22/5/50.
Northwich 1/4/51.
Peterborough 12/10/52.
Plaistow 26/5/57.
Tilbury 31/10/59.

RENUMBERED:
4954 7/7/46.
64954 24/4/48.

CONDEMNED:
15/3/60.
Cut up at Stratford.

1927

Darlington.

To traffic 11/5/38.

REPAIRS:
Don. 26/10/38-10/1/39.**H.**
Gor. 30/3-31/5/41.**G.**
Gor. 11/11/42-27/2/43.**G.**
Gor. 17/10/45-19/1/46.**G.**
Gor. 4/11/47-31/1/48.**G.**
Gor. 29/6-27/8/49.**C/L.**
Gor. 5-22/10/49.**C/L.**
Dby. 8/4-8/6/51.**G.**
Gor. 10/3-11/5/53.**G.**
Gor. 25/7-2/9/55.**G.**
Gor. 11/7-24/8/57.**C/H.**
Gor. 10/11-13/12/58.**L/I.**

BOILERS:
2920.
E1354 *(ex1854)* 31/5/41.
3209 *(new)* 27/2/43.
2720 *(ex1857)* 19/1/46.
2675 *(ex2986)* 31/1/48.
27665 *(ex4959)* 8/6/51.
27757 *(ex4738)* 11/5/53.
27791 *(new)* 2/9/55.
27531 *(ex4840)* 24/8/57.

SHEDS:
Sheffield.
Doncaster 28/2/40.
New England 11/4/42.
Gorton 9/6/43.
Annesley 30/10/43.
Colwick 30/3/47.
Annesley 3/11/57.
Gorton 25/11/60.
Woodford 5/4/62.

RENUMBERED:
4955 11/8/46.
E4955 31/1/48.
64955 27/8/49.

CONDEMNED:
20/7/62.
Cut up at Gorton.

1928

Darlington.

To traffic 14/5/38.

REPAIRS:
Gor. 1/9-19/10/40.**G.**
Cow. 11/3-27/6/43.**G.**
Gor. 12/9-11/11/44.**G.**
Gor. 21/10/45-12/1/46.**G.**
Str. 24/9-20/4/47.**G.**
Gor. 8/6-1/8/47.**L.**
Dby. 12/8-19/10/50.**G.**
Str. 4/5-16/6/53.**G.**
Gor. 25-24/11/56.**G.**
Str. 26/9-2/10/57.**C/L.** *A.T.C. & continuous blow-down fitted.*

BOILERS:
2932.
4915 *(ex1996)* 11/11/44.
4991 *(new)* 19/10/50.
27781 *(ex4893)* 16/6/53.
27776 *(ex4883)* 24/11/56.

SHEDS:
Ipswich.
March 11/5/39.
Grantham 12/5/42.
Retford 13/10/46.
Doncaster 17/8/52.
Plaistow 26/5/57.
Tilbury 31/10/59.

RENUMBERED:
4956 22/9/46.
64956 19/10/50.

CONDEMNED:
15/3/60.
Cut up at Stratford.

1930

Darlington.

To traffic 14/5/38.

REPAIRS:
Gor. 25/7-31/8/40.**G.**
Gor. 9/11/42-16/1/43.**G.**
Str. 9/5-30/6/44.**L.**
Str. 2-3/2/45.**L.**
Gor. 4/6-11/8/45.**G.**
Str. 30/9-16/1/48.**G.**
Gor. 23/8-30/9/48.**L.**
Dby. 10/2-9/4/51.**G.**
Dby. 15/11/51-2/1/52.**C/L.**
Str. 27/1-27/3/53.**G.**
Str. 30/8-8/10/55.**G.**
Str. 8-16/10/57.**C/L.** *A.T.C. & continuous blow-down fitted.*
Str. 21-23/10/57.**N/C.**

BOILERS:
4910.
3211 *(new)* 16/1/43.
2222 *(ex1277)* 11/8/45.
27801 *(new)* 9/4/51.
27747 *(ex4989)* 27/3/53.
27714 *(ex4985)* 8/10/55.

SHEDS:
Sheffield.
Doncaster 28/2/40.
Stratford 5/9/43.
Norwich 7/9/44.
Ipswich 7/11/46.
Plaistow 26/5/57.
Tilbury 31/10/59.

RENUMBERED:
4957 17/3/46.
64957 30/9/48.

CONDEMNED:
14/3/60.
Cut up at Stratford.

1933

Darlington.

To traffic 31/5/38.

REPAIRS:
Gor. 24/8-12/10/40.**G.**
Str. 7/3-26/6/43.**G.**
Str. 8/9-26/10/45.**G.**
Str. 29/9-12/11/46.**L.**
Str. 10/4-19/5/47.**L.**
Gor. 15/2-15/4/48.**G.**
Dby. 6/10-1/12/50.**L/I.**
Dby. 21/4-4/6/52.**G.**
Str. 11/2-26/3/55.**G.**
Str. 29/10-30/11/57.**G.**
Str. 11-14/8/58.**C/L.**
Continuous blow-down fitted.
Bow 16-19/12/58.**N/C.**
Str. 10-19/8/59.**C/L.**

BOILERS:
4911.
E1355 *(ex1856)* 12/10/40.
2102 *(ex1498)* 26/6/43.
2205 *(ex1268)* 26/10/45.
4934 *(new)* 15/4/48.
27433 *(new)* 4/6/52.
27678 *(ex4780)* 26/3/55.
25827 *(new)* 30/11/57.

SHEDS:
Stratford.
Ipswich 11/12/40.
Stratford 14/10/51.
Cambridge 25/9/55.
Plaistow 8/6/58.
Tilbury 31/10/59.

RENUMBERED:
4958 8/9/46.
64958 15/4/48.

All over the LNER the J39s were employed on passenger trains at various times and Nos. 2731-42 which went to Scottish Area were also used equally on main line passenger and goods trains. With a fast train for Edinburgh, 2734 is seen pulling out of Dundee (Tay Bridge) station on 6th August 1939. *WBY collection*

1469, here on 21st June 1936, had been loaned by Leeds Neville Hill to Starbeck shed to work this Sunday excursion from Bradford (Forster Square) to Newcastle and Whitley Bay. Seen at Esholt it is well that the safety valves are lifting because it is faced with the stiff climb out of the Aire valley through Guiseley into the Wharfe valley. *G.H.Butland*

It was not only on main line work that J39s could be seen. 1488 went new to the shed at Ferryhill in December 1934, and on 10th June 1935, they had used it on this branch train to Hartlepool. Five vintage gas lit North Eastern 8-wheelers cannot be really representative of the effort it was making, but this view exudes determination. *WBY collection*

CONDEMNED:
14/3/60.
Cut up at Stratford.

1940

Darlington.

To traffic 30/5/38.

REPAIRS:
Gor. 30/6-3/8/40.**G.**
Cow. 6/6-29/8/43.**G.**
Str. 9-29/7/44.**L.**
Str. 19/10-1/11/45.**L.**
Str. 24/2-2/5/46.**G.**
Str. 15/6-28/8/47.**L.**
Gor. 29/8-16/10/48.**G.**
Dby. 25/8-1/11/50.**H/I.**
Dby. 7/10-3/12/52.**G.**
Dby. 10/12/52-5/1/53.**N/C.**
Dby. 12-21/1/53.**N/C.**
Dby. 29/1-20/2/53.**N/C.**
Gor. 30/8-5/11/55.**G.**

BOILERS:
4912.
4909 *(ex1926)* 3/8/40.
2317 *(ex1477)* 29/8/43.
2684 *(ex2943)* 2/5/46.
3221 *(ex2736)* 16/10/48.
27735 *(ex4833)* 3/12/52.
27797 *(new)* 5/11/55.

SHEDS:
Stratford.
Ipswich 29/1/41.
Lowestoft 6/10/46.
Norwich 26/3/47.
Lowestoft 30/9/51.
Stratford 14/10/51.
Lincoln 22/11/53.

RENUMBERED:
4959 26/4/46.
64959 16/10/48.

CONDEMNED:
1/1/60.
Cut up at Stratford.

1942

Darlington.

To traffic 3/6/38.

REPAIRS:
Gor. 11/10-23/11/40.**G.**
Gor. 21/11/43-29/1/44.**G.**
Gor. 1/2-10/7/47.**G.**
Dby. 15/5-19/7/50.**G.**
Dby. 31/7-7/8/50.**N/C.**
For painting only.
Gor. 19/2-4/4/53.**G.**
Gor. 4/10/55-21/1/56.**G.**
Gor. 5-28/12/57.**C/H.**
Gor. 3-9/1/58.**N/C.**

BOILERS:
4913.
4919 *(ex1984)* 23/11/40.
2301 *(ex2783)* 29/1/44.
2299 *(ex2969)* 10/7/47.
C2032 *(new)* 19/7/50.
27751 *(ex4827)* 4/4/53.
27752 *(ex4974)* 21/1/56.
27662 *(ex4887)* 28/12/57.

SHEDS:
Carlisle.
Sheffield 12/9/38.
Lincoln 15/8/54.
Boston 9/11/58.
Lincoln 7/12/58.

RENUMBERED:
4960 23/6/46.
64960 29/7/50.

CONDEMNED:
1/2/60.
Cut up at Doncaster.

1943

Darlington.

To traffic 9/6/38.

REPAIRS:
Gor. 26/4-28/6/41.**G.**
Gor. 28/2-5/3/44.**L.**
Gor. 14/3-6/5/44.**G.**
Gor. 21/12/46-26/6/47.**G.**
Gor. 13/2-15/4/50.**G.**
Gor. 19-25/4/50.**N/C.**
Str. 22/3-16/5/53.**G.**
Str. 5/8-11/9/53.**N/C.**
Gor. 12/2-29/3/56.**G.**
Gor. 8-19/4/58.**C/L.**

BOILERS:
2767.
2667 *(ex2993)* 28/6/41.
4919 *(ex1942)* 6/5/44.
E1356 *(ex3089)* 26/6/47.
BP134 *(ex4973)* 15/4/50.
27774 *(ex4771)* 16/5/53.
27750 *(ex4827)* 29/3/56.

SHEDS:
Ardsley.
Doncaster 19/10/41.
Ardsley 11/6/44.
Doncaster 30/7/45.

Retford 5/10/47.
Lincoln 4/1/59.

RENUMBERED:
4961 20/6/46.
64961 15/4/50.

CONDEMNED:
21/10/59.
Cut up at Stratford.

1952

Darlington.

To traffic 15/6/38.

REPAIRS:
Gor. 31/10-28/12/40.**G.**
Gor. 30/1-15/4/44.**G.**
Gor. 20/12/46-5/5/47.**G.**
Gor. 14/5-2/6/47.**N/C.**
Gor. 7/11-11/12/48.**G.**
Dby. 10/6-7/9/50.**L/I.**
Dby. 11/9-5/10/50.**N/C.**
Gor. 11/4-6/6/53.**G.**
Gor. 18/1-3/3/56.**G.**
Str. 1-3/9/58.**C/L.** *Spark arrester & cont- blow down fitted.*
Str. 15-17/12/58.**N/C.**
Bow 1-12/1/59.**N/C.**

BOILERS:
2766.
8009 *(ex2967)* 28/12/40.
2146 *(ex2775)* 15/4/44.
8006 *(ex1898)* 5/5/47.
E1354 *(ex3090)* 11/12/48.
27760 *(ex4974)* 6/6/53.
27717 *(ex4734)* 3/3/56.

SHEDS:
Ardsley.
New England 23/2/40.
Stratford 24/6/40.
Doncaster 4/7/40.
New England 11/4/42.
Gorton 8/6/43.
Sheffield 8/4/51.
Stratford 19/5/57.
Plaistow 8/6/58.
Tilbury 31/10/59.

RENUMBERED:
4962 29/6/46.
64962 11/12/48.

CONDEMNED:
16/3/60.
Cut up at Stratford.

1965

Darlington.

To traffic 17/6/38.

REPAIRS:
Don. 7-16/11/41.**G.**
Str. 23/6-18/7/44.**G.**
Str. 20/10-9/11/45.**L.**
Str. 3/2-23/5/47.**G.**
Cow.25/4-10/6/50.**L/I.**
Cow. 6-15/9/51.**C/L.**
Cow. 12/12/51-24/1/52.**G.**
Cow. 24/5-30/6/55.**H/I.**
Cow. 11-12/7/55.**N/C.**
Cow. 24/1-2/3/57.**G.**

BOILERS:
4914.
8023 *(ex2714)* 18/7/44.
8007 *(ex2711)* 23/5/47.
27468 *(ex4858)* 24/1/52.
27596 *(ex4758)* 2/3/57.

SHEDS:
Ardsley.
Doncaster 19/10/41.
March 9/1/43.
Stratford 25/5/43.
Carlisle 20/9/47.
St Margarets 22/3/48.
Dalry Road 11/8/58.
Dunfermline 6/6/60.

RENUMBERED:
4963 20/1/46.
64963 10/6/50.

CONDEMNED:
29/1/62.
Cut up at Inverurie.

1971

Darlington.

To traffic 28/6/38.

REPAIRS:
Gor. 20-27/8/40.**G.**
Gor. 18-27/12/41.**G.**
Str. 21/1-8/2/43.**L.**
Str. 28/4-13/5/44.**G.**
Str. 11/5-17/6/46.**G.**
Cow. 10/8-1/9/48.**G.**
Cow. 18-28/10/48.**L.**
Cow. 23/6-5/8/50.**G.**
Cow. 27/2-21/3/53.**G.**
Cow. 21/2-21/3/55.**H/I.**
Cow. 3/6-6/7/57.**G.**
Cow. 21/5-12/6/58.**C/L.**
Cow. 11/9-9/10/59.**L/I.**

BOILERS:
4915.
E1353 *(ex1828)* 27/8/40.
2920 *(ex1927)* 27/12/41.
2191 *(ex2730)* 13/5/44.
2095 *(ex2706)* 17/6/46.
2129 *(ex4914)* 1/9/48.
27467 *(ex64861)* 21/3/53.
27518 *(ex4927)* 6/7/57.

SHEDS:
Norwich.
Ipswich 1/2/40.
Carlisle 8/4/47.

RENUMBERED:
4964 29/6/46.
64964 1/9/48.

CONDEMNED:
24/4/61.
Cut up at Cowlairs.

1974

Darlington.

To traffic 2/7/38.

REPAIRS:
Gor. 8/10-30/11/40.**G.**
Don. 16/8-22/11/41.**L.**
Gor. 14/5-24/7/43.**G.**
Gor. 15/1-27/8/47.**G.**
Gor. 11/5-9/6/49.**C/H.**
Gor. 29/1-18/3/50.**C/L.**
Gor. 22-24/3/50.**N/C.**
Dby. 22/2-12/4/51.**G.**
Dby. 18/12/51-1/2/52.**C/L.**
Str. 12/10-7/11/53.**G.**
Gor. 7/3-19/5/56.**G.**
Str. 12/5-20/6/58.**G.**
Str. 18-20/8/58.**C/L.** *Spark arrester & cont. blow-down fitted.*
Str. 30-31/12/58.**N/C.**
Str. 31/12/58-6/1/59.**N/C.**
Bow 21-27/1/59.**N/C.**

BOILERS:
4916.
4913 *(ex1942)* 30/11/40.
4906 *(ex1996)* 24/7/43.
3197 *(ex1856)* 27/8/47.
27802 *(new)* 12/4/51.
27660 *(ex64731)* 7/11/53.
27847 *(ex4799)* 20/6/58.

SHEDS:
Norwich.
March 23/6/39.
Norwich 4/9/39.
March 13/10/39.
Grantham 30/4/42.
New England 9/2/47.
Colwick 26/3/50.
Peterborough 12/10/52.
Plaistow 29/6/58.
Tilbury 31/10/59.

RENUMBERED:
4965 23/9/46.
64965 9/6/49.

CONDEMNED:
14/3/60.
Cut up at Stratford.

1977

Darlington.

To traffic 8/7/38.

REPAIRS:
Don. 22/8-21/11/41.**G.**
Gor. 14/10-18/12/43.**G.**
Gor. 17/11/46-22/5/47.**G.**
Gor. 26/9-26/11/49.**G.**
Gor. 22/9-24/10/53.**G.**
Gor. 27-30/10/53.**N/C.**
Gor. 1/12/56-12/1/57.**G.**
Gor. 18/1-20/2/57.**N/C.**
Str. 5/4/60.*Not repaired.*

BOILERS:
4917.
2093 *(ex1493)* 18/12/43.
2146 *(ex1952)* 22/5/47.
2772 *(ex2972)* 26/11/49.
25802 *(ex4911)* 24/10/53.
27761 *(ex4903)* 12/1/57.

SHEDS:
Ardsley.
Doncaster 19/10/41.
Gorton 21/8/43.
Cricklewood 20/1/50.
Stratford 11/3/51.
Cricklewood 1/4/51.
Ardsley 16/3/52.
Doncaster 18/12/55.
Lincoln 4/1/59.

RENUMBERED:
4966 23/6/46.
64966 26/11/49.

CONDEMNED:
11/7/60.
Cut up at Stratford.

1980

Darlington.

To traffic 20/7/38.

REPAIRS:
Don. 10/5-19/7/41.**G.**
Gor. 6/10-12/12/42.**L.**
Gor. 17/11/43-22/1/44.**G.**
Gor. 23/1-18/4/46.**G.**
Gor. 26/1-15/10/47.**G.**
Gor. 6/5-26/7/48.**L.**
Dby. 17/12/50-6/2/51.**H/I.**
Don. 29-30/5/52.**N/C.**
Str. 6/4-30/5/53.**G.**
Gor. 23/11/55-21/1/56.**G.**

BOILERS:
4918.
4917 *(ex1977)* 22/1/44.
4908 *(ex1290)* 15/10/47.
27779 *(ex4803)* 30/5/53.
27735 *(ex4959)* 21/1/56.

SHEDS:
Ardsley.
Bradford 2/12/41.
Ardsley 17/9/44.
Doncaster 30/7/45.

RENUMBERED:
4967 18/4/46.
64967 24/7/48.

CONDEMNED:
15/2/60.
Cut up at Stratford.

1984

Darlington.

To traffic 28/7/38.

REPAIRS:
Gor. 14/9-2/11/40.**G.**
Cow. 14/3-4/9/43.**G.**
Str. 25/3-5/4/44.**L.**
Str. 4/4-8/6/46.**G.**
Gor. 14/11/48-8/1/49.**G.**
Dby. 15/11/51-22/1/52.**G.**
Str. 5/10-6/11/54.**G.**
Str. 15/1-22/2/57.**G.**
Str. 18-20/8/58.**C/L.**
Cont. blow-down fitted.

BOILERS:
4919.
4911 *(ex1933)* 2/11/40.
C1718 *(ex2734)* 4/9/43.
2191 *(ex1971)* 8/6/46.
2317 *(ex2772)* 8/1/49.
27692 *(ex4739)* 22/1/52.
27706 *(ex4763)* 6/11/54.
27821 *(ex4773)* 22/2/57.

SHEDS:
Stratford.
Ipswich 6/9/44.
Lowestoft 22/9/46.
Norwich 26/3/47.
Ipswich 14/6/53.
Norwich 7/10/53.
Melton Constable 12/5/57.
Norwich 28/7/57.
Plaistow 8/6/58.
Tilbury 31/10/59.

RENUMBERED:
4968 7/6/46.
64968 8/1/49.

CONDEMNED:
16/3/60.
Cut up at Stratford.

1996

Darlington.

To traffic 9/8/38.

REPAIRS:
Gor. 8/4-11/5/40.**G.**
Gor. 12/12/42-20/3/43.**G.**
Gor. 30/8-14/10/44.**G.**
Gor. 5/11/46-8/2/47.**G.**
Dby. 11/6-20/9/50.**G.**
Gor. 2/5-13/6/53.**G.**
Gor. 24/6-8/7/53.**N/C.**
Gor. 16/5-23/6/56.**G.**
Gor. 10/6-30/7/59.**G.**
Gor. 18-26/8/59.**N/C.**

BOILERS:
4920.
4906 *(ex1898)* 11/5/40.
4915 *(ex1856)* 20/3/43.
3195 *(ex3095)* 14/10/44.
E1356 *(ex4961)* 20/9/50.
27762 *(ex4755)* 13/6/53.
27729 *(ex4972)* 23/6/56.
27799 *(ex4745)* 30/7/59.

SHEDS:
March.
Grantham 29/4/42.
Boston 18/3/44.
New England 16/4/45.
Grantham 2/8/45.
New England 31/12/45.
Sheffield 22/1/50.
Ardsley 3/2/52.
West Auckland 16/10/60.
Ardsley 17/6/62.

RENUMBERED:
4969 23/11/46.
64969 4/9/50.

CONDEMNED:
30/11/62.
Cut up at Darlington.

1997

Darlington.

To traffic 24/8/38.

REPAIRS:
Gor. 2/12/40-4/1/41.**G.**
Gor. 15-20/1/41.**N/C.**
Gor. 17/6-20/7/43.**G.**
Gor. 2-18/12/43.**H.**
Gor. 4/10/45-12/1/46.**G.**
Gor. 15/8-25/9/48.**G.**
Gor. 25/1-4/3/50.**C/L.**
Dby. 16/3-22/4/52.**H/I.**
Str. 20/6-14/8/54.**G.**
Gor. 28/4-25/5/57.**G.**

BOILERS:
2945.
E1351 *(ex1813)* 4/1/41.
4907 *(ex1926)* 18/12/43.
2097 *(ex2971)* 12/1/46.
3208 *(ex2967)* 25/9/48.
3208 Reno. 27697 22/4/52.
27687 *(ex4830)* 14/8/54.
27884 *(ex4789)* 25/5/57.

SHEDS:
Ipswich.
March 10/5/39.
Grantham 30/4/42.
New England 1/8/45.
Retford 6/10/46.

RENUMBERED:
4970 3/11/46.
64970 25/9/48.

CONDEMNED:
24/5/61.
Cut up at Doncaster.

3081

Darlington.

To traffic 7/2/41.

REPAIRS:
Gor. 12-30/1/43.**G.**
Gor. 28/8-13/9/45.**G.**
Gor. 25/10-13/11/47.**G.**
Dby. 30/11/50-22/1/51.**G.**
Cow. 23/4-19/5/53.**H/I.**
Cow. 29/7-19/9/55.**G.**
Cow. 25/4-30/5/58.**H/I.**
Cow. 3-12/3/59.**C/L.**
Cow. 10/10-18/11/60.**G.**

BOILERS:
3168.
4910 *(ex1930)* 30/1/43.
3211 *(ex1930)* 13/9/45.
2770 *(ex2696)* 13/11/47.
27651 *(new)* 22/1/51.
27572 *(ex65922)* 19/9/55.
27580 *(ex4858)* 18/11/60.

SHEDS:
Doncaster.
Sheffield 30/3/41.
Lincoln 1/7/45.
Immingham 22/12/46.
Lincoln 27/4/47.
Heaton 2/9/51.
Hull Dairycoates 11/2/32.

RENUMBERED:
4971 23/6/46.
64971 12/1/51.

CONDEMNED:
25/6/62.
Cut up at Cowlairs.

3082

Darlington.

To traffic 14/2/41.

REPAIRS:
Gor. 26/2-4/4/44.**G.**
Str. 5/2-13/4/46.**G.**
Gor. 12-22/11/47.**L.**
Gor. 11/4-9/6/48.**G.**
Gor. 12/12/49-18/2/50.**G.**
Gor. 22/2-2/3/50.**N/C.**
Dby. 1/10-10/11/52.**H/I.**
Gor. 10/1-12/3/55.**G.**
Don. 19/9/57.*Weigh.*

BOILERS:
3169.
2617 *(ex1425)* 4/4/44.
2113 *(ex1281)* 13/4/46.
8590 *(ex2702)* 9/6/48.
4901 *(ex2735)* 18/2/50.
4901 Reno. 27729 10/11/52.
27834 *(new)* 12/3/55.

SHEDS:
Doncaster.
Sheffield 30/3/41.
Barnsley 20/10/46.
Gorton 27/4/47.
Sheffield 8/4/51.
Ardsley 23/12/51.
Doncaster 18/12/55.

RENUMBERED:
4972 13/4/46.
64972 5/6/48.

CONDEMNED:
11/12/59.
Cut up at Stratford.

3083

Darlington.

To traffic 28/2/41.

REPAIRS:
Gor. 23/1-22/4/44.**G.**
Gor. 4/9/46-25/1/47.**G.**
Gor. 25/1-18/3/50.**G.**
Gor. 22-23/3/50.**N/C.**
Dby. 11/8-3/10/52.**H/I.**
Str. 21/2-2/4/55.**G.**

BOILERS:
3170.
BP134 *(ex3093)* 25/1/47.
8590 *(ex4972)* 18/3/50.

WORKS CODES:- Cow - Cowlairs. Dar - Darlington. Dby - Derby. Don - Doncaster. Ghd - Gateshead. Gor - Gorton. Inv - Inverurie. Str - Stratford.
REPAIR CODES:- **C/H** - Casual Heavy. **C/L** - Casual Light. **G** - General. **H**- Heavy. **H/I** - Heavy Intermediate. **L** - Light. **L/I** - Light Intermediate. **N/C** - Non-Classified.

2738 worked its first fourteen years from Eastfield shed, and is seen on the West Highland line taking a Class A goods to Fort William.
WBY collection

8590 Reno. 27721 3/10/52.
27432 *(ex4799)* 2/4/55.

SHEDS:
Doncaster.
Sheffield 30/3/41.
Stratford 17/10/54.

RENUMBERED:
4973 16/6/46.
64973 21/1/49.

CONDEMNED:
13/11/59.
Cut up at Stratford.

3084

Darlington.

To traffic 4/3/41.

REPAIRS:
Gor. 9/5-21/8/43.**G.**
Gor. 10-22/9/43.**N/C.**
Str. 20/1-6/4/46.**G.**
Gor. 16/7-28/8/48.**G.**
Gor. 17/3-20/5/50.**G.**
Gor. 25-31/5/50.**N/C.**
Gor. 6-30/6/50.**N/C.**
Gor. 12/2-11/4/53.**G.**
Gor. 13-16/4/53.**N/C.**
Gor. 14/6-13/8/55.**G.**
Gor. 18-27/8/55.**N/C.**
Gor. 10/1-22/2/58.**G.**
Gor. 2-12/3/58.**N/C.**
Gor. 27/6-2/8/58.**C/L.**

BOILERS:
3171.
4913 *(ex1974)* 21/8/43.
2188 *(ex1266)* 6/4/46.
8583 *(ex1492)* 28/8/48.
2667 *(ex2770)* 20/5/50.
27752 *(ex4705)* 11/4/53.
27844 *(new)* 13/8/55.
27795 *(ex4762)* 22/2/58.

SHEDS:
Doncaster.
Sheffield 30/3/41.
Gorton 25/5/44.
Barnsley 20/10/46.
Colwick 27/4/47.

RENUMBERED:
4974 6/4/46.
64974 28/8/48.

CONDEMNED:
31/8/60.
Cut up at Doncaster.

3085

Darlington.

To traffic 17/3/41.

REPAIRS:
Cow. 2/8-18/9/43.**G.**
Cow. 18/9-12/10/45.**G.**
Dar. 31/10-24/11/45.**L.**
Dar. 27/11-8/12/45.**N/C.**
Cow. 2-9/3/46.**L.**
Cow. 4-17/9/48.**G.**
Inv. 5-28/12/51.**L/I.**
Cow. 15/6-8/8/54.**G.**
Inv. 19/7-26/8/55.**C/L.**
Cow. 12/11-3/12/55.**N/C.**
Cow. 4-24/4/59.**G.**
Cow. 6-25/11/59.**N/C.**

BOILERS:
3172.
4909 *(ex1940)* 18/9/43.
3192 *(ex4860)* 17/9/48.
3192 Reno. 27553 28/12/51.
27556 *(ex64978)* 8/8/54.
25805 *(ex4904)* 24/4/59.

SHEDS:
St Margarets.
Carlisle 20/8/45.
Aberdeen 16/10/47.
St Margarets 13/3/59.
Dawsholm 29/8/60.

RENUMBERED:
4975 22/6/46.
64975 17/9/48.

CONDEMNED:
29/12/62.
Sold for scrap to Geo.H.Campbell, Airdrie.

3086

Darlington.

To traffic 22/3/41.

REPAIRS:
Cow. 20/2-2/4/44.**G.**
Gor. 21/8-3/11/45.**G.**
Dar. 26/2-26/4/48.**H.**
Gor. 18/10-24/12/48.**G.**
Dby. 14/11/52-4/2/52.**G.**
Str. 27/7-10/9/54.**G.**
Gor. 4/8-8/10/55.**C/H.**
Gor. 10-19/10/55.**N/C.**
Gor. 2/10-17/11/56.**C/L.**
Gor. 15/7-7/9/57.**C/H.**
Gor. 13-19/9/57.**N/C.**

BOILERS:
3174.
8005 *(ex1429)* 2/4/44.
2945 *(ex1854)* 3/11/45.
3175 *(ex2942)* 24/12/48.
27807 *(new)* 4/2/52.
27823 *(new)* 10/9/54.
27830 *(new)* 7/9/57.

SHEDS:
Doncaster.
Sheffield 30/3/41.
Doncaster 22/9/46.
Colwick 27/4/52.
Tuxford 27/9/53.
Colwick 16/1/55.

RENUMBERED:
4976 9/6/46.
64976 26/4/48.

CONDEMNED:
25/11/59.
Cut up at Stratford.

3087

Darlington.

To traffic 5/4/41.

REPAIRS:
Gor. 27/11/42-27/3/43.**G.**
Str. 15/3-27/6/46.**G.**
Gor. 17/4-29/6/48.**L.**
Gor. 26/9-26/11/49.**G.**
Gor. 10-11/12/49.**N/C.**
Gor. 17/12/49-21/1/50.**N/C.**
Dby. 25/9-1/11/51.**L/I.**
Str. 29/11/53-9/1/54.**G.**
Str. 21/5-15/6/54.**C/L.**
Str. 1/12/54-22/1/55.**C/L.**
Gor. 22/1-16/3/57.**G.**
Gor. 28-29/3/57.**N/C.**

BOILERS:
3175.
4920 *(ex1903)* 27/3/43.
C1718 *(ex1984)* 27/6/46.
3213 *(ex1274)* 26/11/49.
27881 *(ex4781)* 9/1/54.
27781 *(ex4956)* 16/3/57.

SHEDS:
Doncaster.
Lincoln 2/9/51.
Colwick 7/12/58.

RENUMBERED:
4977 27/6/46.
64977 26/6/48.

CONDEMNED:
4/2/60.
Cut up at Gorton.

3088

Darlington.

To traffic 24/4/41.

REPAIRS:
Cow. 24/8-24/9/43.**G.**
Cow. 5/6-8/7/44.**H.**
Cow. 7-21/10/44.**L.**
Cow. 23/6-20/7/46.**G.**
Cow. 14/9-22/11/47.**G.**
Cow. 8-30/12/50.**H/I.**
Cow. 10/2-9/3/51.**C/L.**
Cow. 5/3-8/4/54.**G.**
Ghd. 10/3-25/5/55.**C/L.**
Cow. 14/8-20/9/58.**G.**

BOILERS:
3173.
2686 *(ex2948)* 24/9/43.
E1357 *(ex1547)* 8/7/44.
3212 *(ex2738)* 22/11/47.
3212 Reno. 27556 9/3/51.
27595 *(ex4727)* 8/4/54.
27501 *(ex64814)* 20/9/58.

SHEDS:
St Margarets.
Darlington 22/11/43.
Hull Dairycoates 1/3/48.
West Hartlepool 20/3/49.
Northallerton 19/9/54.
West Auckland 18/11/56.
Gateshead 23/8/59.

RENUMBERED:
4978 26/3/46.
64978 30/12/50.

CONDEMNED:
3/12/62.
Cut up at Darlington.

3089

Darlington.

To traffic 3/5/41.

REPAIRS:
Gor. 26/4-24/6/44.**G.**
Gor. 13/2-23/5/45.**G.**
Gor. 28/1-11/6/47.**G.**
Gor. 29/6-6/7/47.**N/C.**
Dby. 26/11/50-30/1/51.**G.**
Gor. 13/12/53-30/1/54.**G.**
Gor. 2-5/2/54.**N/C.**
Gor. 3/3-6/4/54.**C/L.**
Gor. 11-12/4/54.**N/C.**
Gor. 20/6-10/8/57.**G.**
Gor. 20/12/61.*Not repaired.*

BOILERS:
3176.
E1356 *(ex1813)* 24/6/44.
2093 *(ex1977)* 11/6/47.
27653 *(new)* 30/1/51.
27830 *(new)* 30/1/54.
27833 *(ex4741)* 10/8/57.

SHEDS:
New England.
Grantham 11/5/41.
Colwick 9/10/41.
Annesley 13/10/41.
Colwick 8/8/43.
Ardsley 18/8/46.
West Auckland 16/10/60.

RENUMBERED:
4979 25/8/46.
64979 30/1/51.

CONDEMNED:
5/1/62.
Cut up at Darlington.

3090

Darlington.

To traffic 3/5/41.

REPAIRS:
Gor. 29/7-9/10/43.**G.**
Gor. 1/8-15/9/45.**L.**
Gor. 2/5-27/7/46.**G.**
Gor. 12/10-6/12/48.**G.**
Gor. 14/7-27/8/49.**C/L.**
Gor. 12-25/3/50.**C/H.**
Gor. 29-30/3/50.**N/C.**
Dby. 22/7-10/10/50.**L/I.**
Dby. 25/8-24/10/52.**G.**
Dby. 3-12/11/52.**N/C.**
Dby. 18/11-5/12/52.**N/C.**
Gor. 16/5-9/7/55.**G.**
Gor. 16/8-2/9/55.**N/C.**
Gor. 15/7-31/8/57.**C/H.**
Gor. 6-8/9/57.**N/C.**

BOILERS:
3177.
3171 *(ex3084)* 9/10/43.
E1354 *(ex1495)* 27/7/46.
2684 *(ex1940)* 6/12/48.
BP145 *(ex4890)* 25/3/50.
27726 *(ex4752)* 24/10/52.
27839 *(new)* 9/7/55.
27889 *(ex4987)* 31/8/57.

SHEDS:
New England.
Grantham 11/5/41.
Colwick 9/10/41.
Annesley 13/10/41.
Colwick 30/3/47.

RENUMBERED:
4980 27/7/46.
64980 4/12/48.

CONDEMNED:
30/12/59.
Cut up at Stratford.

3091

Darlington.

To traffic 13/5/41.

REPAIRS:
Dar. 7/5-12/6/42.**L.**
Due to enemy action.
Gor. 24/3-28/4/44.**G.**
Gor. 17/5-21/9/46.**G.**
Gor. 22/10-4/12/47.**G.**
Gor. 26/4-4/6/49.**G.**
Dby. 12/11/51-17/1/52.**G.**
Dby. 21/2-3/3/52.**N/C.**
Str. 24/8-2/10/54.**G.**
In Store.21/10/56-2/6/57.
In Store.23/11/58-4/12/59.

BOILERS:
3191.
8017 *(ex2976)* 28/4/44.
4914 *(ex1898)* 21/9/46.
BP143 *(ex1495)* 4/12/47.
8012 *(ex2724)* 4/6/49.
27688 *(ex4879)* 17/1/52.
27697 *(ex4970)* 2/10/54.

SHEDS:
Grantham.
Colwick 8/10/41.
Ardsley 20/5/51.
Colwick 27/4/52.
Peterborough 12/4/53.
Plaistow 7/4/57.
Doncaster 2/6/57.

RENUMBERED:
4981 21/9/46.
64981 4/6/49.

CONDEMNED:
5/2/60.
Cut up at Stratford.

3092

Darlington.

To traffic 21/5/41.

REPAIRS:
Cow. 10-12/9/42.**N/C.**
Cow. 29/6-23/7/43.**G.**
Cow. 17/6-6/7/46.**G.**
Ghd. 23/11-16/12/47.**L.**
Cow. 11/3-14/5/49.**G.**
Cow. 1-18/7/52.**L/I.**
Cow. 12/8-10/9/55.**G.**
Cow. 19/12/56-18/1/57.**C/L.**
Cow. 16/1-13/2/59.**G.**

BOILERS:
3192.
RS123 *(ex1412)* 6/7/46.
RS123 Reno. 27485 18/7/52.
27587 *(ex64870)* 10/9/55.
27539 *(ex64884)* 13/2/59.

SHEDS:
St Margarets.
Darlington 3/5/44.
Blaydon 29/8/48.
Tweedmouth 23/5/49.
Darlington 19/11/50.
West Auckland 31/8/52.

RENUMBERED:
4982 5/7/46.
64982 14/5/49.

Only rarely can a wartime photograph be included in the Registers, but here on Sunday 8th October 1939, Darlington shedded 1485 is pulling out of Low Fell marshalling yard with an up main line goods. Note that the buffer faces have been painted white to help their visibility in the blackout. *W.B.Greenfield*

CONDEMNED:
3/12/62.
Cut up at Darlington.

3093

Darlington.

To traffic 5/6/41.

REPAIRS:
Gor. 7/5-8/7/44.**G.**
Gor. 3/7-2/11/46.**G.**
Gor. 16/8-2/10/48.**G.**
Gor. 7/12/49-11/2/50.**G.**
Gor. 18-23/2/50.**N/C.**
Gor. 13/1-28/3/53.**G.**
Gor. 31/3-15/4/53.**N/C.**
Gor. 2/6-10/9/54.**C/L.**
Gor. 16/8-20/10/55.**C/L.**
Gor. 24-26/10/55.**N/C.**
Gor. 29/6-15/9/56.**G.**

BOILERS:
3193.
BP134 *(ex1544)* 8/7/44.
8592 *(ex1539)* 2/11/46.
2104 *(ex2973)* 2/10/48.
4929 *(ex4720)* 11/2/50.
27737 *(ex4890)* 28/3/53.
27879 *(ex4838)* 15/9/56.

SHEDS:
Grantham.
Boston 26/7/41.
Colwick 8/10/41.

RENUMBERED:
4983 31/8/46.
64983 2/10/48.

CONDEMNED:
10/11/59.
Cut up at Stratford.

3094

Darlington.

To traffic 18/6/41.

REPAIRS:
Gor. 17/3-5/5/44.**G.**
Gor. 25/10-1/12/45.**G.**
Str. 13/2-11/5/46.**G.**
Gor. 28/1-24/3/48.**G.**
Gor. 16/10-24/12/48.**G.**
Dby. 31/5-10/8/51.**H/I.**
Str. 10/6-31/7/54.**G.**
In Store. 8/5-10/7/55.
In Store. 27/6/58-25/10/59.

BOILERS:
3194.
2691 *(ex2992)* 5/5/44.
2690 *(ex1492)* 11/5/46.
4910 *(ex2971)* 24/12/48.
27673 *(ex4724)* 31/7/54.

SHEDS:
Grantham.
New England 22/7/41.
Boston 26/7/41.
Colwick 8/10/41.
Doncaster 23/8/46.
Retford 28/1/51.
Doncaster 4/3/51.
Lincoln 2/9/51.

RENUMBERED:
4984 11/5/46.
64984 24/3/48.

CONDEMNED:
31/12/59.
Cut up at Stratford.

3095

Darlington.

To traffic 3/7/41.

REPAIRS:
Gor. 31/5-19/8/44.**G.**
Gor. 30/4-3/8/46.**G.**
Gor. 17/8-16/10/48.**L.**
Gor. 17/1-4/3/50.**G.**
Gor. 10-12/3/50.**N/C.**
Dby. 23/6-20/8/52.**G.**
Dby. 25/8-5/9/52.**N/C.**
Str. 7/3-16/4/55.**G.**

BOILERS:
3195.
3193 *(ex3093)* 19/8/44.
3201 *(ex4900)* 4/3/50.
3201 Reno. 27714 20/8/52.
27433 *(ex4958)* 16/4/55.

SHEDS:
New England.
Boston 30/7/41.
Colwick 8/10/41.
Ardsley 18/8/46.
Stratford 22/9/52.
Parkeston 27/11/55.
New England 28/10/56.
Peterborough 14/4/57.
Cambridge 8/6/58.

RENUMBERED:
4985 20/10/46.
64985 16/10/48.

CONDEMNED:
31/12/59.
Cut up at Stratford.

3096

Darlington.

To traffic 18/7/41.

REPAIRS:
Cow. 3/1-18/2/43.**G.**
Cow. 19/8-2/11/46.**G.**
Cow. 18/8-17/9/49.**G.**
Cow. 10-17/3/50.**C/L.**
Cow. 17/3-5/5/52.**G.**
Cow. 1-30/3/55.**H/I.**
Cow. 13-14/4/55.**N/C.**
Cow. 1-23/6/56.**N/C.**
Cow. 27/2-29/3/58.**G.**
Cow. 22/12/61-9/1/62.**C/L.**

BOILERS:
3196.
2719 *(ex4709)* 2/11/46.
27557 *(ex64940)* 5/5/52.
27547 *(ex4939)* 29/3/58.

SHEDS:
St Margarets.
Hawick 20/8/45.
St Margarets 10/2/47.
Carlisle 21/4/47.
St Margarets 22/3/48.
Dalry Road 11/8/58.
Thornton Junction 18/12/61.

RENUMBERED:
4986 7/7/46.
64986 17/9/49.

CONDEMNED:
29/12/62.
Cut up at Inverurie.

3097

Darlington.

To traffic 8/8/41.

REPAIRS:
Gor. 26/2-5/5/45.**G.**
Gor. 21/3-17/5/48.**G.**

Dby. 20/1-12/3/51.**H/I.**
Dby. 24/1-7/3/52.**G.**
Dby. 18/3-1/4/52.**N/C.**
Str. 14/8-24/9/54.**G.**
Gor. 4/6-25/7/57.**G.**
Gor. 31/7-16/8/57.**N/C.**
Gor. 8-20/9/58.**C/L.**

BOILERS:
3199.
3201 *(ex2964)* 5/5/45.
2926 *(ex2978)* 17/5/48.
27805 *(new)* 7/3/52.
27889 *(ex4787 & spare)* 24/9/54.
27687 *(ex4970)* 25/7/57.

SHEDS:
New England.
Grantham 18/1/43.
New England 29/8/43.
Grantham 18/11/45.
Retford 28/9/46.
Doncaster 17/8/52.

RENUMBERED:
4987 8/9/46.
64987 15/5/48.

CONDEMNED:
15/3/61.
Cut up at Doncaster.

3098

Darlington.

To traffic 21/8/41.

REPAIRS:
Gor. 2/6-19/8/44.**G.**
Gor. 30/12/46-14/5/47.**G.**
Gor. 8/4-10/6/50.**G.**
Gor. 14-22/6/50.**N/C.**
Gor. 4-31/7/50.**N/C.**
Dby. 18/10-5/12/51.**H/I.**
Dby. 10-28/12/51.**N/C.**
Gor. 28/4-25/9/54.**C/H.**
Gor. 28/4-25/6/55.**H/I.**
Gor. 26/8-23/9/55.**N/C.**

BOILERS:
3197.
3176 *(ex3089)* 19/8/44.
8013 *(ex2692)* 14/5/47.
E1355 *(ex2945)* 10/6/50.
27681 *(ex4810)* 25/9/54.

SHEDS:
Doncaster.
Colwick 9/9/41.

RENUMBERED:
4988 22/12/46.
64988 10/6/50.

CONDEMNED:
30/12/59.
Cut up at Stratford.

Carlisle's 1875 also on passenger work albeit only on a stopping train to Silloth in Citadel station on 8th April 1946. *H.C.Casserley*

A picture full of nostalgia shows 64763 on 28th May 1955 in Nottingham (Victoria) about to work the 5.06 p.m. to Grantham. On 30th May 1949, and holding a first class return ticket, I was intending to use that train back home by changing at Grantham into one of the King's Cross-Hull trains to get dinner in the restaurant car. The ticket inspector on the bridge at Victoria told me it was not valid that way because "that's not our line". After 25 years of LNER, and 1½ of nationalisation, I thought that really was the peak of loyalty to the Great Central. So instead of waiting an hour to return hungry via Sheffield, I got my ticket punched 'to go to the Victoria refreshment room', then climbed into the Grantham train, and experienced no further difficulty. But it was B1 no.61144 on the train and not a J39. *J.P.Wilson*

Here is an acknowledgement of support given to my Registers by Embsay Steam Railway sales shop, because this pair of J39s would shortly be going through Embsay station. They had taken over this goods at the western side of Skipton station, and had climbed up to this crossing of the Midland main line on their way through Ilkley, and Otley to Starbeck near Harrogate. *WBY collection*

64933 did all its further work from Leeds after it moved to Neville Hill shed in September 1950, and here in April 1957 is bringing an empty stock train through the station at Collingham Bridge. Note that in addition to its 50B shedplate it also has LEEDS on its buffer beam. *M.Mitchell*

With almost three hundred engines in the class, some with a life span of 35 years, it is remarkable how J39 class kept almost completely out of trouble; none were involved in any serious accident. Undoubtedly there would be mishaps, but the only two that I have found recorded pictorially is this to 2982 *(right)* **and 64705** *(below)*. **What, when, and where, are presently unknown to me as regards 2982 can you help please? 64705 is grounded in the Wakefield area and probably towards the end of its career. The classic stances of the railway staff are typical during the early period of recovery operations such as this.** *WBY collection*

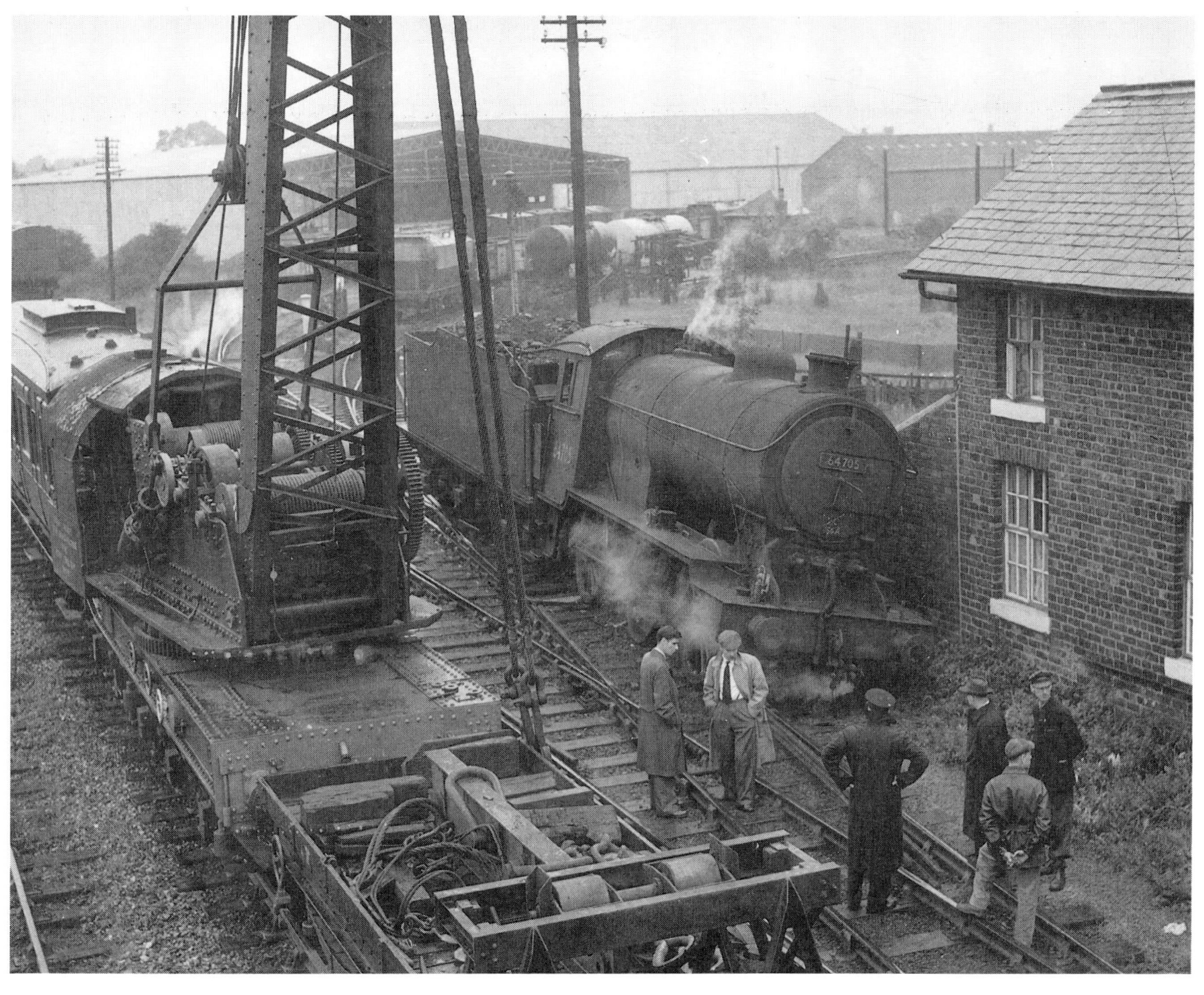

Seven of the class languish 'in store' at March in 1959 alongside one of the former coal dumps. Amongst this woeful line-up are 64764, 64769, 64770, 64771, 64772, 64774 and 64779. None would be reactivated but all made a final journey to either Doncaster or Stratford for scrapping. *N.E.Stead.*

To finish off this volume on a lighter note, we visit the end of a country branch line where Blaydon's 64812 is standing at Alston station, where the complete layout seems to be crammed into the minimum possible space, with single road engine shed included. *WBY coll.*